History
in the
United States
1800–1860

History
in the
United States
1800–1860

Its Practice and Purpose

George H. Callcott

The Johns Hopkins Press
Baltimore and London

The Johns Hopkins Press, Baltimore, Maryland 21218
The Johns Hopkins Press Ltd., London

Library of Congress Catalog Card Number 74–88115

Standard Book Number 8018–1099–X

Contents

Preface

In this book I have tried to explain the remarkable rise of historical consciousness in the United States during the early nineteenth century, to define the standards by which history came to be judged, and to analyze the reasons men of that generation turned to the past. Relying much on biographies and critical analyses of leading historians which have appeared in recent years, I have attempted to venture a step beyond, to explain the meaning of the past itself rather than the contents of particular works. In part, then, this is intellectual history, the anatomy of the idea of history; and in part it is social history, a study of men's need for the past and their use of it.

Americans have always been strangely preoccupied with the future and fascinated with the past. Especially from about 1800 to around 1860, as the future glowed especially bright, a surge of interest in the past swept the young nation. An extraordinary portion of the nation's creative energy went into writing history, but equally important was the sudden prominence of history in the schools, the rise of historical societies, the movement for preservation of historical sites and documents, the fashion for genealogy, and the prominence of historical themes in architecture, painting, sculpture, the theater, fiction, poetry, and oratory. America was finding its identity in history—in the classical and aboriginal past as well as in its own colonial heritage. Even more, the country's first generation with leisure for sustained cultural activity was finding personal fulfillment in history.

Out of this regard for the past developed a highly coherent set of subjects, themes, methods, and uses of history which reflected the preoccupations and aspirations of the nation. The American idea of history combined Hegelian philosophical assumptions and Romantic literary techniques with immediate concerns about morality, God, liberty, progress, and the national mission. Americans were especially convinced of the utility of history, its social use in supporting accepted values, its personal utility in extending human experience, and its philosophical utility in pointing men toward an ultimate reality which was closely akin to melancholy. The idea of history possessed a unity which helped give the Romantic period coherence. However, when the structure weakened at any one point—when historical controversy appeared—the entire edifice collapsed together.

Many people have aided me. Professor Herman Ausubel of Columbia University stimulated my interest in historiography, and Professor Fletcher M. Green of the University of North Carolina guided me in developing this topic as a dissertation. Among the many colleagues who have offered valuable criticism, I am especially indebted to Professor David H. Flaherty of the University of Virginia. The Southern Fellowships Fund and the General Research Board of the University of Maryland provided financial assistance. Portions of this work in earlier form have appeared in the *New England Quarterly,* the *Historian,* the *American Quarterly,* and the *American Archivist.* Most of all, for their helpful criticism and aid, I am grateful to my parents, Professor and Mrs. W. H. Callcott, and to my wife, Peggy.

G. H. C.

University Park, Maryland

History
in the
United States
1800–1860

I

The Intellectual Origins of Romantic History

DURING the first decade of the nineteenth century Americans were gradually maturing a set of attitudes toward the past which paved the way for the great historians they so eagerly awaited. In part the new attitudes developed from the Enlightenment, in part from Romantic currents which were sweeping in from abroad, and perhaps in largest part from developments in America itself. By the 1830's the young nation was confident of its approach to the past and immensely proud of its rising historians—George Bancroft, Washington Irving, John Lothrop Motley, William H. Prescott, Francis Parkman, Jared Sparks, and scores of others.

The Enlightenment Heritage

Eighteenth-century philosophers established history as a meaningful form of knowledge, formulated a scholarly method, and introduced the concept of progress. Enlightenment historians, putting this philosophy into practice, established history as a majestic literary expression. Most important of the philosophers, at least in retrospect, was the Italian rationalist, Giambattista Vico. Though almost unknown in the United States, Vico's principles filtered into the country through the familiar works of

Montesquieu, Voltaire, Condorcet, David Hume, William Robertson, and Edward Gibbon.

Vico argued that history was meaningful only when historians broke away from mere annals of events to describe the essence of a society. When the historian grasped the totality of man's achievement—his laws, manners, institutions, and culture—then the past became understandable and historical knowledge useful. Vico called upon historians to cultivate a self-conscious method —a "scientific" method—for arriving at truth about the past. The method really only amounted to a conscious effort at objectivity. The historian must ask whether a fact were reasonable, if it were relevant to a larger truth, if witnesses were reliable; he must be aware of his own biases and his own standard of judgment.[1]

Vico's theory of history as the essence of society objectively described found its best application in Montesquieu's *Spirit of the Laws* (1748), and in Voltaire's *Age of Louis XIV* (1751), both widely read in America. Boldly, Voltaire subordinated details to the significant essence of the whole culture. "After having read the descriptions of three or four thousand battles," he wrote, "I do not find myself one jot wiser than when I began; because from them I learn nothing but events." He promised his readers "only that which deserves to be known: the spirit, manners and customs of the principal nations." [2] Although Voltaire only partially measured up to his promise, and eighteenth-century American chroniclers like Thomas Hutchinson and David Ramsay fell even farther behind, at least they had established an ideal for the nineteenth century.

Still, while essence history was a great contribution to historical thinking, its limitations stimulated subsequent Romantic thinkers

[1] Thomas Goddard Bergin and Max Harold Fisch, trans. and eds., *The New Science of Giambattista Vico* (New York, 1961); Benedetto Croce, *The Philosophy of Giambattista Vico,* trans. R. G. Collingwood (New York, 1913), especially pp. 268–78; Pardon E. Tillinghast, *Approaches to History* (Englewood Cliffs, N.J., 1963), pp. 117–46.

[2] Cited in Trygve R. Tholfsen, *Historical Thinking: An Introduction* (New York, 1967), pp. 102–3.

almost as much. First of all, the emphasis on essence, combined with the eighteenth-century assumption of the changelessness of human nature, homogenized the past and eliminated uniqueness, the particular, the accidental. Second, essence dehumanized the past, tending to eliminate dramatic conflict and biography. Third, the emphasis on essence intensified the eighteenth-century tendency to judge the past by its own standards, to assume that history had always been the struggle of reason against superstition and authority. "Nature being the same everywhere," said Voltaire, "men necessarily had to adopt the same truths and the same errors." [3] Finally, most significantly, the various corollaries of essence history all contributed to denigrating the importance of the study of the past. Since all history was essentially alike, since it was an abstract study of human nature rather than of real men, and since the historian could hardly sympathize with the past as he unmasked its follies, history could hardly matter very much. For Americans of the nineteenth century, Voltaire's history was not only something to equal but something to improve upon as well.

The concept of a unifying theme for history—particularly the idea of progress—was another contribution of eighteenth-century thought suggested by Vico and developed by Robert Jacques Turgot, Voltaire, Condorcet, and the English historians. For historians who had abandoned the guiding hand of God in human events, history without a central theme was a series of static incidents. To provide a framework for change, Vico postulated a spiraling progress from an age of theocracy to an age of aristocracy to an age of democracy. Turgot urged the idea of progress on historians more explicitly, pointing to the difference between the study of natural phenomena subject to constant laws within "a circle of unchanging revolutions," and the study of history which stretched in an endless unbreakable chain of cause and effect. Historical movement was accounted for, argued

[3] Cited in *ibid.*, p. 117. On Voltaire, see also J. M. Brumfitt, *Voltaire: Historian* (Oxford, 1958); John B. Black, *The Art of History* (London, 1926), pp. 29–75.

Turgot, by man's ability to transmit knowledge to his successors as a cumulative heritage.[4] Voltaire was unable to apply this to political history, but he accepted it as the unifying theme for intellectual history. "All that is needed," he wrote, "is to trace the onward march of the human mind in philosophy, oratory, poetry, and criticism; to show the progress of painting, sculpture, and music; of jewelry, tapestry making, glass blowing, gold-cloth weaving, and watchmaking." [5] For Voltaire, cultural and intellectual history was the easiest kind to write because it had a theme.

Still more pleasing to Americans was Condorcet, who spoke of the unlimited progress of human nature as a natural law and viewed the United States as the extension of the progress of the Old World. An American edition of Condorcet's *Outlines of an Historical View of the Progress of the Human Mind* appeared in Philadelphia in 1796, just one year after the Paris edition, and a second American edition appeared in Baltimore in 1802. Equally popular in America were the English theorists of progress, William Godwin and Joseph Priestly, who viewed the American Revolution as a step in the emancipation and progress of humanity.[6]

The English historians David Hume, William Robertson, and Edward Gibbon came closest to applying progress to history and thus giving the past coherence and sweep. Hume came to history from philosophy, searching particularly for causation— or theme—in the affairs of men. There were conceptual defects in his *History of England from the Invasion of Julius Caesar* (1754–61), for he worked backward from effects to causes and from recent events to earlier ones, but it possessed unprecedented sweep, and imposed on it was the theme of superstition and chaos yielding over the centuries to reason and order. Robertson's *History of Scotland* (1759) told a similar story of barbarism

[4] Ronald V. Sampson, *Progress in the Age of Reason* (London, 1956), pp. 158–82.

[5] Cited in Fritz Stern, ed., *The Varieties of History: From Voltaire to the Present* (New York, 1956), pp. 39–40.

[6] Arthur Alphonse Ekirch, *The Idea of Progress in America, 1815–1860* (New York, 1944), pp. 11–37.

yielding to civilization. Of the three writers, Robertson was far the most popular in America, probably because he never entirely abandoned the suspicion that Providence guided events. Edward Gibbon, of course, turned progress on its head. Accepting a cyclical progress, his *Decline and Fall of the Roman Empire* (1776–88) told the story of fourteen centuries in which superstition triumphed over reason. Though never popular in America because men never fully accepted his anti-Christian standard of judgment, Gibbon's work may have been the most successful thematic history ever written.

While the eighteenth-century concept of progress gave history a unifying theme, it too had limitations, for it seemed to encourage an antihistorical contempt for what had gone before. Historians like Voltaire, Hume, and Gibbon tended to think of progress not organically as youth developing into maturity but mechanically as wrong ideas becoming right. Confidently they judged the past by what they assumed were superior modern standards, brutally exposing the errors of alien ages and cultures. Not until the nineteenth century did Turgot's concept of progress give way to Condorcet's, mechanistic imagery give way to organic, and historians learn to judge the past by its own standards, with sympathy and reverence.

The greatest achievement and greatest failing of Enlightenment history was its literary quality. The achievement was obvious, especially in Gibbon, whose historical works offered some of the most eloquent prose in the language, and whose literary quality, though not style, provided a standard of measurement for all subsequent historians. The failing was that, except as literature, eighteenth-century thinkers were never very successful in establishing a further purpose for history. Enlightenment historians made a display of dismissing their work as "mere amusement," "without serious purpose." Except for its value as literature, history seemed a waste of time, for antiquarians of small mind. Viscount Bolingbroke warned of excessive learning as a "ridiculous affectation," and called for "a temperate curiosity" about history. Scholars below the first rank—such as the eighteenth-century American historians—were duly humble, accepting the general patronizing disdain for their monkish labors and seldom claiming to be more than antiquarians. The eighteenth century valued wit more than learning; it searched for universals rather than the particulars historians found; it supported its values by reason rather than by historical evidence. Despite the popularity of the great historians, their fame was achieved not as scholars but as men of literature, of style, epigram, and wit. In practice, of course, the best historians were doing far more than entertaining. In practice, they were searching curiously for the truth of what had happened, and also they were simply expressing themselves—Voltaire his glorification of the progress of reason, Hume his skepticism, Robertson his love of a dignified story, and Gibbon his distaste for Christianity.[7]

It was, however, for a later age to elevate the search for truth and the joy of self-expression to a legitimate purpose for studying the past, and to make purpose the heart of the idea of history. For Americans in 1800, the Enlightenment heritage—even of the great Voltaire and Gibbon—consisted not only of a tradition to build upon but also one to revolt against.

European Romanticism

Philosophical ideas developing in Germany from 1775 to 1830, along with the eloquent literary history being written in France and England from 1820 to 1860, provided a second source of nineteenth-century American historical thought. These ideas and models all found their way, fairly promptly, into the United States. Americans seldom thought in terms of German philosophy, and seldom directly imitated European historians, but these philosophies and examples helped Americans to know their own thoughts about history.

Most modern scholars believe that the central figure in this period of German historical thought was Johann Gottfried Herder, the father of historicism. He was one of a large school.

[7] See Black, *Art of History,* pp. 14–28; Ronald N. Stromberg, "History in the Eighteenth Century," *Journal of the History of Ideas,* XII (April, 1951), 295–304; James Westfall Thompson, *A History of Historical Writing* (2 vols.; New York, 1942), II, 58–95; G. P. Gooch, *History and Historians in the Nineteenth Century* (Boston, 1959), p. 10.

Gottfried Wilhelm Leibnitz, Johann Joachim Winckelmann, Jean Jacques Rousseau, and Immanuel Kant contributed to Herder's theory, and paralleling or following him were Friedrich Schelling, Friedrich Schiller, Karl von Schegel, Georg Hegel, Johann G. Fichte, A. H. L. Heeren, Friedrich Krause, and Barthold Georg Niebuhr. Even though in 1776 Herder's book on historical theory was one of the first of this group to appear, it seemed appropriate to entitle it *Yet Another Philosophy of History*.

Herder began with the assumption that ultimate reality lay not in the physical world but in the spiritual, not in physical atoms but in Leibnitz' monads of energy, not in eighteenth-century universals but in constant change. It seemed to him to follow that one came to understand reality not through a study of philosophy or science, but of history. His argument, which is immensely complex, laid a new base for historical thinking. "Historical writing was old," said Lord Acton, "but historical thinking was new in Germany." [8] Friedrich Meinecke has called Herder's historicism "the greatest spiritual revolution of the Western world." At any rate, it was the most significant change in historical thought since Vico.[9]

Historicism was the belief that anything in the present must be understood primarily in terms of its historical development, the belief that the past makes and is the primary means of understanding the present. Heretofore men had thought of human events stretching endlessly to the horizon behind and ahead, with the present like a narrow band of light that moves over events and reduces everything behind it to history. The historicists, on the other hand, thought of history as a stream, with the present as the furthermost point it had reached. Everything in the past was in flux, flowing into the present to make it what it is. A study of the many sources of the stream and its meanderings is the only way for a society or a man to know

[8] Cited in Friedrich Engel-Janosi, *The Growth of German Historicism* (Baltimore, 1944), p. 13. Also, Georg G. Iggers, *The German Conception of History* (Middleton, Conn., 1968), pp. 29–43.

[9] Cited in Hans Meyerhoff, ed., *The Philosophy of History in Our Time* (New York, 1959), pp. 9–12.

what he really is. Another image for this concept was organic growth; Germans called it organicism. According to this imagery, the historian studied the roots and the development to understand what the organism had finally become.[10]

History was suddenly immensely important. It did not consist simply of events which passed over people, but was something larger than they were, something that controlled and molded them. History rather than philosophy was the means of understanding man. The purpose of history was to understand reality. While Americans did not think of themselves as "historicists," in the early nineteenth century they were coming to feel the importance of their unique historical experience as the force— more than Locke or Jefferson—that made them what they were. By the mid-nineteenth century, historicism dominated scientific thought, notably Darwinism. In the twentieth century, history as a means of understanding man tended to yield to social statistics, probability theory, and psychology.

For the practicing historian, historicism signified emphasis on the primitive origins of institutions and nations, and on tracing their continuous development into the present. Each age created the next. Instead of emphasizing high spots like the classical world and the Renaissance, the historian should seek the beginning of the modern world. The German philosophers were confident that distinctive national traits and institutions developed primarily from the Middle Ages.

Germans of the early nineteenth century, striving for national unity, were especially concerned with the development of the *Volksgeist*. The historian ought to explain how a distinct history had created a distinct people. In searching for the national spirit, the German historians, even more than Voltaire, were concerned with manners, arts, myths, and culture. While Voltaire was simply curious about the essence of a past age, the Germans were desperately searching for themselves. Knowledge of history would create the nation.

[10] Dwight E. Lee and Robert N. Beck, "The Meaning of 'Historicism,'" *American Historical Review*, LIX (April, 1954), 568–77; Hugh Swinton Legare, "Percival's Clio," *Southern Review*, I (May, 1828), 444.

As for method, Herder called upon the historian to immerse himself in the past. The historian could not stand apart and describe a past age; he had to envelop himself in it, empathize with it, become so absorbed in it that he understood it as he understood himself. The historian must do his research objectively, but then he must go beyond research to become, and make his reader become, the man or period about which he writes. The ultimate test of evidence was in his identifying with the subject and feeling the truth of the fact. Love of a subject was more important than objectivity in gaining true understanding. Only a German could write German history.

Herder's doctrine of change as reality emphasized the uniqueness of every event and every individual in history. The past was constantly changing, and it was the changes rather than the similarities that explained a culture or period and made it meaningful. The *Volksgeist* lay in the *Zeitgeist*. The historian should look for the exotic and the unusual, the local and the peculiar. Since the ultimate unit of society was the individual, and since each individual was distinct and capable of altering the course of events, the historian should emphasize biography.

Finally, Herder and the other German Romantics began and ended with the emotion of spirituality. Behind change and behind all of the *Geists* was human feeling, emotion, yearning. Acts were merely expressions of this inmost being. Behind this was God, who instilled yearning in man. God was the central force in history, its continuity, its direction. In the final analysis, feeling was not only the historian's ultimate method but his ultimate subject as well, for history was the mind of God.[11]

Americans knew about the German philosophers and occasionally read them. Schiller's philosophy of history was available in an English edition in 1799. Herder's in 1800, Schlegel's in 1835, with an American edition in 1841, and Fichte's was available in

---

[11] See Tholfsen, *Historical Thinking*, pp. 127–56; Engel-Janosi, *German Historicism*, pp. 13–50; Thompson, *History of Historical Writing*, pp. 96–146; Herbert Butterfield, *Man on His Past* (Cambridge, 1955), pp. 1–61; Stephen Toulmin and June Goodfield, *The Discovery of Time* (New York, 1965), pp. 135–38; Francis C. Haber, *The Age of the World: Moses to Darwin* (Baltimore, 1959), pp. vii-ix, 98–101, 158, and *passim*.

1848. A recent scholar has found almost a hundred articles on German historians and historical philosophy in American magazines published before 1846.[12] New England students who studied in Germany and returned to spread their doctrines in the early years of the century included Joseph Green Cogswell, Frederick Henry Hedge, George Ticknor, and Edward Everett. In 1818, George Bancroft went to Germany to study German historical philosophy. Returning with his Ph.D., he wrote numerous articles on German thought, including an admiring article on Herder.[13]

The Germans were more influential in writing about history than in writing history itself, but theory found outlet in several works that were well known in the United States. Winckelmann's *History of Art in Antiquity,* originally published in 1764, was translated in 1799 and went through two American editions before the Civil War. Schiller's *History of the Rebellion of the Netherlands* appeared in Germany in 1788, in England in 1799, and in the United States in 1861. By far the most popular of all was Niebuhr's description of Roman origins and the Roman soul. His *History of Rome,* originally published in 1811, went through many English editions and at least three American editions by the time of the Civil War. Friedrich Karl von Savigny's *History of the Middle Ages* appeared in 1815 and was translated in 1829.

The French influence on American historical thought was small, partly because it flowered late, after German philosophy and English romantic literature had made their impact, and partly because it was primarily a lyrical history which lost much in translation. Among the best known of French historians was Augustine Thierry, whose colorful and dramatic *History of the Norman Conquest of England* was published in 1825 and promptly translated. Adolphe Thiers produced an eloquent ten-volume *History of the French Revolution,* which began to appear in 1822, and a twenty-volume *History of the Consulate*

---

[12] Scott H. Goodnight, *German Literature in American Magazines Prior to 1846* (Madison, 1907).

[13] Benjamin T. Spencer, *The Quest of Nationality* (Syracuse, 1957), pp. 90–95; Bancroft, "Herder's Writings," *North American Review,* XX (January, 1825), 138–47; Fred L. Burwick, "The Gottingen Influence on George Bancroft's Idea of Humanity," *Jahrbuch für Amerikastudien,* II (1966), 194–212.

and Empire, which began publication in 1843. Jules Michelet's seventeen-volume *History of France,* the first volume of which appeared in 1833, was an especially powerful and emotional evocation of the Middle Ages. François Guizot, burning with moral fervor, produced a *History of the Revolution in England* in 1826 and a six-volume *History of Civilization in Europe* in 1829. Parts of all of these works were published in the United States before the Civil War and were praised then, as now, more for their language than for their contribution to historical thought.[14]

The other great European influence, besides German philosophy, was English literature, especially the historical romances of Sir Walter Scott. Historicism taught philosophers to think historically, but it was the fine storytelling of Scott that succeeded in recreating the past for the public. He was, by a large margin, the best-selling author in the United States until the Civil War. For a while it seemed that people could not get enough of him. "His works are in everybody's hands and his praises in everybody's mouth," said an observer in 1817. His books "meet with a reception more wide, more prompt, more superstitiously fond than could be believed possible, were it not known to be real," said another. His influence was as great as his popularity. A critic in 1835 believed his "influence on the taste of the age probably exceeds any thing that the world has seen for ages, if not has ever seen." [15] A century later a scholar claimed that "With the exception of Gibbon . . . it is doubtful if any one man so influenced English historical writing as Sir Walter Scott." [16]

Scott heightened the effect of fiction with the drama of real events and exotic settings of history; he heightened the effect of history with the high adventure and emotional warmth of fiction. The historical novel was born late in the eighteenth century when Gothic novelists like Horace Walpole utilized the darkness

[14] Thompson, *History of Historical Writing,* pp. 227–79.

[15] Review, *American Monthly Magazine,* I (May, 1817), 123; review, *North American Review,* XVII (October, 1823), 383; anon., "American Literature," *Knickerbocker Magazine,* V (April, 1835), 319.

[16] G. H. Maynadier, "Ivanhoe and Its Literary Consequences," *Essays in Memory of G. Barrett Wendell* (Cambridge, Mass., 1936), p. 221.

of the past to intensify a mood of horror. Scott, however, flooded the past with color and light, and he ran the gamut of emotions, skillfully combining subject, style, and setting to evoke the response he wanted. Scott's scenes, especially of medieval Scotland, left indelible pictures on his readers' minds—scenes of tournaments and castle grandeur, of pastoral simplicity and peasant dialect, of chivalric kings and noble barbarians.

Scott did real research for his novels, publishing thirteen volumes of sixteenth-century Scottish documents as a by-product. His painstaking research was not undertaken for fear of historical error but in order to add the realism that only authentic detail could provide. For the historian he taught the value of reader involvement in the past, the value of the particular and the exotic, the value of local color and precise detail. Henceforth, readers would expect as much from their historians as they obtained from their novelists.

Scott represented a multitude of forces which influenced each other and in turn influenced historical thinking in the United States. As a poet he represented literary Romanticism and its nearly endless characteristics and definitions—lyricism, idealism, emotion, diversity, restlessness, particularism, individualism, introspection, nationalism, supernaturalism, mysticism, love of nature, and the rest—literary tendencies which doubtless had their impact on serious historians. Scott's historical novels had scores of imitators on both sides of the Atlantic. He represented directly the relatively undistinguished serious historical writing that appeared in England and the United States during the half-century after Gibbon. In England this genre included Sharon Turner's *History of the Anglo-Saxons* (1799), Henry Hallam's *Europe during the Middle Ages* (1818), and Scott's own *Life of Napoleon* (1828). His greatest influence, however, may have been on the abler historians who were reading his novels during their adolescence: Thomas Carlyle, best known for his *History of the French Revolution* (1837); Thomas Babington Macaulay, best known for a *History of England,* which began to appear in 1849; and James Anthony Froude, whose twelve-volume *History of England* began to appear in 1856. In the United

States, Washington Irving explained that it had been Scott who made him into a historian. William H. Prescott, George Bancroft, Charles Gayarré, and Francis Parkman all spoke of him as a direct influence. All added moral purpose to Scott's aim of amusement, but all were attempting to make the past alive with the literary techniques learned from the novelist.[17]

The American Tradition

Distinctly American attitudes toward nationalism, God, and time itself provided what was probably the most important source for American historical thinking in the early nineteenth century. At least as early as the Revolution, American historical writing seemed to have a different tone from its European counterpart, perhaps because of these forces, and these differences grew in the nineteenth century.

The most obvious stimulus to American historical thinking was the brightly burning nationalism of the post-Revolutionary period. Nationalism as something distinct from ordinary love of homeland may have been first born in the Puritan sense of a chosen people; it grew with the common grievances leading to independence, and by the 1780's American nationalism was the most intense in the world. Already Americans were coming to think of their history not as the account of an English colony but as the emergence of a new people with a new way of life. Far more than their European counterparts, Americans were thinking in terms of a distinctive national character, the uniqueness of their own experience, and the ways in which the American soul differed from that of other people. Here was not only nationalism but also a particularism that set the stage for a kind of history different from that of Voltaire and Gibbon.[18]

[17] On Scott's influence, see *ibid.*, pp. 221–33; G. Harrison Orians, "The Rise of Romanticism," Harry Hayden Clark, ed., *Transitions in American Literary History* (Durham, N.C., 1953), pp. 199–216; David Levin, *History as Romantic Art: Bancroft, Prescott, Motley, and Parkman* (Stanford, 1959), pp. 9–13, 236; Michael Kraus, *The Writing of American History* (Norman, Okla., 1953), pp. 139, 145.
[18] See Merle Curti, *The Roots of American Loyalty* (New York, 1946), pp. 3–29; Hans Kohn, *American Nationalism* (New York, 1957), pp. 13–48.

Americans attempted to explain the uniqueness of their national character in terms of liberty, democracy, and individualism—values rooted in the American experience and also values that became central to Romantic thinking. The concept of America as a haven from oppression had flourished since Puritan times. Here, said Tom Paine, is "the asylum for the persecuted lovers of civil and religious liberty from every part of Europe." The Declaration of Independence raised liberty to the realm of a self-evident truth. Democracy also was an intuitive truth, something felt in men's souls. "America's purpose," said David Ramsay, "is to prove the virtues of republicanism, to assert the Rights of Man." [19]

The highest expression of liberty and democracy may have been the cult of individualism which was to evolve in the nineteenth century into something close to the essence of Romanticism. American history was a record of individual achievement and worth, and from individual worth it was only a short step into Romantic cults of heroism, chivalry, diversity, originality, imagination, intuition, subjectivism, and supernaturalism. Historian Russel B. Nye has pointed out that American individualism differed from the European in that it was rooted in the past rather than the future, that it was traditional rather than iconoclastic, that it produced Longfellow rather than Byron, and Emerson's *Self-Reliance* rather than Goethe's *Werther*. American historians were able to combine national spirit with the significance of the individual more easily than Europeans. Instead of subordinating biography to national essence, writers like Mason Locke Weems, John Marshall, and Washington Irving set out to find national essence in the biographies of George Washington. To them, the universal lay in the particular. [20]

American nationalism also intensified the eighteenth-century concept of progress. Europeans saw the improvement of science

---

[19] Russel B. Nye, *The Cultural Life of the New Nation, 1776–1830* (New York, 1960), pp. 46–47.

[20] *Ibid.*, pp. 8–9; Yehoshua Ariele, *Individualism and Nationalism in American Ideology* (Baltimore, 1966), p. 87 and *passim*.

and values, but for Americans progress was also the far more physical reality of the seeds at Jamestown and Plymouth developing into a nation, of wilderness changing into civilization, and of a physical frontier stretching limitlessly ahead. Benjamin Franklin, George Washington, James Madison, Benjamin Rush, Philip Freneau, Thomas Jefferson, and John Adams all saw the nation evolving from primitive origins, and took for granted that society, if not human nature, would be brighter in the years ahead. America's first epic poem, Joel Barlow's "Vision of Columbus," which was written in 1787 and rewritten as "The Columbiad" in 1807, was a long celebration of American progress guided by God. The American idea of progress differed from the European both in its sense of origins and in its sense of God. Evolution from tiny seeds implied an organic growth, a view of the universe that had less in common with Newton's mechanical universe than with Darwin's biological one. Such a growth, moreover, was almost too miraculous to be explained by reason alone. Few Americans ever lost the Puritan belief that somehow behind it all was a divine guidance.[21]

In a somewhat different way, as a force rather than an idea, nationalism stimulated historical writing by its cultivation of a distinctly American culture. Beginning as early as 1750, increasingly after the Revolution, and still more after the War of 1812, Americans exhorted each other to create and support an independent literature. "America must be as independent in *literature*," said Noah Webster in 1783, "as she is in *politics*." [22] It was this sense of patriotic duty to American culture, perhaps more than anything else, that led to the remarkable output of history just after the Revolution. Jedidiah Morse, Hannah Adams, Abiel Holmes, John Marshall, David Ramsay, and Benjamin Trumbull all spoke of their patriotic duty to record the nation's history. By 1837, five years after George Bancroft's first volume had appeared, Ralph Waldo Emerson delivered his

---

[21] Nye, *Cultural Life of the New Nation*, pp. 29–33; Ekirch, *Idea of Progress*, p. 29 and *passim*.

[22] Cited in Spencer, *Quest for Nationality*, p. 27.

address on "The American Scholar," boasting of the maturity of American culture and its independence from Europe.[23]

A second force, besides nationalism, that lay deep in the American tradition and profoundly influenced the nineteenth-century view of the past was a sense of God. Americans never fully rejected their Puritan past, never fully embraced Enlightenment skepticism, never entirely broke the line between the Great Awakening that began in 1740 and the Great Revivals which began in 1757.[24] While Voltaire, Hume, and Gibbon vented their emotions against the Church, similar American feelings found outlet in the development of a pious Unitarianism. Among the American historians who began their careers as clergymen, for the most part Unitarian clergymen, were Jedidiah Morse, Abiel Holmes, Alexander Hewat, Jeremy Belknap, Benjamin Trumbull, Mason Locke Weems, John Gorham Palfrey, Jared Sparks, Frank Lister Hawks, George Bancroft, and Richard Hildreth.

Jonathan Edwards more than anyone else was responsible for bringing seventeenth-century Puritanism through the Enlightenment and into nineteenth-century historical thought. Though Edwards never wrote history himself, historian Peter Gay has shown that he may have dealt with the philosophical problems of history more profoundly than any American has ever done. Edwards insisted on the presence of God in history, as both the force behind progress and the essence of the national spirit. He accepted the eighteenth-century search for universals in history, but he insisted on the importance of every detail, the significance of every individual and the uniqueness of every particular event. Above all, Edwards insisted that the study of history had a serious purpose, the glorification of God. Writing history was demonstrating truth and thus was an act of worship.[25] The archetype American Romantic historian, George Bancroft, grounded in both Enlightenment historiography and German Romanticism, insisted that despite all other influences "Edwards' was his

---

[23] Nye, *Cultural Life of the New Nation*, pp. 42–43; Spencer, *Quest for Nationality*, p. 158 and *passim*.

[24] See Oliver Wendell Elsbree, *Rise of the Missionary Spirit in America, 1790–1815* (Williamsport, Pa., 1928).

[25] Peter Gay, *A Loss of Mastery* (Berkeley, 1966), pp. 88–117.

creed." Bancroft hoped that "Each page of history may begin with Great is God and marvellous are his doings among the children of men." [26]

Religion also flowed into nineteenth-century historical thought through the American adoption of Scottish "common sense" philosophy. It was only Platonism updated, an affirmation of the reality of inner ideas. In reaction to the skepticism and empiricism of Locke and Hume, common sense advocates talked of the "self-evident principles" felt by all men. Reason and experience provided knowledge of the external world, but the internal senses—the dictates of the heart—provided knowledge of God, of beauty, and of good and evil. By 1800 most American universities were teaching this metaphysics through the Scottish philosophy textbooks by Thomas Reid, Dugald Stewart, Sir James Beattie, and Lord Kames. American spokesmen included John Witherspoon at Princeton, Timothy Dwight at Yale, and David Tappan at Harvard. Common sense philosophy laid the basis for American acceptance of German Romantic thought and for Transcendentalism; more immediately, it gave historians a sense of the reality of God and the importance of moral standards in history—values often more important than the facts themselves.[27]

Along with a powerful sense of nationalism and religion, nineteenth-century Americans possessed a distinct concept of time which may have worked to strengthen the consciousness of history and to sharpen its aim. Daniel Boorstin has explained that while the European condemned past time for creating present muddles, the American felt freed from the errors of history and consequently glorified his ancestors, remolded them in his own image, and celebrated a simple happy past. Another brilliant scholar, Fred Somkin, has suggested that a sense of historical unprecedentedness was the source of American nationalism.

[26] Russel B. Nye, *George Bancroft: Brahmin Rebel* (New York, 1945), p. 28; Bancroft to wife, 31 December 1847, Mark A. DeW. Howe, *The Life and Letters of George Bancroft* (2 vols.; New York, 1908), II, 77.

[27] Herbert W. Schneider, *A History of American Philosophy* (New York, 1963), pp. 216–20; Nye, *Cultural Life of the New Nation,* pp. 33–36; Leon Howard, "The Late Eighteenth Century," Clark, ed., *American Literary History,* pp. 51–70.

Americans assumed that the nation was not created by the past but was a unique entity, chiefly one yet to be realized; the nation was still becoming what she was. Somkin suggests that, ironically, this sense of unprecedentedness resulted in an American fascination with the past. Partly, this was an eagerness to survey all history in order to expropriate as models anything they wished. Even more, the attention to their own past was an effort to identify traits which they believed characterized themselves in the present and for the future. Still another scholar, studying nineteenth-century political rhetoric, has suggested that men of both sides in every dispute—tariff, improvements, expansion, slavery, secession—argued in terms of retaining the faith of the founding fathers or of renewing that faith. Nineteenth-century conservatism and liberalism, he seems to say, had less to do with privilege and democracy than with nostalgia for the past and hope for the future.[28]

Recent analyses of the American preoccupation with time reached a peak in the work of the literary critic R. W. B. Lewis, who has shown that one of the most pervasive themes in American literature after the Revolution was the theme of Adam in the Garden, of America standing innocent in the New World, unsullied by the past, beginning anew. Adam is the American hero—Natty Bumppo, Billy Budd, the Yankee of *Leaves of Grass,* Huck Finn, Daisy Miller, and Holden Caulfield. The American response to this freedom from the past, suggests Lewis, created a basic division in American thought. On one hand, the absence of a long history created what Emerson first called "The Party of Memory," which glorified Eden, waxed nostalgic about the passage of time, and yearned to retain the present into the future. On the other hand, the absence of a past created a "Party of

[28] Daniel Boorstin, *The Genius of American Politics* (Chicago, 1958), pp. 10–22 and *passim;* Fred Somkin, *Unquiet Eagle: Memory and Desire in the Idea of American Freedom, 1815–1860* (Ithaca, 1967), pp. 55–90 and *passim;* Major L. Wilson, "The Concept of Time and the Political Dialogue in the United States, 1828–1848," *American Quarterly,* XIX (Winter, 1967), 619–44; also William R. Taylor, *Cavalier and Yankee* (New York, 1961), pp. 240–78; Georges Poulet, *Studies in Human Time,* Elliott Coleman, trans. (Baltimore, 1956), pp. 323–41.

Hope"—the belief that time constantly renewed and improved all that went before.[29]

In Lewis' scheme, the Party of Memory was represented in historical writing by Prescott, Motley, and, generally, Parkman. Because they felt totally freed from the distant past, they were able to study it with detachment and sympathy. History may flourish most when men are not overwhelmed by it. Men like Prescott could recreate the past, revel in it, and use it legitimately as a vehicle for their own enthusiasms—Prescott his love of heroic adventure, Parkman his love of nature and struggle.

The Party of Hope, meanwhile, represented by Bancroft and generally by Hildreth, turned to history to interpret an experience characterized by incessant change. Eagerly, they seized upon the idea of progress, the idea that the present constantly renewed the past. American liberty, for example, was renewed at Plymouth, in the overthrow of Edmund Andros, in the Revolution, in the election of Andrew Jackson. "Everything is in motion, and for the better," said Bancroft, "The last system of philosophy is always the best." Men could simultaneously have history and be free from it. They stood at the furthermost point in time, able to move in any direction into the future; yet the past was a record of what men really were, a record of the purpose behind change, an explanation of the purpose of America. Bancroft maintained that the purpose of America was liberty, and he more than anyone else made Americans conscious of their history as the constant reassertion of liberty. This awareness, more than philosophical theory, shaped their concept of time, of history, and of themselves. Such awareness was close to what the Germans arrived at philosophically as historicism.[30]

The New History

There was, of course, no clear break between eighteenth- and nineteenth-century historical writing. No one can accurately

---

[29] R. W. B. Lewis, *The American Adam: Innocence, Tragedy and Tradition in the Nineteenth Century* (Chicago, 1955), p. 2 and *passim*.

[30] *Ibid.*, pp. 159–73.

identify a work as "Enlightenment" or "Romantic." As the scholar Arthur O. Lovejoy has shown, there is no archetype "romanticism"; the definition of the word exists primarily in the mind of each critic. In fact, it refers to little more than a period, generally from 1800 to 1860 in the United States, along with whatever generalizations can be established about ideas and culture during that period.[31]

In both Europe and the United States, new attitudes toward history developed at about the turn of the century, well before the appearance of historians who fully exemplified them. After Robertson and Gibbon in the 1780's, there came a pause in great historical writing, except perhaps in Germany, until the flowering of French, English, and American literary historians in the 1820's and 1830's. Critics found the old writers increasingly out of date. "Hume, Robertson and Gibbon are no longer acceptable," said a critic in 1815: "It is time," said another, "that we have a more worthy school." [32] During the transitional period chroniclers continued to pour forth material—in the United States as actively as anywhere. Slowly, perhaps, the chroniclers were accepting the new German philosophy and English literary techniques. For reviewers, meanwhile, nothing quite measured up to their standards.

Despite the patriotic impulse to praise things American, reviewers impatient for the American Gibbon were cool toward their own post-Revolutionary historians. Almost everything seemed too biased, too local, too lacking in coherence and style. By eighteenth-century standards these historians did not deal with universals, and by nineteenth-century standards they were dull. Almost automatically, critics condemned the works by loyalist or English historians—Thomas Hutchinson, Alexander Hewat, Robert Proud, George Chalmers, and William Gordon.[33]

---

[31] Arthur O. Lovejoy, "The Meaning of Romanticism for the Historian of Ideas," *Journal of the History of Ideas*, II (June, 1941), 257–78.

[32] Reviews, *Analectic Magazine*, VI (August, 1815), 92; *Monthly Anthology*, II (October, 1805), 538–41; also, *American Review*, I (January, 1810), 1–16.

[33] Thomas Hutchinson, *The History of the Colony and Province of Massachusetts Bay* (3 vols.; London, 1764–1828); Alexander Hewat, *An Historical Account . . . of South Carolina and Georgia* (London, 1779); Robert Proud,

Other works, often studies later judged to be outstanding, seemed too local and provincial. This especially applied to the state histories of David Ramsay, Jeremy Belknap, Benjamin Trumbull, and John Daly Burk.[34] Hannah Adams' *A Summary History of New England* (1799) seemed hopelessly dry, and Mercy Otis Warren's *History of the American Revolution* (1805) antagonized both Federalists and southerners. Critics were especially disappointed by John Marshall's much-publicized history of the country written around a five-volume *Life of George Washington* (1805–07). It angered Jeffersonians and bored Federalists. "A mausoleum," said John Adams. Abiel Holmes's two-volume *American Annals* (1805) was equally dull. Critics despaired of their historians. "The most of them are respectable writers," said a reviewer dejectedly, "but America has not yet produced historians who can vie with the first class." [35]

Actually, such an output for the young nation was impressive in quantity, and if it had been accepted as its authors intended —as simply the gathering of materials for some future historian —then the production was respectable in quality as well. The great eagerness to write history, like the dissatisfaction with the result, was part of the transition in historical thinking. After

The History of Pennsylvania (2 vols.; Philadelphia, 1797); George Chalmers, *Political Annals of the Present United Colonies* . . . (London, 1780); William Gordon, *The History of the Rise, Progress, and Establishment of the Independence of the United States of America* . . . (3 vols.; London, 1788).

[34] David Ramsay, *The History of the Revolution of South Carolina* . . . (2 vols.; Trenton, N.J., 1785); Jeremy Belknap, *History of New Hampshire* (3 vols.; Philadelphia, 1784–92); Benjamin Trumbull, *A Complete History of Connecticut . . . to the Year 1764* (New Haven, 1797); John Daly Burk, *The History of Virginia* . . . (3 vols.; Petersburg, 1804–5).

[35] Samuel Miller, *A Brief Retrospect of the Eighteenth Century* (2 vols.; New York, 1803), II, 140, 397. For typical reviews of these works as unimportant and old-fashioned, see *Portfolio,* I (May, 1816), 369–74; *Portfolio,* IV (November, 1807), 331; *Monthly Anthology,* VIII (March, 1810), 206; *Monthly Anthology,* V (May, 1808), 262; *Monthly Anthology,* V (August, 1808), 441; *Monthly Anthology,* IV (February, 1807), 98–101; *American Review,* I (September, 1799), 445; *Boston Review,* IV (December, 1807), 663; *American Review,* II (October, 1802), 406; *American Review,* I (January, 1801), 1–16; *North American Review,* XXVI (January, 1828), 39; *The Columbian,* I (February, 1800), 105; *Gazette of the United States,* I (December, 1789), 176; *American Museum,* II (February, 1792), 43–6.

Bancroft and Prescott in the 1830's, the compilers could be accepted on their own terms, and they were widely acclaimed. "We misjudged," said a critic in 1832 reviewing a reprint of Jeremy Belknap. Americans have learned to "revere" their early compilers, he noted. "This however is a late love."[36]

While critics abused most turn of the century historians for being old-fashioned, they were puzzled and angered by other historians who were radically different. This was especially true of Mason Locke Weems's *Life of Washington*. First appearing in 1800, it combined a multitude of literary forms in unprecedented manner—history, biography, epic, lyric, sermon—and was immediately a best seller. One reviewer called it an outrage, "unique in the annals of literature." Another, torn between outrage and delight, called it "as entertaining and edifying matter as can be found in the annals of fanaticism and absurdity."[37] Perhaps it was the first "Romantic" history published in the United States. Jedidiah Morse bothered reviewers almost as much. His *American Geography* (1789) and *History of New England* (1805) were infused with a style and moral purposefulness that evoked wildly varying and passionate reviews. Other books that puzzled reviewers and delighted the public were Washington Irving's Knickerbocker *History of New York* (1809), Henry Trumbull's *History of the Discovery of America* (1810), and William Wirt's *Life of Patrick Henry* (1817).[38] Critics felt these books were either very bad or very good; they knew that they were different.

By the 1830's Americans were fully aware that a new era of historical writing had come. Whatever had been lacking in the idea of history was now emerging in towering new works. Washington

---

[36] Reviews, *American Monthly Review*, I (June, 1832), 437; also, *New England Magazine*, I (August, 1831), 170; *North American Review*, XXIX (October, 1829), 429; *North American Review*, XXXVIII (January, 1834), 134–58.

[37] Reviews, *Monthly Anthology*, IX (December, 1810), 414–19; *Monthly Magazine*, III (September, 1800), 210–11; also *Panoplist*, V (April, 1810), 525. See Mason Locke Weems, *The Life of Washington*, ed. Marcus Cunliffe (Cambridge, Mass., 1962), pp. xxiv–liii.

[38] For example, reviews in *American Review*, II (October, 1802), 457–61; *Portfolio*, VIII (November, 1812), 440–53; *Monthly Anthology*, II (October, 1805), 541–44; *Monthly Anthology*, VIII (February, 1810), 123–28.

Irving's *The Life and Voyages of Christopher Columbus* (1828) and *A Chronicle of the Conquest of Granada* (1829) were received with almost unanimous acclaim. "This country seems to be fairly arrived at a new era," exulted a reviewer. When Bancroft's first volume appeared in 1834 critics were beside themselves with delight: "He is the instrument of Providence"; "He is worthy of his country and his age"; "At length we Americans are to have a history"; "We have come of age!" [39] Within three years came Jared Sparks's twelve-volume *Life and Writings of Washington,* Peter Force's four volumes of settlers' memoirs, William H. Prescott's three-volume *Ferdinand and Isabella,* and Timothy Flint's *Daniel Boone.* The great Romantic works from abroad were pouring in—the histories of Thierry, Thiers, Guizot, Macaulay, and Carlyle. Not far behind was an almost endless list of American writers—Gayarré, Headley, Hildreth, Howe, Hawks, Motley, Paulding, Parkman, Randall, Sabine, Shurtleff, Ticknor, Tucker, and many more. Theirs was a new approach to the past. With unusual clarity they were able to explain exactly what they were doing and their reasons for doing it.

[39] Reviews in *Southern Review,* II (August, 1828), 1; *Christian Examiner,* XVI (November, 1834), 281; *North American Review,* XL (January, 1835), 101; *American Quarterly Review,* XVI (September, 1834), 212; *DeBow's Review,* XV (August, 1853), 163.

II

The People Discover the Past

THE new idea of history in the United States began with the supposition that the past was immensely important. Never before or since has history occupied such a vital place in the thinking of the American people as during the first half of the nineteenth century. Architecture, painting, theater, fiction, poetry, and oratory were filled with historical themes. About one-third of the best-selling books were historical, double the proportion it has ever been since. Popular magazines ran huge quantities of material on history and popular historical journals flourished. At least seventy-two historical societies were active on the eve of the Civil War, when there were only fifty-five towns in the country with a population over 15,000. Americans first became conscious of family heritage and began to cultivate genealogical trees. National and state governments established archives, supported historical restorations, and subsidized historical publications in unprecedented fashion; history first emerged as a prominent discipline in the schools; and at no other time has the historian's place been so eminent among men of letters.

The American people were fully aware of the unusual popularity of the past and gloried in it as a sign of cultural maturity. Observers marveled that "no department of literature amongst us is cultivated with more assiduity than history"; "there never has

been a period in which Antiquities were so intensively and actively cultivated"; "historical Studies receive more attention than
ever before." [1] Critics labeled the new interest "immense," "vast,"
"unbelievable." [2] Regardless of whether history books are good or
bad, they "have to be purchased by the fifties or hundreds by our
circulating libraries"; "still they come, and they will continue to
come, a swelling host." [3] Sometimes observers were critical, especially if they happened to be advocating some other form of expression. One was "struck with the seeming disproportion between
historical treatises and any other branch of knowledge." Others
believed "the intensity of our historic strain is disproportionate";
"we have come so entirely to depend on it for general amusement,
that . . . conversation as an art has about ceased to exist." [4]

Art and Literature

Of all the arts, architecture from the 1790's until well after the
Civil War was most completely dominated by the past. Thomas
Jefferson led the way, both as critic and as practicing architect,
demanding a cultural declaration of independence, repudiation of
colonial Georgian styles, and the creation of buildings expressing

[1] Reviews, *American Monthly Review*, I (June, 1832), 437; *American Re-
view and Literary Journal*, I (January, 1801), 1; Samuel Miller, *A Brief
Retrospect of the Eighteenth Century* (2 vols.; New York, 1803), I, 148; *Pro-
ceedings of the Antiquarian and Historical Society of Illinois . . . 1827*
(Edwardsville, 1828), p. 8; also anon., "Historic Speculations," *Southern
Literary Messenger*, VI (September, 1840), 606; anon., "Historical Studies,"
Church Review, IV (April, 1851), 9.

[2] *Transactions of the Historical and Literary Committee of the American
Philosophical Society*, I (1819), xvi; reviews, *Southern Quarterly Review*, V
(April 1844), 266; *North American Review*, XV (October, 1822), 319; also
Jared Sparks, "History," *American Museum of Science, Literature and Art*,
II (March, 1839), 123; anon., "History," *New York Mirror*, II (October 23,
1824), 123; anon., "Education," *Portfolio*, I (June, 1813), 567; review, *DeBow's
Review*, XV (August, 1853), 163.

[3] Anon., "The Art of History Writing," *Littell's Living Age*, XLVIII (January, 1856), 243; reviews, *Christian Examiner*, LX (March, 1856), 248; also
Atlantic, VII (April, 1859), 442.

[4] Anon., "The Philosophy of History," *North American Review*, XXXIX
(July, 1834), 31; reviews, *Atlantic*, VII (April, 1859), 442; *Westminster Review*,
LXII (July, 1854), 140; anon., "Impostures of History," *Portfolio*, I (May,
1816), 369.

republican virtues in symbols of the classical past. To Jefferson and his successors for over half a century, buildings were designed not so much to be beautiful as to represent the values which the nation wished to express. Architects sought to call to mind the grandeur and civic virtue of Rome, the purity and liberty of Greece, and the faith and charity of the Middle Ages. In terms which R. W. B. Lewis applied to literature, the nation beginning in the New World was freed from the past, and consequently was able to recreate it at will.[5]

The first purely Roman temple in America was Jefferson's own design for the state capitol building in Richmond, completed in 1789; it was a firm statement of political creed, anti-English, expressing a return to the purity of the original classic virtues. Jefferson spoke explicitly of the analogy between the classic grandeur of the Roman republic and the bright future of his own. For the next thirty years, in a period of feverish government building, Roman revival architecture became almost as official as the adopted Roman eagle. In 1792 William Thornton won the competition for the national capitol building with a Roman design, and in 1809 Benjamin Latrobe in Baltimore completed the nation's first cathedral on the model of the Roman Pantheon. Americans saw the Roman revival as a revolt against the artificiality of England, a statement of grandeur and heroism and liberty reborn in the wilderness, of stability and confidence and patriotism. Federalist New England, consciously resisting the Jeffersonian tide, modified the Roman expression into a "Federal" style, but the inspiration and symbolism were the same. Alongside old towns like Jerusalem, Bethlehem, Salem, and New Zion appeared new place names like Rome, Carthage, Pompeii, and Syracuse.

From the 1820's to the 1840's the Greek revival dominated American architecture. As the Roman became tiresome, and as its association with the Jeffersonian and the Napoleonic grew too close, men were deciding that Greece rather than Rome was the

[5] Talbot Hamlin, *Greek Revival Architecture in America* (New York, 1944), pp. 3–19; Alan Gowans, *Images of American Living* (Philadelphia, 1964), pp. 243–328.

source of classical virtue. Towns like Athens, Sparta, Corinth, and Troy appeared. The Greek revival probably produced the greatest flowering of American architectural talent until the twentieth century. Benjamin Latrobe led the transition from Roman to Greek and did his best work in it, notably the Bank of Philadelphia (1818). Other Greek revivalists were Robert Mills, noted for his Treasury Building, Patent Building, and Washington Monument, all begun in the capital in the 1830's. William Strickland began the Tennessee State Capitol in 1845, Thomas U. Walker began Girard College in 1850, authors like Asher Benjamin and Minard Lefever produced carpenters' handbooks that spread Greek motifs to almost every workbench in the country, and a thousand southern planters added columns and porticos to make farmhouses into mansions. The symbolism was different, North and South. To the Yankee the Greek temple meant individual freedom, civic enterprise, and the nobility of the common man; to the southerner it meant aristocracy, conservatism, stability, and reason. In the difference lay problems, both for art and for politics.[6]

During the 1840's and 1850's Greek styling gave way to a Gothic revival and also to a broad eclecticism. Still, architecture was symbolic, a kind of literary reference to a mood or set of values from the past. Typical of the best Gothic was James Renwick's Smithsonian Institution, built in Washington in 1846, and his St. Patrick's Cathedral, built in New York in 1850. In a period of great church building, Gothic became a semiofficial church style. Romantic landscape architects claimed to be inspired by the Gothic when they called for natural rather than formal gardens, the use of curves, irregular lines, natural colors, wistaria, and trumpet vines. Eclectic architects boasted of their ability to match the function of each particular building to specific ideals from the past, and to combine the best ideals from different periods. One advertized his specialities: "English Cottage, Collegiate Gothic, Manor House, French Suburban, Swiz Chalet, Swiz Mansion, Lombard Italian, Tuscan from Pliny's

[6] Oliver W. Larkin, *Art and Life in America* (New York, 1960), pp. 77–99; Hamlin, *Greek Revival Architecture, passim.*

Villa at Ostia, Ancient Etruscan, Suburban Greek, Oriental, Moorish, Round, Castellated . . . ." [7]

The historic theme was almost as prominent in painting and sculpture as in architecture. In England a "Historical School" was established in the 1770's by two Americans, Benjamin West, especially famous for his *Death of Wolfe* (1771), and John Singleton Copley. By the turn of the century historical themes were dominating painting at home. Artists in revolt against banal portraiture turned to the past for drama and heroism. John Trumbull delighted his countrymen with scenes from the Revolution, and in 1817 he received $24,000 from Congress to adapt four of his scenes to murals for the national Capitol. Among the most famous pictures of the historical school were Washington Allston's *Belshazzar's Feast* (1818), John Vanderlyn's *Marius Musing Among the Ruins of Carthage* (1807) and *Landing of Columbus* (1837), and Samuel F. B. Morse's *Dying Hercules* (1813). By the 1820's landscapes and family scenes became common subjects, but history continued to be a major inspiration. Emanuel Leutze's *Washington Crossing the Delaware* (1850) may be the most frequently reproduced picture of the period. Other painters of the mid-century who used historical themes include Rembrandt Peale, Thomas Cole, George Catlin, Robert Walker Weir, William Dunlap, William Henry Powell, Daniel Huntington, and Caleb Bingham. [8]

In sculpture, the five works that may be the most famous of the period were all historical: Hiram Power's *Greek Slave* (1832), Horatio Greenough's *George Washington,* dressed like a Roman senator (1839), Clark Mills's *Andrew Jackson* (1853), Thomas Crawford's *Past and Present of America* (1856), and William Rimmer's *Falling Gladiator* (1860). [9]

[7] Cited in Gowans, *Images of American Living*, p. 303.

[8] Larkin, *Art and Life in America*, pp. 127–34, 189–209; Virgil Barker, *American Painting* (New York, 1950), pp. 323–28, 463–77; Lloyd Goodrich, "The Painting of American History, 1775–1900," *American Quarterly*, III (Summer, 1951), 283–94.

[9] Larkin, *Art and Life in America*, pp. 99–107, 177–87; Albert T. Gardner, *Yankee Stonecutters, The First American School of Sculpture, 1800–1850* (New York, 1945).

In literature, as perhaps in painting, history was primarily a device to gain public interest. It was more common in popular than in serious literature, and it was more often a setting than a subject of immediate concern. Authors knew that settings from the past excited their audiences, and they learned to use the particular moods which the past evoked, like the architects, to symbolize and heighten their own expressions.

The historic theme entered American fiction through the Gothic novel, in which authors used exotic settings from the past, or ancient ruins, to heighten a mood of horror or suspense. Charles Brockden Brown, perhaps the first professional writer and the first true novelist in the United States, used the technique in his novels *Arthur Mervyn* and *Edgar Hundley,* both published in 1799. The Gothic tradition continued in the novels of Hugh Henry Breckenridge, John Neal, and Richard Henry Dana, and in such works of Edgar Allan Poe as "The Fall of the House of Usher." Nathaniel Hawthorne, though too important to be limited by any single tradition, carried on the Gothic mood in *The Scarlet Letter* (1850) and *The House of the Seven Gables* (1851).

The historic theme was especially important in the enormous number of historical romances that stemmed directly from Sir Walter Scott. Reading about the past made readers forget themselves and brought wonder into their lives. James Fenimore Cooper introduced the genre in American writing in 1818 with his novel *The Spy.* Set during the Revolution, it was a rousing adventure story which made the most of local legends and dialects, picturesque scenes, and dramatic action. Historical romances flooded the market. Important writers like Washington Irving, James Kirke Paulding, William Gilmore Simms, and John Pendleton Kennedy adopted it as a vehicle, and the number of lesser imitators reached into the hundreds. Although the historical romance was beginning to run dry by 1860, it accounted for one of the richest, and certainly one of the largest, themes in American literature.

Closely related to the historical romance was the theme of the Indian in American history, savage, heroic, free, and doomed.

Novelists and poets like Joel Barlow and Henry Whiting launched the subject. Cooper combined it with his historical romances in the Leatherstocking tales, notably in *The Last of the Mohicans* (1826), and Paulding and Simms followed. The movement reached its peak in Henry Wadsworth Longfellow's poems of the 1850's, "Evangeline," "Hiawatha," and "The Courtship of Miles Standish." "Hiawatha" is often called trite by critics, but it was probably the most popular poem ever written in the United States. Scores of literary imitators followed, reveling in the bittersweet theme of lost Indian glory. Serious historians like Benjamin Drake and Francis Parkman were among those so inspired.[10]

History was even more prominent in the theater than in fiction and poetry. To begin with, Shakespeare was easily the most popular dramatist on the American stage, and most of his plays had become historical in setting; this, in fact, may have been an important reason for their revival in the early nineteenth century. Beginning with William Dunlap in the 1790's, Gothic melodramas abounded. During the 1820's dramatists like John Howard Payne and Robert Montgomery Bird adapted the historical romance to the stage, including many adaptations of Scott's novels, as well as biblical and classical settings. Soon, the most common historical setting was America, however. One scholar has found some 150 plays performed from 1825 to 1860 with an American historical background. The favorite theme was the Indian, especially the Pocahontas story, but many plays were based on Columbus, Plymouth, the Revolution, the Daniel Boone legend, and the Barbary wars.[11]

The most impressive evidence of the place of history in popular thought is statistical: of the 248 best-selling books in the United States from 1800 to 1860, ninety of them, or 36 per cent,

[10] Harry Hayden Clark, ed., *Transitions in American Literary History* (Durham, N.C., 1953), pp. 80–244; Robert E. Spiller *et al.*, eds., *Literary History of the United States: History* (2 vols.; New York, 1963), I, 242–636.

[11] Arthur H. Quinn, *History of the American Drama from the Beginning to the Civil War* (New York, 1923), especially pp. 269–91; Richard Moody, *America Takes the Stage* (Bloomington, Ind., 1955), especially pp. 26–30, 79–87.

dealt with history. By comparison, about 15 per cent of the most popular books before 1800 were historical, and about 15 per cent have been historical since 1860.[12]

12 The following list is taken from Frank Luther Mott, *Golden Multitudes: The Story of the Best Seller in the United States* (New York, 1947), pp. 305–25. An *asterisk* indicates nonfiction:

1800, *M. L. Weems, *Life of Washington;* 1804, Jane Porter, *Thaddeus of Warsaw;* 1807, *[Paul Jones], *Life and Adventures;* 1809, *[Washington Irving], *History of New York.*

1810, Jane Porter, *Scottish Chiefs;* *Henry Trumbull, *Discovery of America;* *Peter Horry and M. L. Weems, *Francis Marion;* 1811, *William Robertson, *History of Scotland;* Isaac Mitchell, *Alonzo and Melissa;* 1815, Walter Scott, *Guy Mannering;* Walter Scott, *Waverly;* 1817, Archibald Robbins, *Loss of Brig Commerce;* *William Wirt, *Patrick Henry;* 1818, Walter Scott, *Heart of Midlothian;* Walter Scott, *Rob Roy.*

1820, Walter Scott, *Ivanhoe;* Walter Scott, *The Monastery;* Walter Scott, *The Abbot;* 1821, J. F. Cooper, *The Spy;* Walter Scott, *Kenilworth;* 1822, J. F. Cooper, *The Pilot;* Walter Scott, *The Pirate;* Washington Irving, *Bracebridge Hall;* 1823, Walter Scott, *Peverill of the Peak;* J. F. Cooper, *The Pioneers;* 1824, *James E. Seaver, *Mrs. Mary Jemison;* Washington Irving, *Tales of a Traveller;* Walter Scott, *Redgauntlet;* J. F. Cooper, *Lionel Lincoln;* 1825, Walter Scott, *The Talisman;* 1826, J. F. Cooper, *Last of the Mohicans;* 1827, J. F. Cooper, *The Prairie;* Catherine Sedgwick, *Hope Leslie;* 1828, George Croly, *Salathiel;* 1829, *Washington Irving, *Chronicle of the Conquest of Granada.*

1830, *G. P. R. James, *Richelieu;* 1831, J. K. Paulding, *The Dutchman's Fireside;* 1832, Edward Bulwer-Lytton, *Eugene Aram,* *Benjamin Thatcher, *Indian Biography;* 1833, *G. P. R. James, *Mary of Burgundy;* *Timothy Flint, *Daniel Boone;* 1834, Edward Bulwer-Lytton, *Last Days of Pompeii;* Victor Hugo, *Hunchback of Notre Dame;* *George Bancroft, *History of the United States;* 1835, Edward Bulwer-Lytton, *Rienzi;* *David Crockett, *Martin Van Buren;* W. G. Simms, *Yemassee;* 1836, J. H. Ingraham, *LaFitte;* Richard Hildreth, *The Slave;* 1837, R. M. Bird, *Nick of the Woods;* *W. H. Prescott, *Ferdinand and Isabella;* Samuel Lover, *Rory O'More;* Nathaniel Hawthorne, *Twice-Told Tales;* William Ware, *Zenobia;* 1838, *Benjamin Drake, *Life of Black Hawk;* 1839, *Jared Sparks, *Life of Washington;* *D. P. Thompson, *Green Mountain Boys.*

1840, J. F. Cooper, *The Pathfinder;* Charles E. Hoffman, *Greyslayer;* G. P. R. James, *King's Highway;* 1841, J. F. Cooper, *Deerslayer;* Charles Dickens, *Barnaby Rudge;* W. H. Ainsworth, *Old St. Paul's;* 1842, Edward Bulwer-Lytton, *Zanoni;* 1843, *W. H. Prescott, *Conquest of Mexico;* Edward Bulwer-Lytton, *Last of the Barons;* 1844, Alexandre Dumas, *Three Musketeers;* *W. G. Simms, *Francis Marion;* 1845, Eugene Sue, *Wandering Jew;* 1846, *J. T. Headley, *Napoleon and His Marshalls;* 1846, Nathaniel Hawthorne, *Mosses from an Old Manse;* 1847, *William H. Prescott, *Conquest of Peru;* *H. Montgomery, *Zachary Taylor;* 1848, Edward Bulwer-Lytton, *Harold;* 1849,

HISTORICAL BEST SELLERS

Period	Nonfiction	Fiction	Total	Best Sellers Percentage
1750–1789	2	4	48	12
1790–1799	4	6	32	31
1800–1809	3	1	12	33
1810–1819	4	6	15	66
1820–1829	2	18	24	88
1830–1839	10	12	55	40
1840–1849	6	13	67	28
1850–1859	6	11	73	24
1860–1899	7	32	256	15

Although such figures are too small to be conclusive for any one decade, the over-all trend is striking: historical interest emerged rapidly in the 1790's to reach a peak in the 1820's when three out of every four of the most popular books were historical. After that, when historical societies, history in the schools, and the best historical writing were just appearing, the popular interest in the past began to decline. Public interest was ahead of educators and scholars both in acclaiming the past and in tiring of it.

The historical romance, of course, easily led the list of most popular books. Scott alone had eleven historical best sellers, Cooper wrote eight, and Irving five. Other novelists with at least two titles were Edward Bulwer-Lytton, G. P. R. James, William Gilmore Simms, Jane Porter, Alexandre Dumas, and Victor

---

*T. B. Macaulay, *History of England;* Alexandre Dumas, *Man in the Iron Mask.*

1850, Giovanni Boccaccio, *The Decameron;* Nathaniel Hawthorne, *The Scarlet Letter;* 1852, W. M. Thackeray, *Henry Esmond;* 1853, *E. S. Creasy, *Fifteen Decisive Battles of the World;* Charles Kingsley, *Hypatia;* *J. G. Baldwin, *Flush Times in Alabama and Mississippi;* 1854, G. P. R. James, *Ticonderoga;* *Charles Dickens, *Child's History of England;* *Thomas Bulfinch, *Age of Fable;* 1855, Charles Reade, *Cloister and the Hearth;* A. S. Stephens, *The Old Homestead;* *Washington Irving, *Life of Washington;* J. H. Ingraham, *Prince of the House of David;* Charles Kingsley, *Westward-Ho!;* 1857, *J. T. Headley, *Washington and His Generals;* 1859, Charles Dickens, *Tale of Two Cities;* W. M. Thackeray, *The Virginians.*

Hugo. Some books on the list, often by historical novelists, barely crossed the line into nonfiction. These included some of the works of Mason Locke Weems, Washington Irving, Edward Bulwer-Lytton, and Daniel Thompson. More surprising than the popularity of historical fiction, however, was that of serious history. The most popular books included three multi-volume works by William H. Prescott, the long sets by George Bancroft and Jared Sparks, and works by William Robertson, William Wirt, Joel T. Headley, Thomas Bulfinch, and Thomas Babington Macaulay.

The content of popular magazines confirmed the appeal of history on best-seller lists. In a sampling of seven magazines of the period, selected for their prominence and breadth of coverage, an average of approximately 30 per cent of their space was devoted to historical events. The *North American Review* averaged 35 per cent; the *Christian Examiner,* 30 per cent; *Portfolio,* 27 per cent; the *New York Mirror,* 14 per cent; *Eclectic Magazine,* 40 per cent; *Harper's Magazine,* 25 per cent; and the *Atlantic Monthly,* 32 per cent. The popular magazines emphasized historical fiction and curious incidents from the past, while more serious journals concentrated on essay reviews and reprints of historical documents. There appeared to be a slight increase in the quantity of history in popular magazines until the 1840's, and a slight decline thereafter.[13]

Publishers discovered that the very word "history" helped to sell books. Novelists used such titles as *The History of Henry Esmond, Esq.,* and *The History of Margaret Catchpole,* though neither were truly historical novels. Word-conscious artists like Prescott, Parkman, and Irving contrived to use the word in ways that now seem redundant: *The History of the Conquest of Mexico, The History of the Conspiracy of Pontiac,* and *The History of the Life and Voyages of Christopher Columbus.* Publishers

---

[13] This sampling is from every fifth year of the *North American Review,* 1815–60; every tenth of the 70 volumes of *Christian Examiner,* 1824–61; every fifth year of *Portfolio,* 1810–25; every tenth of the 50 volumes of *Eclectic,* 1844–60; every fifth volume of the *New York Mirror,* 1823–42; volumes I and X of *Harper's* (1850, 1855); and volume I of *Atlantic* (1858). In this sampling, no material is counted as "historical" unless it is ten years past; memoirs, literary biography, and chiefly religious material are excluded.

chose the word for current events periodicals: the *American Review of History and Politics* (1811–12) and the *Historical Register of the United States* (1812–14), neither of which were in any way historical journals. Editors made up historical double-crostics games for their readers, and publishers commonly recommended history books "as holiday gifts." [14] History was fun.

Historical Societies

For people who wanted to indulge their taste for the past more fully than in casual reading, the local historical society provided one of the most active cultural endeavors in ante-bellum America. These societies were not for professionals, of course, for there were none, but for ordinary men who took history seriously. For most society members, no doubt, a general desire for intellectual companionship plus a general interest in the past preceded any more definite purpose. Here men gathered to talk about the past, to collect historical documents, and, eventually, to stimulate historical writing. Here, more than in the colleges, was the origin of historical association and professionalism.

The first historical society in America, and the most prominent one for almost a century, was the Massachusetts Historical Society, organized in 1791 by Jeremy Belknap, the Boston minister who was writing the history of New Hampshire in his spare time. Around Belknap gravitated like-minded people, gentlemen-scholars, book collectors, and antiquarians. The association fulfilled a need for both companionship and service, and it flourished far beyond original expectations. In 1794 the state recognized the services of these men by granting them a charter, and the town of Boston provided rooms in a new city building.[15] The Connecticut Historical Society arose in a similar way in 1799, and one appeared in New York in 1804. Soon it was a movement; at least 111 historical societies had been organized by 1860, of which at

[14] For example, anon., "Moot Points in History," *Portfolio*, XX (September, 1825), 257; review, *North American Review*, LXXXI (July, 1855), 26.

[15] Leslie W. Dunlap, *American Historical Societies, 1790–1860* (Madison, 1944), pp. 165–67; David D. Van Tassel, *Recording America's Past: An Interpretation of the Development of Historical Studies in America, 1607–1884* (Chicago, 1960), pp. 59–62.

least 90 published some proceedings. Five existed in 1800, 6 more
appeared in the 1810's, 15 more in the 1820's, 19 in the 1830's, 30
in the 1840's, and 36 in the 1850's.[16]

Although the movement began in New England, the societies
spread almost evenly over the country: 22 in New England, 38 in
the Middle Atlantic States, 20 in the South, and 21 in the West.
Especially surprising was the western enthusiasm for the past; as
for all America, the lack of heritage seems to have made the past
more important than the abundance of it. Iowa, Michigan, Minnesota, and New Mexico all had active historical societies before
they were admitted as states. The Minnesota Historical Society is
today the oldest chartered institution in the state. In addition to
his eagerness to display the evidences of culture, the pioneer carried with him a sense of destiny as he crossed the continent.
Aware that he was making history, he was anxious to preserve his
deeds for the future historian, who, he was confident, would be
interested. Eagerly the pioneers urged each other "to preserve in
an authentic form those rich materials . . . which would otherwise perish with the first settlers." [17]

The organization and operation of the societies was fairly uni-
form. Usually there was a single moving spirit brimming with
enthusiasm for collecting and studying history. Some of these
leaders, such as Henry Stevens in Vermont, Lyman Draper in
Wisconsin, and Isaiah Thomas of the American Antiquarian Society, were primarily bibliophiles, fondly collecting and curating
any kind of historical material. Sometimes the founder of the
new society was writing a history himself and wanted aid in collecting materials, as was the case with Jeremy Belknap in Massachusetts, John Haywood in Tennessee, and William Stevens in
Georgia; and sometimes he was an organizer and patriot like
John Pitkin, founder of the New York Society, who wanted to
establish a club where men of similar interests could talk about
history as a means of promoting state and national pride. Typi-

[16] Appleton Prentiss Clark Griffin, *Bibliography of American Historical
Societies* (Washington, 1907), lists 90 publishing societies; Van Tassel, *Recording America's Past*, pp. 181–85, lists 21 more.

[17] Editorial, *Firelands Pioneer*, I (June, 1858), 46; also editorial, *Western
Monthly Review*, I (April, 1828), 563.

cally, these leaders met with a few sympathetic friends. They sent out a circular letter to the leading men of the community, explaining their aims and calling for a meeting. A few dozen men attended, listened to a speech by the founding father, elected him president, drew up a constitution, and published an appeal for all kinds of historical documents for the society library.

The membership of the historical societies included a cross section of the prominent men of the community. In classifying its members according to profession, one society listed "statesmen, Physicians, attorneys, and ministers," and another listed the "legal, medical, mercantile, and mechanical professions." [18] Of the 238 members of the Maine Historical Society before 1860, there were 140 lawyers, 56 clergymen, 16 doctors, and 26 miscellaneous merchants, teachers, and gentlemen.[19] "The typical member," said one scholar, was "a young, successful professional man, probably a lawyer." [20] The societies attracted able men. John Marshall, John Quincy Adams, Albert Gallatin, DeWitt Clinton, Gouverneur Morris, and Edward Everett all served as presidents of historical societies in their states. Among the 29 founders of the Essex Institute Historical Society were 3 United States senators, 15 congressmen, and 2 cabinet members. The list of active members of the Massachusetts Historical Society reads like an index of New England's greatest names, with such figures as John Adams, Charles Francis Adams, Daniel Webster, Edward Everett, Caleb Cushing, and Henry Wadsworth Longfellow, plus the historians Belknap, Sparks, Bancroft, Prescott, Motley, Palfrey, Ticknor, and Parkman.[21]

[18] Zachary T. Leavall, "The Ante-Bellum Historical Society of Mississippi," *Publications of the Mississippi Historical Society*, VIII (1904), 228; John Lea, "History of the Tennessee Historical Society," *American Historical Magazine*, VI (October, 1901), 353.

[19] "Catalogue of Past and Present Members of the Maine Historical Society," *Collections of the Maine Historical Society*, VII (1876), 5–17.

[20] Dunlap, *Historical Societies*, p. 27.

[21] *Ibid.*, p. 24; Robert Samuel Rantoul, "The Seventy-fifth Anniversary of the Founding of the Essex Historical Society," *Essex Institute Historical Collections*, XXXII (1896), 106–7; "Members of the Society," *Collections of the Massachusetts Historical Society*, Fifth Series, I (1871), xiii–xvii.

The size of any one of the societies depended both on its success and on the purpose of its founders. The original plan of the Massachusetts Historical Society, for example, was to limit membership to 7 members, on the theory that an intimate body could be most active. Soon its membership was raised to 25, and then successively to 30, 60, and 100, but membership remained limited, and election by the society was a coveted honor. In most cases, however, membership was less exclusive. The South Carolina organization expressed the hope "that every man of fair character who claims the name of a Carolinian shall join us," and in Pennsylvania membership was "unlimited." While most groups had from 25 to 100 members, the Maryland society, with a $10 initiation fee, boasted 500 members in 1858, and the New York Historical Society in 1860 had 1,500 resident members.[22]

Most of the historical societies were state-wide organizations with interests limited primarily to state boundaries. The constitutions of many societies restricted them "only" to their state, and in practice the collections and publications of most other societies were similarly limited. Historical activity was a matter of state pride, and people felt that a society should glorify the past of its state, memorialize its ancestors, and reflect distinction upon itself. Sometimes the societies expressed an interest in a particular region of the country. The Michigan society, for example, was curious about "the Country of the Lakes," and the Louisiana and Kentucky societies expressed an interest in the Mississippi Valley. Southern localism seems to have been stronger than southern nationalism, for neither southern societies nor southern historians seemed concerned with the region. Some very active societies were even more restricted. Such fine organizations as the Essex, Worcester, Dorchester, Firelands, and Jeffersonville

[22] "Original Plan for the Society," *Proceedings of the Massachusetts Historical Society,* IV (1858–60), 110; Frederick Adolphus Porcher, "Address," *Collections of the South Carolina Historical Society,* I (1857), 14; William Rawle, "Inaugural Discourse," *Memoirs of the Historical Society of Pennsylvania,* I (1826), 29; *Annual Report of the President of the Maryland Historical Society . . . 1858* (Baltimore, 1858), p. 7; Dunlap, *Historical Societies,* p. 186.

societies devoted their attention to a single town or county. The idea of a national society seems to have been stronger in the early part of the nineteenth century than in the decades approaching the Civil War. The three most notable national organizations were the American Antiquarian Society, founded in 1812, the Historical Committee of the American Philosophical Society, of 1819, and the short-lived American Historical Society of 1835.

A few of the historical societies were devoted to special topics such as religion, genealogy, Indian antiquities, and numismatics. A nondenominational Religious Historical Society was founded in Philadelphia in 1817. In 1839 the Methodists established an active national historical society to study their past, and they were soon followed by the Lutherans, Episcopalians, Presbyterians, Moravians, and Baptists. The American Indians were a source of fascination for almost all societies, and at least three, the New Confederation of the Iroquois, the Red Jacket, and the American Ethnological Societies, devoted full attention to them. The relationship between coins and history was studied by the American Numismatic and Archaeological Society, and the Numismatic and Antiquarian Society. One of the most active groups was the New England Historical and Genealogical Society. Although this was the only strictly genealogical society, other organizations, including the New England Society of Charleston, the Old Dominion Society of New York, the Society of California Pioneers, and the Pilgrim Society, were similar associations of old settlers.[23]

The desires of the large historical societies to curate and publish were expensive ambitions, and finances were an ever-present problem. Usually there was an initiation fee of $5 and annual dues of about $3. The wealthy Chicago society, however, charged $20 for initiation and $10 per year, and by the 1850's was collecting over $1,500 a year in dues. The large societies earnestly sought endowments from donations, bequests, and life memberships. The American Antiquarian Society had an endowment

[23] Dunlap, *Historical Societies*, pp. 133–219.

of $41,700 by 1860, and the Maryland Historical Society was trustee of the George Peabody fund of more than $300,000.[24]

Some of the societies became semi-official state agencies, gaining state support and assuming responsibility for state record keeping. The western states were most generous in aiding the societies. Wisconsin made an appropriation of $1,000 to its society annually after 1856, and by 1860 New York, Minnesota, Iowa, South Carolina, Connecticut, Indiana, and Rhode Island had made substantial grants to their state societies. Occasionally, as the societies undertook supervision of state records and the state library, they obtained quarters in government buildings and the use of state printing facilities. The New Hampshire society moved its offices into the state capitol. South Carolina by 1860 had spent over $57,000 through its historical association for the preservation of official records. The societies frequently petitioned Congress for aid, but while the federal government supported individual publishing ventures sponsored by particular societies, it never provided a general subsidy to local historical organizations.[25]

The constitutions of the historical societies elaborately outlined their goals and their idea of history. By far the most important aim was the collection and preservation of the materials of American history. The need for materials was intense, and if Americans were to have the written history they wanted, the gathering of documents must come first. Societies typically listed as their "chief object," "to discover, procure, and preserve what-

[24] "Biennial Report of the Chicago Historical Society," *Reports Made to the General Assembly of Illinois . . . 1863* (Springfield, 1863), I, 452; *Proceedings of the Semi-Annual Meeting of the American Antiquarian Society . . . 1860* (Boston, 1860), p. 21; George Peabody, *Letter from George Peabody, Esq., to the Trustees for the Establishment of an Institution in the City of Baltimore* (Baltimore, 1857), pp. 4–12.

[25] Dunlap, *Historical Societies*, pp. 48–64; Alexander Samuel Salley, "The Preservation of South Carolina History," *North Carolina Historical Review*, IV (April, 1927), 145–51; *Proceedings of the American Antiquarian Society, 1812–1849* (Worcester, 1912), p. 216; *Proceedings of the Massachusetts Historical Society, 1791–1834* (Boston, 1879), pp. 396–97; *Proceedings of the Massachusetts Historical Society, 1835–1855* (Boston, 1880), pp. 418, 550.

ever may relate to the natural, civil, literary, and ecclesiastical history of the United States in general and of this State in particular." [26] "The authentic history will soon be beyond our reach," cried men frantically. "Preserve it now while we may." [27]

The societies did save invaluable material from destruction. Countless collections of manuscripts became the property of the societies, and some of the best research libraries in the country were assembled. By 1860, for example, the Massachusetts Historical Society had 14,000 books and 15,000 pamphlets, plus the papers of such men as Jonathan Trumbull, Jeremy Belknap, Thomas Hutchinson, James A. Otis, John Winthrop, and Cotton and Increase Mather.[28] The Chicago society owned 31,000 volumes, and the American Antiquarian Society owned 28,000.[29] By comparison, the largest university library, at Harvard, had 15,000 volumes in 1812 and 40,000 in 1850. At least four societies, and probably several others, had full-time paid librarians.[30] In 1849 the New York Historical Society could boast of "the best American History collection in the country." [31] America was conscious that to the societies and collectors "the public owes a great debt of gratitude." "They have excited a spirit of inquiry among educated men generally," said one writer, "and many of the

[26] *Constitution and By-Laws of the New York Historical Society* (New York, 1805), p. 3; *Act of Incorporation, The Laws, and the Circular Letter of the Massachusetts Historical Society* (Boston, 1794), p. 5; also Dunlap, *Historical Societies,* pp. 137–219.

[27] Cited in Zachary T. Leavell, "The Ante-Bellum Historical Society of Mississippi," *Publications of the Mississippi Historical Society,* VIII (1904), 235.

[28] *Catalogue of the Library of the Massachusetts Historical Society* (Boston, 1860), p. iii.

[29] "Biennial Report of the Chicago Historical Society," *Reports Made to the General Assembly of Illinois . . . 1863* (Springfield, 1863), I, 445; *Proceedings of the American Antiquarian Society, 1812–1849* (Worcester, 1912), p. 252.

[30] *Proceedings of the American Antiquarian Society* (Worcester, 1912), p. 252; *Annual Report of the President of the Maryland Historical Society* (Baltimore, 1858), p. 17; *Proceedings of the Massachusetts Historical Society, 1835–1855* (Boston, 1880), p. 538; Robert W. G. Vail, *Knickerbocker Birthday: Sesqui-Centennial History of the New York Historical Society* (New York, 1954), pp. 58, 97.

[31] Vail, *Knickerbocker Birthday,* p. 93.

valuable contributions to . . . literature owe their existence
. . . to the inspiring efforts of these societies." [32]

After collection, the "diffusion" of history was the next most
important objective of the historical societies, and increasingly
they added publication to their activity. Typically, the Massachusetts Historical Society declared that while preservation was
its primary aim, it would seek "not only to collect, but to *diffuse* the various aspects of historical information"; the New
Jersey society believed its duty was "to disseminate as widely as
possible the historical information it may gather." [33] One reason
for diffusion was that "the surest way to preserve a record is to
multiply the copies." [34] Perhaps a deeper reason for publication
was to "serve" and "improve" the public. The printing of
records would advance "the promotion of useful knowledge"; it
would be of "vital importance to the people of the state." [35]

About 184 major volumes were published by the historical
societies, along with over 650 pamphlets containing minutes of
meetings, lists of members, annual addresses, and the like.[36]
Many of the large volumes contained rare and, occasionally, interesting material. The state societies of New York, New Jersey,
Louisiana, and South Carolina, for example, published copies
and indices of European manuscripts relating to their history.
Often they published papers of colonial founders, including
those of William Penn, Roger Williams, James Oglethorpe, and
Henry Hudson. The Massachusetts society printed William Bradford's *History of Plymouth Plantation* for the first time. Reminiscences of early settlers were favorite subjects of the western
societies, and accounts of town origins, settlers' genealogies, and

[32] Anon., "Recent Historical Revelations," *Eclectic Magazine*, XLIV (July,
1858), 356; review, *Southern Quarterly Review*, III (January, 1844), 41.

[33] *Collections of the Massachusetts Historical Society*, I (1792), 3; *Proceedings of the New Jersey Historical Society*, V (1850–51), 40.

[34] *Collections of the New York Historical Society*, I (1811), iv.

[35] Anon., "Transactions of the Historical and Literary Committee of the
American Philosophical Society," *Analectic Magazine*, XIII (March, 1819), 243;
also Dunlap, *Historical Societies*, p. 139.

[36] Griffin, *American Historical Societies*. "Major volumes" is an arbitrary
category which includes documentary collections and original works of more
than 200 pages.

Indian "antiquities" consumed much space. Today, few of these volumes are of great use. Intended to please the reader as well as serve the historian, most of the material is by modern standards far too obscure for entertainment and too incomplete to be relied upon for research. Most of the collections were published irregularly, as money appeared, but the large societies maintained annual publications, and some material appeared in the form of monthly or quarterly historical journals. Small societies often utilized the town newspaper or the pages of a sympathetic magazine editor to "diffuse" their most significant material. Magazines which served societies included the *American Apollo, DeBow's Review,* the *Southern Literary Messenger,* and the *North Carolina University Magazine.*

The societies sought to encourage interest in the past in many ways besides collecting and publishing. The Historical Society of Cuyahoga County, in Neuburg, Ohio, sponsored annual picnics to popularize history. In 1858, an "army of wagons, carriages, and vehicles of every name and style" poured into the little town of 2,000 people. Five thousand people gathered for a public picnic, songs, and historical addresses. It was, suggested one historian, more like a camp meeting or a county fair than a gathering of antiquarians.[37] During the 1830's the Massachusetts Historical Society stimulated popular interest in the past and realized a profit of several hundred dollars each winter from a series of public lectures featuring such speakers as Ralph Waldo Emerson and George Bancroft. Other societies conducted pilgrimages to historic sites, held commemorative banquets, marked graves, built monuments, encouraged state publication and archive care, or crusaded for more history in the schools.[38]

[37] Charles C. Baldwin, "Notice of Historical and Pioneer Societies in Ohio," *Publications of the Western Reserve Historical Society,* I, no. 27 (1870–71), 5; Dunlap, *Historical Societies,* pp. 90–91.
[38] *Proceedings of the Massachusetts Historical Society, 1791–1835* (Boston, 1879), p. 478; *Proceedings of the Massachusetts Historical society, 1835–1855* (Boston, 1880), p. 34; Hampton Carson, *History of the Historical Society of Pennsylvania* (Philadelphia, 1940), p. 247; Edwin Martin Stone, "Review of the History of the Society," *Proceedings of the Rhode Island Historical Society,* II (1872–73), 68; J. G. DeRoulhac Hamilton, "The Preservation of North Carolina History," *North Carolina Historical Review,* IV (January,

Perhaps even more important than collecting or publicizing history were the general literary and philosophical purposes of the societies. The societies were literary clubs where men of similar interests could come to read and smoke and talk. The Maryland society provided "a resort" for its members, with a chess room and a periodical room containing current newspapers and magazines. Most societies held formal meetings annually or quarterly, though some held "monthly Soirées." [39] Frequently the societies served as museums and circulating libraries. Eight of the organizations were entitled "Historical and Philosophical" societies, four were called "Literary," seven made reference to "Geology" or "Natural History," and ten used the word "Antiquities," which implied a nonpolitical sort of history. History often served as an entrée to men who really wished to talk about about archaeology, literature, or philosophy. Any poem with a historical allusion had a claim for inclusion in the society's publications. The Arkansas society, for example, collected "not only specimens of natural and artificial curiosities, but also a library . . . a chemical laboratory and apparatus for making experiments in natural philosophy." The Missouri society urged doctors "to aid the cause of science by preparing at their leisure and depositing the skeletons of such wild and domestic animals as may be convenient, with the society, for a museum of anatomy." Almost all societies had cabinets of fossils, Indian artifacts, coins, and historical curios, so that the societies became, as the president of one organization said, "a receptacle of antique trash." [40]

1927), 9; Theodore Henly Jack, "The Preservation of Georgia History," *North Carolina Historical Review*, IV (July, 1927), 243; Thomas H. Donaldson, *Fourth Annual Address to the Maryland Historical Society* (Baltimore, 1849), p. 8.

[39] *Annual Report of the President of the Maryland Historical Society* (Baltimore, 1858), p. 8; *Annual Report of the President of the Maryland Historical Society* (Baltimore, 1854), p. 8.

[40] William B. Buchanan, *Baltimore, A Long, Long Time Ago* (Baltimore, 1853), pp. 3–5; Myra M. Vaughn, "The First Historical Society of Arkansas," *Publications of the Arkansas Historical Association*, III (1908), 347; "First Annual Meeting of the Missouri Historical and Philosophical Society," *Annals of the Missouri Historical and Philosophical Society*, I (1848), 13; William Bradford Reed, *Address before the Historical Society of Pennsylvania . . . 1848* (Philadelphia, 1848), p. 7.

Frequently, too, the societies served as art galleries. The societies of Maryland, New York, Wisconsin, and Chicago possessed some of the finest collections in the country. The exhibition held by the Chicago Historical Society in 1859 was the first art exhibit in Illinois and was attended by some 12,000 people.[41] Sometimes members worried about the nonhistorical activities of the societies: "the Gallery should be kept in subordinate relations . . . it should not swallow up the Historical Society." [42] The significant fact, however, was that history was so often paramount, and that art, literature, and science were relegated to lesser roles.

Members of the societies took their work very seriously, crusading for history with the earnestness that characterized expansionists and abolitionists. "One of the greatest benefits of our age has been conferred in the establishment of a properly run historical society," said one enthusiast. "Historical associations," said another, "should direct the destinies of humanity." [43] At any rate, the excitement they generated, and their successes, indicated a remarkable interest in the past and an assumption that history was somehow important.

Journals, Government, Genealogy, and Preservation

A multitude of miscellaneous historical activities developed in the early nineteenth century—historical magazines, official record keeping, hereditary societies, concern with genealogy, and historical restorations—in part inspired by the historical societies, but each one an important expression of growing concern with

[41] "Biennial Report of the Chicago Historical Society," *Reports Made to the General Assembly of Illinois . . . 1863* (Springfield, 1863), p. 445.

[42] *Annual Report of the President of the Maryland Historical Society* (Baltimore, 1850), p. 11.

[43] Brantz Mayer, *A Discourse Delivered at the Dedication of the Baltimore Athenaeum* (Baltimore, 1848), p. 33; Levi Silliman Ives, *Introductory Address of the Historical Society of the University of North Carolina* (Raleigh, 1845), p. 18; also, Introduction, *Historical Family Library*, I (June, 1835), 1. See Julian Parks Boyd, "State and Local Historical Societies," *American Historical Review*, XL (October, 1934), 11–12; Clifford L. Lord, ed., *Keepers of the Past* (Chapel Hill, 1965).

the past. Each revealed something of the society which gave rise
to it, and each has itself become a tradition.

Historical journals, sometimes sponsored by the societies and
sometimes launched as commercial ventures, were designed for
people who wanted to delve into history more than was possible
in popular magazines. The first and one of the finest was the
sixty-page *Collections Historical and Miscellaneous and Monthly
Literary Journal,* begun in Concord, New Hampshire, in 1822
by two amateur historians, Jacob B. Moore and John Farmer. By
1840, five more journals had appeared, an additional five by
1850, and six more by the time of the Civil War. The magazines
were scattered all over the country, with some of the most successful published in the smallest towns. Although the lifetime
of most of the journals was short, thirteen lasted two years, five
lasted over twelve years, and two, which still exist, are among the
oldest publications in the country. The magazines usually contained from thirty to sixty pages. Eight were issued monthly,
three bimonthly, and six quarterly.[44]

The journals, like the historical societies with which they were
often affiliated, considered it their duty to collect and disseminate historical information. "Our main object," said one, "is to
collect and diffuse useful and entertaining information relating

[44] *Collections Historical and Miscellaneous and Monthly Literary Journal*
(monthly, Concord, N.H., 1822–24); *Worcester Magazine and Historical
Journal* (monthly, Worcester County Historical Society, Worcester, Mass.,
1825–26); *The Albany Quarterly* (quarterly, Albany Historical Society, 1832–
34); *Historical and Scientific Sketches* (monthly, Historical Society of Michigan,
Detroit, 1834); *Historical Family Library* (bimonthly, Cadiz, Ohio, 1835–36);
American Historical Magazine (monthly, New Haven, 1836); *American Pioneer* (monthly, Logan Historical Society, Cincinnati, 1842–43); *Antiquarian
and General Review* (monthly, Schenectady, 1845–47); *The Olden Time*
(monthly, Pittsburgh, 1846–47); *New England Historical and Genealogical
Register* (quarterly, New England Historic and Genealogical Society, Boston,
1847–current); *Virginia Historical Register and Literary Companion* (quarterly, Richmond, 1848–60); *American Historical Magazine* (monthly, New
York, 1850); *Historical Magazine and Notes and Queries* (monthly, Boston,
1857–75); *Historical and Genealogical Researches and Recorder of Passing
Events of the Merrimack Valley* (quarterly, Haverville, Mass., 1857–58);
Firelands Pioneer (quarterly, Firelands Historical Society, Sandusky, Ohio,
1858–72, 1882–1918); *Historical Collections of the Essex Institute* (bi-
monthly, Essex Institute Historical Society, Boston, 1860–current); *Vermont
Quarterly Gazette* (quarterly, Ludlow, Vt., 1860–63).

to the History of our State," and another announced its aim, "to serve as a repository of minute and authentic facts . . . on . . . antiquities, history, statistics, and genealogy." [45] The journals, like the societies, would make a contribution to knowledge. They would "preserve for the use of posterity rich historical materials which would otherwise perish." Their contents would be "not merely amusing for the present moment" but would serve "for the use of the future historian." [46]

Although the journals were usually labors of love and service, edited by devoted antiquarians, they kept a business eye to the profitable as well and tried to appeal to a wide audience by being interesting as well as valuable. There appeared to be no contradiction between "useful and entertaining information," or between "furnishing materials for the elaboration by the future historian" and serving "for the gratification . . . of the curious reader." [47] "We trust we are not over sanguine in expecting to *interest* our readers, while preserving for them curious matters of history," said one editor. Another editor felt assured of success, for he was certain the public would agree that "there is no higher mental pleasure than that produced in tracing the footsteps of past existence." He warned bluntly, however, "We shall not . . . be lavish of labor to our own disadvantage." [48] The *Historical Magazine,* one of the most successful journals, was a purely commercial venture, edited by a succession of professional publishers.[49]

[45] Introduction, *Virginia Historical Register,* III (January, 1850), i; Preface, *New England Historical and Genealogical Register,* I (January, 1847), v; also, editorial, *Firelands Pioneer,* I (January, 1842), 3; Introduction, *Historical Collections of the Essex Institute,* I (April, 1859), 1–2.

[46] Editorial, *American Pioneer,* I (January, 1842), 3; editorial, *Firelands Pioneer,* I (June, 1858), 46; editorial, *Hazard's Register of Pennsylvania, Devoted to the Preservation of Facts and Documents, and Every Other Kind of Useful Information Respecting the State of Pennsylvania,* I (January 5, 1828), 1.

[47] Introduction, *Virginia Historical Register,* III (January, 1850), i; Introduction, *Historical Collections of the Essex Institute,* II (February, 1860), 1.

[48] Introduction, *Historical Magazine,* I (January, 1857), 1; Preface, *Collections Topographical, Historical and Biographical,* I (January, 1822), vii.

[49] Frank Luther Mott, *A History of American Magazines, 1850–1865* (Cambridge, Mass., 1938), p. 176.

In an attempt to be interesting and to appeal to the general public, these magazines sometimes enlivened their contents with illustrations, poetry, historical anecdotes, and historical fiction. The *Virginia Historical Register* assured its readers that history would be kept "exciting" and "entertaining." "We have no thought, certainly, of going out of the warm and sensible world around us, to bury ourselves amidst the rubbish of antiquity—to dote upon dust." Another publisher with a view to the public's taste promised that he would emphasize Indian wars with especial detail on "the adventures and sufferings of the captives." [50] The *Historical Family Library* furnished abridged, serialized reprints of the most popular history books.

The contents of the magazines were divided about evenly between local history, biography, and collections of primary source material. The articles on local history were often reprints of rhetorical speeches made before the local historical societies, or the researches of local antiquarians on some phase of the town's or state's past. Biography ranged from genealogies of the state's leading families to philosophical apostrophes to the great men of history. Favorite subjects were the early settlers of the state, Revolutionary heroes, and eulogies delivered at the death of prominent men. Most valued as a "contribution," however, were the sections devoted to primary documents. This included selections from the papers of famous men, town and church records, lists of college graduates, tombstone inscriptions, reprints of early travel accounts in America, abstracts of wills and deeds, or proceedings of early governmental bodies. One journal systematically collected "personal reminiscences" by interviewing "the first settlers of this region, who are now rapidly passing away." Such materials, the editors believed, were the "lumber-yards" of history for "the future historian." [51] A few pages in the journals were usually devoted to the proceedings of historical societies, a few brief notes, usually anecdotal, on non-American history, a bit

[50] Introduction, *Virginia Historical Register*, III (January, 1850), ii; Preface, *Collections Topographical, Historical and Biographical*, I (January, 1822), i.

[51] Editorial, *Firelands Pioneer*, I (June, 1858), 46; editorial, *American Pioneer*, II (September, 1843), 400; also, editorial, *American Pioneer*, I (January, 1842), 3.

of historical fiction or poetry, and perhaps a page or two of book reviews. Comprehensive coverage of current historical literature and long essay-reviews usually were left to the literary journals, however. General magazines could be relied upon to cover historical works rather thoroughly, and it was for the special historical journals to furnish something additional. If this something happened to be history, many Americans were apt to find it exciting.

Gradually, too, state and federal governments began to reflect the growing concern with history, both in the care of their own records and in the subsidy of important historical projects. Beginning in about the 1820's, often at the urging of historical societies, most states authorized a particular state agency to care for current records and to begin the collection of official records from the past. Georgia, in 1823, authorized a clerk to compile an index of some one hundred historical volumes, and Massachusetts, in 1836, employed a binder to compile and bind some 240 volumes of loose historical materials. By 1860 at least a dozen states had supported publication of documents from the past. New York was perhaps most ambitious, employing a copyist who spent four years in Europe transcribing documents on the state's colonial backgrounds, and then supporting the publication of fourteen volumes of this material. Georgia, South Carolina, Louisiana, and New Jersey also hired European copyists. The Massachusetts legislature urged town councils to "grant and vote such sums as they judge necessary for . . . procuring the writing and publishing of their town histories." [52]

Congress also turned to the problems of record keeping and history. In 1800 the Library of Congress was established, although it was not until the 1850's that the Library began to serve as an important depository of historical materials and started a

[52] Ernest Posner, *American State Archives* (Chicago, 1964), pp. 13–16 and *passim;* G. Philip Bauer, "Public Archives in the United States," William B. Hesseltine and Donald R. McNeil, eds., *In Support of Clio: Essays in Memory of Herbert A. Kellar* (Madison, Wisc., 1958), pp. 49–75; Edmund Bailey O'Callaghan, ed., *Documents Relative to the Colonial History of the State of New York* (14 vols.; Albany, 1853–87), I, vi–xlv; *General Statutes of the Commonwealth of Massachusetts . . . 1853 . . .* (Boston, 1873), p. 158.

systematic collection of manuscripts.[53] In 1810 Congressman Josiah Quincy of Massachusetts, a member of the Massachusetts Historical Society, headed a committee to investigate the government's care of its records. Quincy's committee reported that records were scattered in attics all over Washington "in a state of great disorder and exposure; and in a situation neither safe nor convenient for the nation." [54] Congress responded immediately with the first Archives Act, providing fireproof quarters for government records within the new post office building. In 1859 Congress established a Public Documents Bureau in the Department of Interior to keep files of all government publications. The present National Archives Bureau was not established until 1934.[55]

The government's greatest service to history came through remarkably generous subsidy of the publication of historical documents. As in the states, publication was in part an archival policy, based on the theory that multiple copies would guarantee preservation. Partly, too, subsidy of historical projects was intended as an encouragement to "useful" reading habits. "An enlightened legislature will always regard these things as important," declared one editor, and another believed that "There is no expenditure of public money more creditable to the country." [56]

From 1815 to 1857 Congress launched at least sixteen major historical projects, comprising a total of 184 volumes. Most of these, such as *The American State Papers* and Peter Force's *American Archives,* were official proceedings and documents from an earlier period, chiefly from the Revolution. Five of the projects included the biographies and correspondence of the founding fathers—Washington, Adams, Madison, Jefferson, and

---

[53] Lucy Salamanca, *Fortress of Freedom, The Story of the Library of Congress* (Philadelphia, 1942), pp. 23–194.

[54] Cited in *First Annual Report of the Archivist of the United States* (Washington, 1936), p. 2.

[55] *Ibid.,* pp. 5–10.

[56] Editorial, *Niles' Weekly Register,* XII (June 21, 1817), 263–64; review, *North American Review,* XXXIII (October, 1831), 484.

Hamilton.[57] For Congress it was seldom a clear-cut matter of direct appropriation but rather one of assigning government employees to a project, parceling out subsidies to editors, and purchasing editions for gratuitous distribution. John Spencer Bassett, tracing the perambulations of Force's nine-volume *American Archives,* estimated that the project cost the government over $225,000.[58] At this arbitrary but apparently typical figure of $25,000 a volume, Congress would have spent over $4,500,000 for subsidies to historical projects during the period.

Hereditary patriotic societies were fraternal and political as well as historical, but all encouraged a sense of history and genealogy. The first and most active was the Society of the Cincinnati organized in 1783 by officers in the Revolutionary army and their heirs. A New England Society of New York was established in 1805 "for literary purposes," and a Society of the War of 1812 was founded by veterans "to perpetuate the memories and victories of the War." At least half a dozen similar as-

---

[57] *State Papers and Publick Documents* . . . (8 vols.; Boston, 1815); *Journal of the Senate* . . . *1789–1815* (5 vols.; Washington, 1820); *Secret Journals of Acts and Proceedings of Congress* . . . [1775–89] (4 vols.; Boston, 1821); *Journal of the House* . . . *1789–1815* (9 vols.; Washington, 1826); Jonathan Elliot, ed., *Debates . . . on the Adoption of the Federal Constitution* . . . (5 vols.; Washington, 1827–30); Jared Sparks, ed., *Diplomatic Correspondence of the American Revolution* (12 vols.; Boston, 1829–30); *American State Papers* . . . (38 vols.; Washington, 1832–61); Francis P. Blair, ed., *Diplomatic Correspondence . . . 1783 to 1789* . . . (7 vols.; Washington, 1833–34); *Debates and Proceedings in the Congress* . . . *1789–1824* (42 vols.; Washington, 1834–56); Jared Sparks, ed., *The Writings of George Washington* (12 vols.; Boston, 1834–37); Peter Force, ed., *Tracts and Papers* . . . (4 vols.; Washington, 1836–46); Peter Force, ed., *American Archives* . . . (9 vols.; Washington, 1837–53); Henry D. Gilpin, ed., *Papers of James Madison* . . . (3 vols.; Washington, 1840); Charles Francis Adams, ed., *The Works of John Adams* . . . (10 vols.; Boston, 1850–56); H. A. Washington, ed., *Writings of Thomas Jefferson* . . . (9 vols.; Washington, 1853–54); John Charles Hamilton, ed., *History of the Republic . . . as Traced in the Writings of Alexander Hamilton* . . . (7 vols.; New York, 1857–64). This list is taken from *Checklist of United States Public Documents, 1789–1909* . . . (Washington, 1911), and Benjamin Perley Poore, *Descriptive Catalogue of the Government Publications of the United States* . . . (Washington, 1885).

[58] John Spencer Bassett, *The Middle Group of American Historians* (New York, 1917), pp. 239–302.

sociations of veterans or old settlers had appeared by the time of the Civil War.[59]

Genealogical interest was slow to develop after the Revolution, probably because family prominence implied an unfashionable association with loyalism and aristocracy. The first significant interest seemed to parallel Jacksonian democracy. In 1829 the New Hampshire apothecary and antiquarian John Farmer published the first collected work on genealogy in America, noting that recently "there has been a curiosity among many of the present generation to trace back their progenitors, in an uninterrupted series, to those who first landed on the bleak and inhospitable shores of New England." In 1844, one year before the Native American Party was formed, James Savage, a Massachusetts antiquarian who is generally called "The Father of American Genealogy," organized the New England Historic and Genealogical Society, launched the first genealogical journal, and began his four-volume *Genealogical Dictionary of the First Settlers of New England.*[60]

The preservation of historic sites usually stemmed from popular enthusiasm over particular sites rather than from the initiative of societies or historians. The first successful preservation came in 1813 when citizens' petitions moved the city of Philadelphia to appropriate $70,000 to save Independence Hall from the wrecker. A few years later the city appropriated additional funds for restoration. Private citizens took the initiative in saving Fort Ticonderoga in the 1820's and Monticello in the 1830's. In 1850 New York State contributed $8,000 to a private group which was making George Washington's Neuburg, New York, headquarters into the first historical museum. In 1856 Tennessee appropriated $48,000 to buy Andrew Jackson's home, The Hermitage.[61]

The most important preservation enterprise came in the 1850's

[59] Frederick Adams Virkus, ed., *Handbook of American Genealogy* (Chicago, 1937), pp. 1000–1006.

[60] *Ibid.,* pp. 1–5; William C. Hill, *A Century of Genealogical Progress* (Boston, 1945); John Farmer, *A Genealogical Register of the First Settlers of New England* (Lancaster, Mass., 1829), p. iii.

[61] Charles B. Hosmer, Jr., *Presence of the Past, A History of the Preservation Movement before Williamsburg* (New York, 1965), pp. 29–40.

with efforts to purchase Mount Vernon from Washington's heirs, who kept raising the price. A Charleston, South Carolina woman, Ann Pamela Cunningham, established the Mount Vernon Ladies' Association, one of the first women's organizations in the country, to raise whatever sum was necessary. At first she appealed to the South to make Mount Vernon a southern symbol, but later she changed the direction of her appeal to the entire nation to make Washington's home a symbol of union. The association named women vice-presidents in thirty states and began a newspaper, the *Mount Vernon Record*. Edward Everett made 139 appearances for the association, raising an average of $500 at each appearance with his unionist oration on "The Character of Washington." By the end of the decade, with the aid of several state appropriations, the association had raised the $200,000 purchase price, plus a fund for upkeep.[62]

The enthusiasm for things historical—from art and literature to societies to genealogy and preservation—obviously reflected the feeling that history was a great deal of fun. Beyond that, however, Americans of the early nineteenth century were also persuaded that history was enormously important for the well-being of society. They were concerned particularly that history occupy a larger place in the school curriculum so that the younger generation might gain the benefits of the past.

[62] *Ibid.*, pp. 41–62.

III

History Enters the Schools

THE most accurate measure of the rise of history in the early nineteenth century was its entrance into the schools. At the time of the Revolution almost no one studied history academically, but by the time of the Civil War it was at least as prominent in the elementary and secondary schools—though not in the colleges—as it is today.

The New Curriculum

The entrance of history into the curriculum was part of a dramatic transformation taking place in both the theory and practice of education. Men like Benjamin Franklin, Noah Webster, Thomas Jefferson, and DeWitt Clinton denounced the ancient concept of training a few men to be philosophical gentlemen; instead, they called for a democratic education which would elevate all society by preparing men for an occupation and for the duties of citizenship. Specifically, the old curriculum of philosophy and the classics had to yield to new utilitarian subjects like spelling, rhetoric, modern languages, geography, and history. The movement for more useful courses gained momentum in the 1820's as men like Henry Barnard and Horace Mann began to establish public schools throughout much of the nation. A standardized curriculum, prescribed largely by state legislators, replaced the haphazard offerings of local church schools and academies.[1]

Of course, each generation believes the curriculum changes it makes are practical ones; recently, traditional subjects like history have had to defer to typing and automobile mechanics. As Americans have repeatedly searched for a broader definition of democracy, they have also sought a broader definition of practicality. The changing justifications of history have been an index of its utility in society. Sixteenth-century travelogue history became impractical for seventeenth-century Puritans, who wanted history to manifest God; this, in turn, appeared irrelevant to eighteenth-century gentlemen, who imagined that history might expand their knowledge of human nature; and that seemed of little use to men of the nineteenth century, who wanted history to buttress the truths in which society believed and to probe for ultimate reality. After the Civil War this last view seemed hopelessly vague to scientific historians who thought that history should explain the present, predict the future, and offer guidance on specific problems. Finally, this attitude appeared impractical to men of the twentieth century who often approached the past because, like Mount Everest, it was there, and because historical knowledge supplied at least a partial answer to many questions, personal and social. In the twentieth century a partial answer was enough.

The study of the past first entered the elementary school curriculum as part of the reading exercises. As early as 1749 Benjamin Franklin urged that for children, "History be made a constant Part of their Reading." [2] With the nationalistic impulse of the Revolution, leading educators like Benjamin Rush and Samuel Harrison Smith maintained that primary readers should include history "above all," and that the quantity of history in

[1] See the various histories of education, for example, Stuart G. Noble, *A History of American Education* (New York, 1930), pp. 110–31; Lawrence Arthur Cremin, *The American Common School: An Historic Conception* (New York, 1951), pp. 83–218.

[2] Benjamin Franklin, *Proposals Relating to the Education of Youth in Pensilvania* [sic] (Philadelphia, 1749), p. 19.

readers should be "greatly increased." [3] Thomas Jefferson, in planning for a public school system, said, "the books which shall be used therein for instructing the children to read shall be such as will at the same time make them acquainted with Grecian, Roman, English, and American history." [4]

The man who probably did more than any other in the elevation of history to a prominent place in the primary school readers was Noah Webster, the compiler of the dictionary. Webster maintained that "a selection of essays" on history, particularly American history, "should be the principal school book in the United States," and that "every child . . . as soon as he opens his lips . . . should lisp" the lessons of the past.[5] Webster supplied the needed volume in 1790. Entitled *The Little Reader's Assistant,* it was a primer intended for use at about third grade level. Over half of the volume, 139 out of 239 pages, was devoted to ancient, modern, and American history. Soon other educators, anxious to share Webster's success, were emulating his approach. By 1860 about one-fifth of the average primer was devoted to history. The famous *McGuffey's Fifth Reader* devoted over a third of its space to history lessons.[6]

Gradually, history entered the elementary schools as an inde-

[3] Benjamin Rush, *A Plan for the Establishment of Public Schools and the Diffusion of Knowledge in Pennsylvania* . . . (Philadelphia, 1786), p. 29; Samuel Harrison Smith, *Remarks on Education Illustrating the Close Connection between Wisdom and Virtue* (Philadelphia, 1798), p. 6.

[4] Thomas Jefferson, "A Bill for the More General Diffusion of Knowledge," Julian Parks Boyd *et al.,* eds., *The Papers of Thomas Jefferson* (Princeton, 1950), II, 528; see also Clifton Johnson, *Old Time Schools and School Books* (New York, 1917), pp. 252–74.

[5] Noah Webster, *On the Education of Youth in America* (Boston, 1788), p. 23; also Allen Oscar Hansen, *Liberalism and Education in the Eighteenth Century* (New York, 1926), p. 153 and *passim;* John T. McManis, "History as a Study in the American Elementary School," *The Educational Bi-Monthly,* VI (November, 1911), 150–52.

[6] A sample of twelve of the most popular primers gives the following amounts of space to history: American Society for the Diffusion of Useful Knowledge, *The American Reader* (New York, 1848), 23 per cent; Lyman Cobb, *Cobb's Juvenile Reader* (Pittsburgh, 1831), 12 per cent; Samuel Griswold Goodrich, *Goodrich's Fifth Reader* (Louisville, 1857), 6 per cent; William H. McGuffey, *McGuffey's Newly Revised Third Reader* (Cincinnati, 1848), 13 per cent; William H. McGuffey, *McGuffey's Newly Revised Rhetori-*

pendent subject as well. In Connecticut in 1839, Henry Barnard reported that within the past two decades history had come to be taught as a separate subject in "nearly all" of the elementary schools of that state.[7] By 1840 history was taught in at least half of the primary schools of Massachusetts, and in 1857 the Massachusetts legislature required that history be taught in all of its public elementary schools.[8] By 1860 about one-sixth of the normal school teacher-training curriculum for elementary teachers was history.[9]

In the secondary schools history came to have an even more important place than in the primary. First entering the private academies through the study of the Latin and Greek classics, it quickly emerged as an independent subject.[10] The typical pattern was evident in New York: in 1825, 33 per cent of the academies taught some form of history; in 1830 the figure had risen to 77 per cent; and by 1860, 92 per cent of the private academies offered history as an independent subject.[11] The public high

---

cal Guide, or Fifth Reader (Cincinnati, 1853), 35 per cent; Lindley Murray, The English Reader (Utica, 1821), 20 per cent; John Pierpont, The American First Class Book (Boston, 1828), 13 per cent; J. Russell Webb, Webb's Normal Reader (New York, 1850), 12 per cent; Noah Webster, An American Selection of Lessons (Philadelphia, 1787), 60 per cent; Marcius Willson, The Fifth Reader (New York, 1861), 9 per cent; Samuel Worcester, A Third Book for Reading (Boston, 1857), 19 per cent.

[7] Connecticut, First Annual Report of the Board of Commissioners of Common Schools (Hartford, 1839), p. 41.

[8] Alexander James Inglis, The Rise of the High School in Massachusetts (New York, 1911), pp. 72–76; also McManis, "History in the American Elementary School," pp. 150–52.

[9] United States Bureau of Education, The Inception and Progress of the American Normal School Curriculum to 1860 (Washington, 1891), p. 279.

[10] See Agnew O. Roorbach, The Development of the Social Studies in the American Secondary Education Before 1861 (Philadelphia, 1937), passim. Sampling 300 catalogues from 238 academies in 23 states from 1820 to 1860, Prof. Roorbach found (pp. 102, 237, 242) 632 courses offered in history. Also, see William H. Cartwright, "Evolution of American History in the Curriculum," Richard E. Thursfield, ed., The Study and Teaching of American History (Washington, 1946), passim; Edith W. Osgood, "The Development of Historical Study in the Secondary Schools of the United States," School Review, XXII (September, 1914), 449.

[11] New York, Thirty-ninth, Forty-ninth, and Seventy-fourth Annual Reports of the Regents of the University of the State of New York (Albany, 1825, 1830, 1860), pp. 201–20; 195–217; 242–72.

schools, which were most responsive to popular pressures, were
ahead of the classically oriented private academies in the adoption of new, practical subjects. During the 1820's, soon after the
establishment of the high schools, Massachusetts, Vermont, New
York, Virginia, and Rhode Island required by law that history be
taught in tax-supported institutions.[12] By 1860 the typical high
school student was studying approximately three full years of
history.[13] Secondary-school history became an entrance requirement of New York University in 1832, and soon most colleges
made it part of their published entrance requirements.[14]

In the colleges, history began earliest but developed slowest,
for higher education long remained wedded to the classical
tradition of producing enlightened gentlemen.[15] Generally, until after the time of the Civil War the colleges tolerated history
as men of the eighteenth century had done, as a literary amusement for the students, taught by a professor whose major concern was languages or philosophy. Jared Sparks complained in
1830 that "No professorships of history have hitherto been established on such a scale and upon such principles as in any degree
to answer to the public demands." [16] As late as the Civil War the
typical instructor was "Professor of Moral Philosophy, Classics
and Antiquities," or "Professor of Belle Lettres and History." [17]

Nevertheless, the place of history did expand in the colleges
as it had in the elementary and secondary schools, for students
eventually have their way in spite of educators. The precise

[12] See Bessie Louise Pierce, *Public Opinion and the Teaching of History*
(New York, 1926), pp. 6–7.

[13] Emit Duncan Grizzell, *Origin and Development of the High School in
New England Before 1860* (New York, 1923), pp. 290–329; John Elbert Stout,
*The Development of High School Curricula in the North Central States from
1860 to 1918* (Chicago, 1921), p. 263.

[14] Theodore Francis Jones, *New York University, 1832–1932* (New York,
1933), p. 36; Herbert Baxter Adams, *The Study of History in American Colleges and Universities* (Washington, 1887), p. 91.

[15] See Richard Hofstadter and C. DeWitt Hardy, *The Development and
Scope of Higher Education in the United States* (New York, 1952), pp. 9–28.

[16] Sparks' Journal, June, 1830, cited in Herbert Baxter Adams, *The Life
and Writings of Jared Sparks, Comprising Selections from his Journals and
Correspondence* (2 vols.; Boston, 1893), II, 361–62.

[17] For example, at Georgia, Pennsylvania, Michigan, Virginia, Missouri,
Yale, New York, Columbia. See various college histories.

"firsts" lie buried in college records and obscured by controversy. In 1643 Harvard offered the first course in history; it was entitled *Historia Civis* and was taught for one hour a week to seniors in their final semester.[18] Yale, Columbia, Pennsylvania, Princeton, Brown, and North Carolina provided similar offerings to their students before 1800.[19] The first independent "chair" of history may have been that held by Robert Davidson at Pennsylvania in the 1780's.[20] John Hall was professor of history at Maryland in 1813, and Ruel Keith held that title at William and Mary in 1821.[21] The first courses in American history were probably those at William and Mary in 1821 and the College of Charleston in 1828.[22] Especially significant was the appointment of Francis Lieber as "Professor of History and Political Economy" at South Carolina in 1835, for this indicated that history was being treated as a social science rather than as part of the classical education, probably for the first time in an American college.[23] At Harvard in 1839, Jared Sparks offered one of the first specialized courses, a series of twelve lectures on the American Revolution, which was required of all seniors. Three years later Harvard offered the first elective, in English constitutional

[18] Adams, *History in American Colleges*, pp. 11–14.

[19] *Ibid.*, pp. 51, 59; Edward Potts Cheyney, *History of the University of Pennsylvania* (Philadelphia, 1940), pp. 31, 84, 134; Thomas Jefferson Wertenbaker, *Princeton, 1746–1896* (Princeton, 1946), p. 93; Walter Cochrane Bronson, *The History of Brown University* (Providence, 1914), p. 105; George A. Beebe, "One Hundred and Fifty Years of History in the University of North Carolina" (Master's thesis, University of North Carolina, 1946), pp. 1–5.

Ancient history was taught at Harvard, Yale, Columbia, Pennsylvania, Princeton, Brown, North Carolina, Virginia, Delaware, College of Charleston, South Carolina, and Amherst. World history was taught at Delaware, Pennsylvania, New York University, South Carolina, Harvard, Princeton, and North Carolina. By no means all inclusive, this list is compiled from published histories of these institutions.

[20] Cheyney, *University of Pennsylvania*, p. 134.

[21] George H. Callcott, *A History of the University of Maryland* (Baltimore, 1966), p. 32; Lyon Gardiner Tyler, "A Few Facts from the Records of William and Mary College," *Papers of the American Historical Association*, IV (New York, 1890), 467.

[22] Tyler, "Records of William and Mary," p. 467; Coyler Meriwether, *History of Higher Education in South Carolina* (Washington, 1889), p. 60.

[23] Daniel Walker Hollis, *University of South Carolina* (2 vols.; Columbia, 1951), I, 120–23.

history.[24] Finally, the first separate "departments" of history were probably those at North Carolina in 1853 and at Michigan two years later.[25] In summary, a one-semester history course was common in the colleges by 1830, and by 1860 the typical student received about three semesters of history.

The best evidence of the emergence of history in the schools and colleges was the appearance of history textbooks. Several bibliographies have been compiled, together showing 439 editions of history texts in use in the United States before 1860. Of these, about 2 per cent appeared before 1800, about 30 per cent from 1800 to 1830, and about 65 per cent from 1830 to 1860.[26]

[24] Adams, *History in American Colleges*, pp. 18–22.
[25] *Catalogue of the Trustees, Faculty, and Students of the University of North Carolina* (Raleigh, 1854), p. 134; Adams, *History in American Colleges*, pp. 16–17, 92–97.
[26] At least three laborious and fairly complete compilations have been made of the history textbook editions that were used in this country before the Civil War. (Henry Barnard, "American Text-Books," *American Journal of Education*, XIII [June, 1863], 202–22; [September, 1863], 401–8; [December, 1863], 626–40; XIV [December, 1864], 751–57; XV [September, 1865], 639–75; William F. Russell, "Historical Text-Books Published Before 1861," *History Teacher's Magazine*, VI [April, 1915], 122–25; Roorbach, *Development of Social Studies in the American Secondary Schools*, pp. 246–78.) Together they have found the following number of editions:

TEXTBOOK EDITIONS BY SUBJECT

	Ancient	U.S.	World	England	Local	Church	Modern	France	Medieval	Biography	Other	Total
Before 1775	2		2									4
1775–1799	3	1	3									7
1800–1809	8	3	7	1	3							22
1810–1819	13	1	15	7	1	1	1	1				40
1820–1829	16	23	19	5	5	4						72
1830–1839	9	23	15	3	2	1	1			2	1	57
1840–1849	19	23	15	5	3		6	1			1	73
1850–1859	33	35	31	13	3	4	2	5	4	1	1	132
n.d.	12	4	6	5		2	1	1		1		32
Total	115	113	113	39	17	12	11	8	4	4	3	439

Methods of Teaching History

The same educational revolution that brought a new curriculum and public schools in the early nineteenth century also brought important changes in teaching methods. The result was that history entered the schools not as a dry and dreaded subject but as an enjoyable one. The changes in teaching methods were based on the theories of Rousseau and Johann Heinrich Pestalozzi. Protesting against the formal, eighteenth-century methods which treated the child as an adult, forcing him to memorize facts and principles he did not understand, Rousseau declared that a child must be stimulated, not forced; he should find learning natural, pleasant, and enjoyable.[27] Pestalozzi set out to apply this theory, to discover just how learning could be made pleasant and the student's curiosity aroused. This must be done, he said, by abolishing the long-established practice of rote instruction, by substituting student participation for memorization, and by the use of stories, discussions, projects, and games as part of the teaching process.[28] The new methods appealed to American educators and were spread throughout the country by such men as Joseph Neef, John Griscom, Henry Barnard, Horace Mann, and Calvin E. Stowe (whose better-known wife applied the theories in her book, *Uncle Tom's Cabin*).[29]

The change came slowly, for the old system was well entrenched. In 1807 the typical history textbook still called for every student *"to commit all the historical facts to memory* and at the end of every section to repeat the whole of what has been learnt,"* and as late as 1840 another called for the student to recite "exactly in the language of the textbook."* [30] The teacher

[27] W. H. Payne, ed. and trans., *Rousseau's Émile; or, Treatise on Education* (New York, 1893), see especially pp. 54, 137.

[28] Eva Channing, ed. and trans., *Pestalozzi's "Leonard and Gertrude"* (Boston, 1885), pp. 129–31 and *passim*.

[29] For example, John Griscom, "A Year in Europe," and Calvin Ellis Stowe, "Report on Elementary Public Instruction in Europe," Edgar W. Knight, ed., *Reports on European Education* (New York, 1930), pp. 16–115, 248–317. See Noble, *History of American Education*, pp. 197–217.

[30] John Robinson, *An Easy Grammar of History, Ancient and Modern* (Philadelphia, 1807), p. 4; *Fifty-Fourth Annual Report of the Regents of the University of the State of New York* (Albany, 1840), p. 94.

would read questions from the textbook on the day's assignment, and the student, with books closed, and upon threat of the birch, would recite the answers verbatim. Many of the earliest textbooks were written in the question and answer style of a religious catechism.[31] As rote instruction came under attack, its advocates tried desperately to streamline their procedures to keep up with the times. Textbooks appeared in rhyming verse to facilitate memorization, and one author devised a memory aid whereby syllables were substituted for numbers and nonsense words made of the syllables, in order to help in the memory of dates.[32] Advocates of rote claimed that memory in itself was an essential part of education, that it would "improve the mind," that any other kind of learning was "superficial," and that the traditional methods of instruction had "stood the test of time."[33]

Advocates of new subjects like history led the way in calling for newer methods of instruction. They attacked rote instruction on at least four counts: it made history dull, the facts were soon forgotten, true wisdom was not the accumulation of information, and the entire principle of drilling to improve the mind was falacious. As early as 1795, Oliver Goldsmith criticized "the dry mode of question and answer," suggesting that it was a refuge for schoolbook authors who could not write and teachers who could not teach.[34] Other historians took up the attack: mere facts "chill and disgust the mind"; they "neither amuse nor instruct the reader"; they leave the student "as ignorant as a poet who has learned a grammar by heart"; students must "learn to think."[35]

[31] For example, Frederick Butler, *A Catechical Compend of General History, Sacred and Profane* (Hartford, 1817); William Mayor, *The Catechism of Universal History* (Boston, 1814).

[32] For example, Hannah Townsend, *History of England in Verse* (Philadelphia, 1852); Richard Valpy, *A Poetical Chronology of Ancient and English History* (Boston, 1813); Robinson, *Easy Grammar of History*.

[33] *Fifty-Second and Fifty-Third Annual Report of the Regents of the University of the State of New York* (1838, 1839), pp. 94, 103, 126; Robinson, *Easy Grammar of History*, p. 6.

[34] Oliver Goldsmith, *Dr. Goldsmith's Roman History* (Philadelphia, 1795), p. 1.

[35] Samuel Whelpley, *An Historical Compend, Containing a Brief Survey of*

By the 1830's most history textbooks were imploring teachers to "make the time of study pass pleasantly," "excite rather than gratify the curiosity," "feed the child's imagination," "stimulate a desire for more," and "inspire the pupil with a sense of the value and importance of knowledge." [36] Frequently this meant minimizing the importance of the textbooks which were the chief vehicle for this sentiment. "School books are at best elementary tools," said one author. Lectures, projects, and class discussion ought to be employed.[37] Teachers would be especially rewarded for the effort of a lecture, promised one educator, for "the marked attention . . . the starting tear, and the heaving bosom will testify to his success." [38]

History textbook authors struggled to make their own books interesting. One way was through style, "eloquence of manner which reveals pictures to the imagination [and] excites sympathies in the heart." There should be as many "incidents and anecdotes" as in a novel; words should be used as felicitously as in a poem.[39] Another method of pleasing readers was in care-

---

the Great Line of History from the Earliest Times . . . (2 vols.; Morris Town, N.J., 1806), II, 1; Samuel Griswold Goodrich, The First Book of History for Children and Youth (Boston, 1833), p. iii; George T. Manning, Outlines of the History of the Middle Ages . . . (London, 1853), p. 12; Fifty-Second Annual Report of the Regents of the University of the State of New York (1838), p. 103; also Samuel Griswold Goodrich, Peter Parley's Universal History on the Basis of Geography (Boston, 1837), p. 2.

[36] Emma Hart Willard, Universal History in Perspective . . . (New York, 1858), p. v; Salma Hale, History of the United States (New York, 1837), p. 6; Jesse Olney and John Warner Barber, The Family View of History . . . (Philadelphia, 1839), p. 6; John Frost, Pictorial History of the World (Richmond, 1848), p. ix; Fifty-First Annual Report of the Regents of the University of the State of New York (1837), p. 97; also anon., Tales from American History (New York, 1844), p. 5; Charles A. Goodrich, A History of the United States (Hartford, 1831), p. 1.

[37] Manning, History of the Middle Ages, p. 13; also Francis Lister Hawks, History of New England . . . (Boston, 1831), p. 5; Emma Hart Willard, History of the United States (New York, 1845), p. iii.

[38] Fifty-Third Annual Report of the Regents of the University of the State of New York (1838), p. 107.

[39] A. H. L. Heeren, History of the States of Antiquity (Northampton, Mass., 1828), p. iii; S. G. Goodrich, Universal History, p. 2; Olney and Barber, Family View of History, p. 5; also, Whelpley, An Historical Compend, I, vi; Goldsmith, Roman History, p. 1; Samuel Griswold Goodrich, Pictorial History of

ful selection of the kinds of history to be studied. Writers especially called for large amounts of military history, since battlefield events seemed particularly full of adventure and heroic drama, and for social history, which allowed students to identify with the daily life of men in the past. Chiefly because educators believed these subjects were most interesting, about a third of the typical textbook after 1830 was devoted to military history and a tenth to social history.[40] Above all, authors struggled to enliven their books by introducing ideas as well as facts. Endlessly, they promised "to exercise the . . . habit of thinking" and "to fill the narrative with reflection rather than details . . . in order to make the work more interesting." [41]

To be sure, few textbooks actually contain very stirring narrative or do much to stimulate excitement for a modern reader. The point is, however, that most historians ardently championed the new educational methods, and, according to all evidence, history emerged as a favorite subject for the students. As is often the case, technology was ahead of theory. The formats of textbooks changed notably after about 1820, with more pages, larger type, topical headings, maps, and pictures. "Everything must, if possible, be presented to the eye," said an educator.[42] One of the most popular histories of Greece contained 200 pages of pictures in 400 pages of text; and one of the most widely used histories of the world contained 1,100 pictures in 1,000 pages of text.[43] Despite the difficulty of reproduction, textbook maps and charts may have been in greater use by the mid-nineteenth

the United States (Philadelphia, 1845), p. iv; William Cooke Taylor, *A Manual of Ancient History* (New York, 1855), p. vii.

[40] See below, p. 102.

[41] John Bigland, *Letters on French History* (Baltimore, 1819), p. 4; Joseph Emerson Worcester, *Elements of History* (Boston, 1840), p. v; also, Eliza Robbins, *English History* (New York, 1839), pp. 7–8; Manning, *History of the Middle Ages*, p. 12; Taylor, *Manual of Ancient History*, pp. iv, vii; Heeren, *History of the States of Antiquity*, p. iv.

[42] *Fifty-Third Annual Report of the Regents of the University of the State of New York* (1838), p. 97; also Willard, *History of the United States*, p. iii; Marcius Willson, *American History* . . . (New York, 1855), p. ix.

[43] Samuel Griswold Goodrich, *A Pictorial History of Greece* (New York, 1851); Frost, *Pictorial History of the World*.

century than they are today. Colored maps appeared in almost every text, and fold-out charts of vast ingenuity sometimes made historical facts appear more complex than they were in reality.[44]

History, then, made its way prominently into the schools during the early nineteenth century, primarily because it seemed useful, but also because it seemed interesting. Along with the new aims and methods in education came a definite concept of what history was supposed to be—a pleasant and exciting subject of stirring narrative and intellectual adventure.

[44] For example, Willard, *Universal History;* Elizabeth Peabody, *Chronological History of the United States* (New York, 1856); Joseph Emerson Worcester, *Elements of History . . . With a Chart and Tables of History Included Within the Volume* (Boston, 1848); Manning, *History of the Middle Ages.*

IV

The Writers of History

I N 1809, in one of the most famous parodies of American literature, Washington Irving drew a caricature of the contemporary historian. To Irving the historian was a slightly ridiculous
figure, a good-natured soul, abhorring publicity, too much in
love with pedantic toil ever to complete his work, and so wedded
to the past as to be oblivious to the realities of the present.[1]
There was much truth in the portrait. The pre-Civil War historian turned to the past almost entirely as an avocation, secure
in the knowledge that he was serving a useful purpose, and he
often resembled modern cartoons of the absent-minded professor.

Who They Were

There are 145 historians listed in *The Dictionary of American Biography*—a surprisingly large number—who did a major
portion of their work between 1800 and 1860, and from their
lives a more thorough, if less colorful, portrait than that of
Irving emerges.[2]

[1] Diedrich Knickerbocker [Washington Irving], *A History of New York,
from the beginning of the world to the end of the Dutch Dynasty . . . being
the only authentic history of the time that hath ever been, or ever will be
published* (2 vols.; New York, 1809), I, 1–8.

[2] Allen Johnson and Dumas Malone, eds., *The Dictionary of American Biography* (22 vols.; New York, 1928–44). The *Dictionary* is remarkably accurate

The early nineteenth-century historian was, first of all, likely to be a New Englander. Although comprising only 10 per cent of the population in 1860, the region produced 48 per cent of the historians, and Massachusetts alone produced over half of those. The Middle States produced 25 per cent of the historians; the South, 17 per cent; and 10 per cent were from abroad. Areas with rich historical heritages seemed to breed a consciousness of the past; only six historians were born in the trans-Appalachian region, but over twice that number were immigrants from the Old World.[3]

The historians were an extremely well-educated group. Although considerably less than 1 per cent of the population was educated beyond high school, 70 per cent of the historians had attended college. Several had done graduate work at European universities, though only George Bancroft had earned the Ph.D. degree.[4] Naturally, the New England colleges produced the largest number of historians, with twenty-six from Harvard, fifteen from Yale, five from Brown, four from Princeton, and three or less from each of thirty other colleges. Although the publicly supported city colleges and state universities emphasized history considerably more than the private classical colleges, the classical institutions produced by far the greater number of

---

and thorough in its index listing of the various occupations of its subjects, and most of these 145 men are to be found under the listing "Historians." Nevertheless, related occupations such as antiquarians, authors, biographers, chroniclers, church historians, editors, educators, medical historians, and writers have also been checked, and these occupations yielded a few other names.

For a similar statistical analysis of contemporary historians based on 2,979 replies to a questionnaire, see J. F. Wellemeyer, Jr., "Survey of United States Historians, 1952, and a Forecast," *American Historical Review*, XLI (January, 1956), 339–52.

[3] Birthplaces of 145 historians: Massachusetts, 38; New York, 18; Connecticut, 16; Pennsylvania, 13; Virginia, 10; Maine, 6; England, 6; Ireland, 5; North Carolina, 5; Maryland, 4; New Hampshire, 4; Rhode Island, 4; New Jersey, 3; Georgia, 2; Kentucky, 2; South Carolina, 2; Bermuda, 1; Germany, 1; Louisiana, 1; Mississippi, 1; Switzerland, 1; Tennessee, 1; and Vermont, 1.

[4] Today 99 per cent of the historians have at least one college degree, and 57 per cent have the Ph.D. Wellemeyer, "Survey of United States Historians," p. 346.

historians.[5] The kind of student who would become a historian was evidently attracted to the classical college. Possibly a classical education encouraged the study of history, while the additional history courses offered in publicly supported schools dampened further historical investigation.

Generally, it was not the young man just out of college who turned to history but rather the mature man with time and leisure for a hobby. Less than one-fourth of the historians published their first books before they were thirty years old, and over one-fourth published their first works after they were fifty. These men reflected the benefits of a good classical education, being able to turn to cultural pursuits such as the writing of history in the leisure of middle age.

The most striking contrast with the twentieth century was, of course, the nonprofessional character of the early nineteenth-century historian, for almost every one claimed something besides history as his chief profession or livelihood.[6] The primary professional occupation of the 145 major American historians was as follows:

Clergyman	34
Lawyer-statesman	32
Printer, editor, bookseller	18
Physician, scientist	17
Gentleman of wealth	9
Teacher	9
Writer, journalist	7
Librarian, archivist	7
Businessman	5
Engraver, artist	4
Planter	2
Historian	1

The clergymen and lawyer-statesmen, by far the most numer-

[5] See Richard Hofstadter and C. Dewitt Hardy, *The Development and Scope of Higher Education in the United States* (New York, 1952), pp. 9–28.

[6] In 1952 only 135 out of 2,979 historians were not professors, and many of these were retired or were still college students. Wellemeyer, "Survey of United States Historians," p. 340.

ous groups, were generally the least distinguished as historians. Although these included statesman John Marshall and clergymen Abiel Holmes and Francis Lister Hawks, men in these professions generally produced only one or two modest works, usually of local history. Similarly, other occupations which were not closely related to history writing—medicine, teaching, business, farming—produced a large number of relatively minor writers, though physician David Ramsay and educator George Ticknor provided something of an exception.

Professions that stood closer to the literary life produced a more eminent group. Printers, editors, and librarians easily combined an interest in the past with their occupations, and such men as Jared Sparks and Peter Force compiled and edited large masses of historical material. Professional writers and journalists also produced able histories. Their historical works were usually exciting narratives as opposed to the compilations of documents that preoccupied editors and librarians. Eminent novelists like Washington Irving, James Fenimore Cooper, Nathaniel Hawthorne, and William Gilmore Simms produced outstanding works of serious history. Three men listed as writers—James Parton, Joel Tyler Headley, and Benson John Lossing—might almost be called historians by profession, for they were among the most prolific writers about the past. Their best works were historical; however, they wrote much else besides, and essentially their purpose was to serve the muses of literature, biography, and journalism rather than Clio.

Clearly the outstanding historians were among the small body of men with no real profession at all, gentlemen of wealth and leisure. Writing chiefly for love of the subject and from a sense of service to society, they had little concern for profit or acclaim. They approached history as an avocation rather than as a profession or means of livelihood. In this category were the nation's most eminent historians—William Hickling Prescott, Francis Parkman, and John Lothrop Motley. Others such as John Gorham Palfrey, George Ticknor, and George Bancroft might also be included in this group, for while they are listed as editor, educator, and historian, they too were men of wealth who wrote

history for love of the subject rather than as a means of livelihood. Most of these outstanding historians were of the Boston
Brahmin caste which contributed so richly to American culture
and could claim to have returned with large dividends the
fortunes society had created for them. Many of the Brahmins
devoted themselves to literary pursuits in ante-bellum America,
and a remarkable number chose to write about history. Only
slightly less eminent were Samuel Eliot, Mercy Otis Warren, and
Isaiah Thomas of Boston, Charles Etienne Gayarré of New Or-
leans, and Henry Charles Lea of Philadelphia, all of whom had
a position, if not a profession, of leisure which permitted them
to indulge in the writing of history.

The interest of historians in the past came surprisingly late in
the prewar period. While the peak of public interest in history
had come in the 1820's and was on the decline by the 1850's,
the interest of writers in the past was only beginning in the
1830's, and they were rapidly increasing their output at the
end of the period. The 145 important historians between 1800
and 1860 published 625 significant historical volumes which
appeared by decades as follows:

1800–1809	26
1810–1819	42
1820–1829	50
1830–1839	158
1840–1849	123
1850–1859	226

The great increase in historical writing in the 1830's can be
explained largely by the publication of historical documents,
with Jared Sparks's documentary and biographical works alone
accounting for 47 volumes. Generally instigated and financed by
the national and local governments, these ponderous documentary publications were products of the popular demand for history. Many of the best narrative histories came even later; writers
such as Bancroft, Motley, Prescott, Parkman, and Lea, whose
early work relates them to the first part of the century, actually
brought out many of their works in the 1860's, the 1870's, and

even the 1880's, by which time their Romantic concept of history was generally considered old-fashioned.

Thus the writers of history appeared to be the product, not the cause, of the new historical interest which was manifest in the schools, in the establishment of historical societies and government archives, in architectural revival styles, and in popular reading. The historians' lag can partly be explained by the age of the writers, for while their interest in and view of history was formed early in life when the Romantic movement was at its peak, they were often past middle age when their major works appeared, and by then their concepts were often dated. Perhaps there is a consistent pattern in the lag of historical scholarship. With the coming of intellectual currents like rationalism in the eighteenth century, Romanticism in the early nineteenth, realism in the mid-nineteenth, and relativism in the early twentieth —history seemed to trail behind literature, art, philosophy, science, and possibly even behind the temper of the public mind.

Why They Wrote

History was primarily a hobby in ante-bellum America, and by far the greatest number of historians were motivated simply by a love of the past, a desire to amuse themselves and occupy their hours of leisure. Men of leisure like the Brahmins could afford to devote full time to their hobby, and this was one reason for the pre-eminence of their work. Often their interest in the past was whetted by a rich family heritage and intensified by European travel. Jared Sparks explained that history had been an "absorbing passion" since youth. Francis Parkman, John Lothrop Motley, George Ticknor, and Charles Etienne Gayarré wrote of how history, as a pleasant diversion, had been a great love and hobby at least since college days.[7] As Prescott explained:

[7] Sparks to George Bancroft, December 26, 1825, cited in John Spencer Bassett, *The Middle Group of American Historians* (New York, 1917), p. 137. Prescott's Journal, 1822, cited in George Ticknor, *Life of William Hickling Prescott* (Boston, 1863), p. 70. Parkman to F. P. Martin Brimmer, October 28, 1886, quoted in Henry Dwight Sedgwick, *Francis Parkman* (Boston, 1904), p. 328; Motley to William Amory, February 26, 1859, quoted in Oliver Wendell

Pursuing the work in this quite leisurely way, without overexertion or fatigue, or any sense of obligation to complete it in any given time, I have found it a continual source of pleasure. It has furnished food for my meditations, has given a direction and object to my scattered reading, and supplied me with regular occupation for hours that would otherwise have filled me with *ennui*.[8]

Other men, less fortunate financially, could turn to writing history only in their spare time. "I felt the necessity of something, which, by occupying my mind, should relieve me" from the tedium of my profession, explained a historian-doctor.[9] Another declared that writing history had been "one of the cherished projects of his youth," and that "very early in the period of his professional life he began the task of collecting and arranging the materials," which only now, during retirement, he was able to narrate.[10] John Gorham Palfrey discovered in retirement that the subject which had "been long a favorite occupation of my leisure" would be "a suitable employment for what may remain in my life." [11] Many a book was "the fruit of days and nights stolen from other pursuits," and many historians explained that their work was written "whenever the author's occupation in life would permit his indulgence in any literary pursuit," or "during those hours of leisure that could be found in the intervals of the regular practice of medicine" or the duties of a clergyman.[12]

Holmes, *John Lothrop Motley: A Memoir* (Boston, 1879), pp. 63–65; Anna Ticknor, *Life, Letters, and Journals of George Ticknor* (2 vols.; Boston, 1877), pp. 243–44; Charles Gayarré, *Romance of the History of Louisiana* (New York, 1848), pp. 9–10.

[8] Prescott's Diary, June 26, 1836, cited in G. Ticknor, *Life of Prescott*, p. 103.

[9] Henry Reed Stiles, *The History of Ancient Windsor, Connecticut . . .* (New York, 1859), p. v.

[10] John Van Lean McMahon, *An Historical View of the Government of Maryland, From Its Colonization to the Present Day* (Baltimore, 1831), pp. iii–iv.

[11] John Gorham Palfrey, *History of New England* (5 vols.; Boston, 1859–90), I, x–xi.

[12] Henderson Yoakum, *History of Texas from Its First Settlement in 1685 to Its Annexation to the United States in 1846* (2 vols.; New York, 1856), I, 3; John Leeds Bozman, *A Sketch of the History of Maryland during the First Three Years after Its Settlement* (Baltimore, 1811), p. v; Robert Breckinridge

To some hobbyists the process of writing history was, as Washington Irving suggested, a labor of love which the author so relished that he hated to complete his work. George Ticknor called his work "a task I cannot find it in my heart to hurry, so agreeable it is to me." [13] Another writer declared: "If the reader shall derive from its perusal the same satisfaction which I have found in its compilation, I shall feel myself abundantly remunerated for this labor of love." [14]

To other historians it was not so much the process of writing as the romance of the past itself that was exciting. The devoted antiquarian felt a warm and melancholy glow in musing on antiquity and wandering in graveyards. It was not the particular subject that mattered, these men would say, but simply "the love of olden time" gratified by dwelling on the past.[15] "All antiquity is environed by some halo of romance—by a mystic veil that greatly engages our curiosity." [16] Young men went abroad to indulge a love of antiquity, or sometimes they first discovered a love of the past in the ruins found there. Motley, alone in Holland, wrote of his delight in ruins, tombs, old castles, and ancient art. "The dead men of the place are my intimate friends," he wrote. "I am at home in any cemetery." [17]

McAfee, *History of the Late War in the Western Country* . . . (Lexington, Ky., 1816), p. iii; Samuel Prescott Hildreth, *Pioneer History: Being An Account of the First Examination of the Ohio Valley, and the Early Settlement of the Northwest Territory* (Cincinnati, 1848), p. iv; see also John Hill Wheeler, *Historical Sketches of North Carolina, from 1584 to 1851* (2 vols.; Philadelphia, 1851), I, xvii; Clifford Kenyon Shipton, *Isaiah Thomas, Printer, Patriot and Philanthropist, 1749–1831* (Rochester, 1948), pp. 74–80.

[13] Cited in A. Ticknor, *Life of George Ticknor*, I, 244.

[14] Alexander Young, *Chronicles of the Pilgrim Fathers of the Colony of Plymouth from 1602 to 1625* (Boston, 1841), p. xi; see also, Hildreth, *Pioneer History*, p. iv.

[15] John Hammond Trumbull, *The Public Records of the Colony of Connecticut, Prior to the Union with the New Haven Colony, May, 1665* . . . (3 vols.; Hartford, 1850–59), I, iii.

[16] David Hoffman, *Chronicles Selected from the Originals of Cartaphilus, the Wandering Jew* (3 vols.; London, 1853), I, v; see also Charles Colcock Jones, *Monumental Remains of Georgia* (Savannah, 1861), p. 7.

[17] Motley to Oliver Wendell Holmes, November 20, 1853, cited in Holmes, *John Lothrop Motley*, p. 69; see also Chester Penn Higby and Bindford Toney Schantz, *John Lothrop Motley* (New York, 1939), p. xxiii.

Another writer told how he "loved to meditate among old tombs," how he "would rather hold converse with old books, and old epitaphs, and old ruins, than with the living." [18] One author compiled five volumes of graveyard epitaphs, explaining that "from an early age, I have been in the habit, as opportunity presented, of copying from stones, erected to the memory of the dead." He believed that it would "afford religious gratification and advantage to every heart fraught with christian [sic] sensibility, to meditate among the tombs." [19]

To others it was the love of a particular subject rather than writing or antiquity that gave to history its attractiveness. "I had not first made up my mind to write a history, and then cast about to take up a subject," wrote one scholar. "My subject had taken me up, drawn me on, and absorbed me into itself." [20] Francis Parkman also came to history not because of fondness for the past or a literary life, but through fascination with the colors and fragrance of the western forest and the drama of the conquest of a continent. "Delving into dusty books and papers," he said frankly, was "a kind of work I detested." [21] Prescott, too, though he loved writing, was much more interested in the excitement of the subject itself than in research. Cheerfully he admitted that mere digging into the past was something he "destested—hunting up latent, barren antiquities." [22] Many local historians, especially those of religion, explained that it was affection for the subject itself that led them to explore its background and history, to "dwell lovingly upon her conflicts and triumphs, her sufferings and joys, her thoughts, words, and deeds." [23]

[18] Philip Slaughter, *A History of Bristol Parish, Virginia, with Genealogies of Families Connected Therewith, and Historical Illustrations* (Richmond, 1846), p. x.

[19] Timothy Alden, *A Collection of American Epitaphs and Inscriptions with Occasional Notes* (5 vols.; New York, 1814), I, 5–6.

[20] Motley to William Amory, February 26, 1859, cited in Holmes, *John Lothrop Motley*, p. 63.

[21] Parkman to F. P. Martin Brimmer, October 28, 1886, cited in Sedgwick, *Francis Parkman*, p. 330.

[22] Cited in G. Ticknor, *Life of Prescott*, p. 75.

[23] Philip Schaff, *History of the Apostolic Church: With a General Introduction to Church History* (New York, 1854), p. iii. See also Frank Lister Hawks,

The man with the avocation of history often cared little for the product of his labor. "I don't care for the result," wrote Motley; "The labor is in itself its own reward and all I want." [24] Many writers began with no thought of publication and agreed to it reluctantly so that "it might afford the reader half the pleasure I had in its compilation," or so that "others may share" the delight the author found in the subject.[25] After he had completed his first manuscript on Spain, Prescott hesitated long before allowing it to be published. The work, he explained, had been for his own amusement, not for the public. When finally persuaded to let it go to press, he wrote again, "I must confess that I feel some disquietude at the prospect of coming in full bodily presence, as it were, before the public . . . . When I saw my name—harmonious Hickling and all [in a prepublication advertisement], it gave me . . . quite a turn;—anything but agreeable." [26]

Whether historians were motivated by a fondness for writing, a feeling for past time, or a particular subject, few men in pre-Civil War America turned to writing history for profit, and most of those who did so were disappointed. Although the public bought history books in proportions which have not been equaled since, little writing of any kind was profitable to American authors of the early nineteenth century. The book-buying public was small, printing was expensive, and copyright laws were ineffective. Authors seldom expected royalties, for

---

Contributions to the Ecclestiastical History of the United States of America (2 vols.; New York, 1836–39), I, ix; John Leeds Bozman, *A Sketch of the History of Maryland,* p. 349; Lorenzo Sabine, *The American Loyalists . . .* (Boston, 1847), p. 372; William Leete Stone, *Life of Joseph Brant . . .* (2 vols.; New York, 1838), I, xix.

[24] Motley to Oliver Wendell Holmes, November 20, 1853, cited in Holmes, *John Lothrop Motley,* p. 70.

[25] Yoakum, *History of Texas,* I, 3; McMahon, *Historical View of Maryland,* p. iv; see also William Henry Prescott, *The Diplomatic History of the Administrations of Washington and Adams, 1789–1801* (Boston, 1857), p. viii; Alexander Young, *Chronicles of the Pilgrim Fathers of the Colony of Plymouth, from 1602 to 1625* (Boston, 1841), p. xi; George Ticknor, *History of Spanish Literature* (3 vols.; New York, 1849), I, x.

[26] Prescott to Ticknor, April 11, 1837, cited in G. Ticknor, *Life of Prescott,* p. 105.

writing was generally considered the polite occupation of a gentleman.

That few men could have been writing for profit seems evident from the small royalties which even the most successful historians realized. If such men as Irving, Bancroft, Prescott, and Sparks, with the most popular subjects, could not make a living at writing history, the ordinary hobbyist could not hope to acquire much profit. The greatest single income from history royalties was probably that of Washington Irving. Including such works as the Knickerbocker history of New York which is semifictional, and *The Legend from the Alhambra* which is largely travel, his total income from writing history was probably about $100,000. Distributed over the fifty years from 1809 to 1859, during which his twelve volumes of history appeared, Irving's total income from the subject was about $2,000 a year.[27]

George Bancroft's royalties varied from a peak of about $4,250 in 1841 to $1,448 in 1865.[28] Bancroft reported that he had actually spent $100,000 on collecting and writing his history, and if he averaged $2,500 a year in profits, it would have taken forty years to pay his actual costs.[29] Jared Sparks, an experienced editor with an eye to profits, earned about $75,000 during a lifetime of publishing more than sixty volumes, chiefly from editing the twenty-five-volume *Library of American Biography* in a manner that was, to say the least, shrewd.[30] Prescott's income from history was probably about $60,000, and from this he paid secretaries and European copyists, in addition to the cost of the library he was forced to purchase. Like many of the gentleman-authors, he expected financial loss, observing that "lucre is

[27] Pierre Munroe Irving, *The Life and Letters of Washington Irving* (4 vols.; New York, 1864), IV, 410–11; Stanley Thomas Williams, *The Life of Washington Irving* (2 vols.; New York, 1935), II, 338 and *passim;* Bassett, *Middle Group of American Historians,* pp. 313–14. These figures, like the following ones, are estimates at best.

[28] Russel B. Nye, *George Bancroft: Brahmin Rebel* (New York, 1944), pp. 121, 227.

[29] Michael Kraus, *The Writing of American History* (Norman, Okla., 1953), p. 122. Bancroft's profits are estimated at $2,500 a year in Donald E. Emerson, *Richard Hildreth* (Baltimore, 1947), p. 143.

[30] Bassett, *Middle Group of American Historians,* pp. 308–12.

not my object." [31] Marshall received about $20,000 from his life of Washington; Hildreth made less than $5,000 on his massive volumes; and Parkman received no royalties on his work until after the Civil War.[32] The journalist James Parton, called by his biographer the first American to make a living entirely by writing, earned about $2,000 on each of his three popular histories which appeared before 1860.[33]

To the great body of part-time antiquarians—the hundreds of retired clergymen and lawyers who became local chroniclers—profit was no object at all. The most popular of the scholarly state histories, that of Jeremy Belknap, cost the author so dearly that he was forced to delay publication of the last volume for eight years.[34] Local histories and local biographies had to be subsidized by the town, state, or local historical society, or else were published by the author as a service.

Although spectacular royalties did not materialize and the profit motive could only have applied to a few, such an incentive at least helped produce some of the most popular volumes. Authors like Bancroft, Sparks, Irving, and Marshall undoubtedly kept an eye to profit, and even if they were generally disappointed, a small income from their avocation helped reconcile them to spending the time on it.[35] Journalists, printers, and literary adventurers like Parton, Headley, Abbott, Lossing, and Bulfinch eagerly sought the modest royalties available in historical publishing. While few in number, these men produced numerous exotic historical studies, popular surveys of religion

[31] Prescott to Ticknor, December 29, 1835, cited in G. Ticknor, *Life of Prescott*, pp. 107, 105. Prescott sold approximately 60,000 copies of his works at a profit of about one dollar a copy. See Bassett, *Middle Group of American Historians*, pp. 312–13; Harry Thurston Pack, *William Hickling Prescott* (New York, 1905), p. 95.

[32] Albert Jeremiah Beveridge, *The Life of John Marshall* (4 vols.; Boston, 1919), III, 226, 251; Emerson, *Richard Hildreth*, pp. 143; Charles Haight Farnham, *A Life of Francis Parkman* (Boston, 1901), p. 189.

[33] Milton Embick Flower, *James Parton: The Father of Modern Biography* (Durham, N.C., 1951), pp. 4, 33.

[34] Bassett, *Middle Group of American Historians*, pp. 306–7.

[35] See *ibid.*, pp. 303–14; Nye, *George Bancroft*, pp. 121, 227; Williams, *Life of Washington Irving* (2 vols.; New York, 1935), II, 338 and *passim;* Beveridge, *Life of Marshall*, III, 223–25.

and of battles, and popular biographies. Even for the most mercenary, however, it took a genuine love of history to turn men to the past.

Another motive, perhaps deeper than pleasure or profit, that caused men to write history was a sense of service, a sincere conviction of the duty of man to utilize his time and talents in activity beneficial to mankind. Writing history was a service to the communtiy that would educate and uplift the masses, rescue the worthy from oblivion, memorialize a beloved town or state, and make a contribution as literature to American culture. Like the ideals which Romantic educators inculcated in history textbooks, this concept of service was really more Victorian than Romantic. Perhaps this attitude stemmed from a Puritan heritage, perhaps it was *noblesse oblige,* but certainly it was genuine and powerful. In the twentieth century men are often suspicious of elevated motives. To many historians of ante-bellum America, however, it was far more than hypocrisy or desire for acclaim that led them to express their eagerness to serve, and far more than self-seeking that led them to the past. Albert James Pickett, an Alabama planter-historian, analyzed his reasons for writing history:

> About four years since, feeling impressed with the fact that it was the duty of every man to make himself, in some way, useful to his race, I looked around in search of some object, in the pursuit of which I could benefit my fellow-citizens; for although much interested in agriculture, that did not occupy one-fourth of my time. Having no taste for politics, and never having studied a profession, I determined to write a History.[36]

One writer declared that he wrote "for the pleasure of contributing his mite to the service of the community"; another insisted that *"Public Utility* has been the predominant object of my labour." [37] Men really believed, in the nineteenth century, that "man subserves the purpose of moral existence, when he

[36] Albert James Pickett, *History of Alabama, and Incidentally of Georgia and Mississippi, from the Earliest Period* (Sheffield, Ala., 1851), p. 10.

[37] Benjamin Trumbull, *A Complete History of Connecticut . . . to the Year 1764* (2 vols.; New Haven, 1818), I, 5. Humphrey Marshall, *The History of Kentucky* (2 vols.; Frankfort, 1824), I, iii.

does what is a real benefit to his Country"—and writing history
was such a subservice of existence.[38] The Brahmin historians
were particularly aware of their obligations in this respect.
Mercy Otis Warren explained that she had devoted herself to
history in order "to improve the leisure that Providence has
lent"; Parkman expressed a similar sentiment.[39] Prescott explained his search for an occupation:

> A person in our country who takes little interest in politics or in
> making money—our staples, you know—will be thrown pretty much
> on his own resources, and if he is not fond of books he may as well
> go hang himself, for as to a class of idle gentlemen, there is no
> such thing here.[40]

Such an attitude drove historians to continue their labors long
after writing had ceased to be a pleasure. Man must work hard
to be useful, must utilize all his talents, must force himself on
when he would prefer to rest. "I held that the true aim of life
was not happiness but achievement," wrote Parkman.[41] When
Prescott lapsed into idleness or fell behind schedule he imposed
fines upon himself, amounting to as much as $1,000 a year, which
he contributed to charity.[42] "The end of being was best answered," he believed, "by a life of active usefulness, and not by
one of abstract contemplation, or selfish indulgence, or passive
fortitude." [43]

American historians of this period, then, may be classified

[38] William Durken Williamson, *The History of the State of Maine; From
its First Discovery, A.D. 1602 to the Separation, A.D. 1820, Inclusive* (2 vols.;
Hallowell, Me., 1839), I, iv. See also Sabine, *American Loyalists*, p. iv; Samuel
Green Arnold, *The Life of Patrick Henry of Virginia* (Auburn, N.Y., 1854), p.
14.

[39] Mercy Otis Warren, *History of the Rise, Progress and Termination of the
American Revolution . . .* (3 vols.; Boston, 1805), I, iii. Parkman to F. P.
Martin Brimmer, October 28, 1886, cited in Sedgwick, *Francis Parkman*,
pp. 329-35.

[40] Prescott to Nicolaus Heinrich Julius, May 20, 1839, Roger Wolcott, ed.,
The Correspondence of William Hickling Prescott, 1833–1847 (Boston, 1925),
pp. 71-72.

[41] Parkman to F. P. Martin Brimmer, October 28, 1886, cited in Sedgwick,
Francis Parkman, p. 329.

[42] Ticknor, *Life of Prescott*, pp. 135-37.

[43] William Hickling Prescott, *Biographical and Critical Miscellanies* (Philadelphia, 1865), p. 93.

into three or four distinct types with different interests. First of all there were the gentlemen of leisure. Ablest of the historians and fairly numerous, they were men of inherited wealth or were retired from a successful career. They were likely to be from Boston, or at any rate from one of the older eastern states. Highly educated, with a degree from a classical college, they undertook ambitious subjects to amuse themselves and to serve the public. Perhaps they chose an exotic subject such as Spain or Peru, perhaps a history of America or some broad, cultural topic. Their works combined art and scholarship, for they were interested in history in its grandest sense, as art and truth.

A similar group of historians were the lawyers, doctors, and clergymen who throughout their lifetimes had turned to collecting historical materials and who in their retirement, devoted themselves to compiling a single grand opus. They, too, were prominent citizens, highly educated, often from New England or the East. Numerically they were the largest group of historians, but they were modest in aims and accomplishments. Almost invariably they were interested in a local subject—the history of their native town or state or the biography of a local man of eminence. Their volumes were generally compilations of myriad facts, evincing laborious scholarship but little philosophy or art.

A few professional journalists, printers, and novelists also turned to history to find an exciting story, to meet the public demand for a short and dramatic, simple and informative narrative. Men of little education, perhaps from New York, they were younger, few in number, but prolific in works and in sales. Biography was their favorite topic, for that is what the public wanted to buy, though sometimes they would bring out a history of religion, an episode from the Revolution, or a tale of exotic peoples. They did not pretend to scholarship; they sought chiefly to popularize what others had done, and their art was the art of journalism.

Finally, there were the patient professional archivists, editors, and collectors. They were the smallest group, and least eminent in society, education, and ability. A few, such as professional publishers, undertook these compilations for profit; some were salaried state employees; all, however, were devoted antiquarians who looked upon their projects as labors of love and service.

In all America not a book was written to earn a man a degree, and scarcely one was written to earn its author professional recognition. Perhaps the distinguishing characteristic of historians was their internal motivation. As the historians of that generation were different from their professional progeny, the kind of history they produced was different also.

V

The Subject Matter of History

THE fashion for various fields of history changes. In 1957 the school board of Houston, Texas, revised its social studies curriculum, eliminating world history and striking all mention of the United Nations. The board substituted one year of Houston history, two years of Texas history, and two years of American history "with emphasis on the Southwest." Americans in the nineteenth century preferred somewhat different fields.

History presented such an unexplored panorama at the beginning of the nineteenth century that choosing the correct subject seemed especially important. Later historians moved methodically into what "needed to be done," but men of the Romantic era did not take the subject so much for granted. Schoolmasters argued endlessly whether "universal," ancient, or American history best presented the lessons of the past. Authors agonized over possible topics before they began to write. Reviewers debated angrily which author had been most felicitous in choice of subject.[1]

Since men thought of history as story, the historian's duty was to select a subject that served as a narrative tale, unified and

[1] See reviews in *Atlantic Monthly*, III (January, 1859), 122; *Living Age*, XXIV (February, 1850), 202; *Christian Examiner*, XXX (July, 1841), 310–12; *Christian Examiner*, XXIV (March, 1838), 99; *North American Review*, XC (January, 1860), 23.

complete. Charles W. Botta decided to write a history of the American Revolution after listening to a discussion in a Paris salon about the most appropriate topic for an epic poem. If the Revolution was the grandest theme for a poem, he reasoned, it was certainly the grandest for a history. Sometimes writers decided upon subjects for their inherent drama, claiming that their choice included "all that is wild and wonderful in history . . . so much that is strange and romantic." [2] Other times they emphasized significance, a topic which "changed the direction of history," or the one which "shaped the modern world." [3] At still other times the skillful writer justified his choice by arguing its relevance to the daily life of his readers, guaranteeing that Dutch independence, Spanish expansion, or Austrian feudalism were intimately "bound up with the everyday affairs" of contemporary Americans.[4]

Critics, especially, assumed that the historian chose his topic in much the same way that an artist selected the subject for his painting, deliberately matching it to his personality, literary style, ideas, and purpose. Just as the color, line, and feeling of Titian were suited to sensuous nudes, so the style, philosophy, and feeling of Bancroft were suited to depicting the glory of the United States. Gainsborough should not paint nudes, and Prescott should not write about Puritans. "The first indication of the degree to which the historian possesses the power of judgment is to be seen in his choice of subject." Keeping in mind the theme he wished to develop, his stylistic abilities, his taste, ideas,

---

[2] John Stevens Cabot Abbott, *The Empire of Austria* (New York, 1859), p. v; also Humphrey Marshall, *The History of Kentucky* (2 vols.; Frankfort, 1811), I, viii.

[3] Samuel Green Arnold, *History of the State of Rhode Island* . . . (2 vols.; New York, 1859), I, v; James Parton, *Life of Andrew Jackson* (3 vols.; New York, 1820), I, vi; Samuel Eliot, *History of Liberty* (4 vols.; Boston, 1853), I, v; John Lothrop Motley, *The Rise of the Dutch Republic* (3 vols.; New York, 1856), I, iii–v.

[4] Motley, *Dutch Republic*, I, v; Prescott's Journal, 1825, cited in George Ticknor, *Life of William Hickling Prescott* (Boston, 1863), p. 72; Abbott, *Empire of Austria*, p. vi; Benjamin Trumbull, *A Complete History of Connecticut . . . to the Year 1764* (2 vols.; New Haven, 1818), I, v.

and emotional attachments, he should "choose his subject, so as to do most justice to his own abilities." [5] Critics declared that an artist like Francis Parkman, with his style "redolent with forest fragrance," had to write about the American frontier; that William H. Prescott's dramatic style was ideally suited to "memorials of vanished greatness" of the Incas and Aztecs; and that George Bancroft's sweeping style suited him to the epic of America's growth.[6] Later historians could hardly quarrel with the theory, but few were so conscious of putting it to practice.

The following table indicates the areas of history to which schoolboys were most exposed, in which writers were most productive, and to which the reading public was most responsive.

POPULARITY OF VARIOUS FIELDS [7]

Field	Percentage of Textbooks	Percentage of Works by 145 Leading Writers	Percentage of Most Popular Books
United States			
General	25	13	22
Regional	2	10	4
State	3	13	4
Local	0	5	2
Western civilization			
General	25	5	6
Ancient	26	1	4
Medieval	1	1	11
Since 1500	12	4	24
Non-Western	0	13	3
Biography	2	26	17
Religion	3	8	2

[5] John Hill, "An Essay upon the Principles of Historical Composition," *Portfolio*, IX (April, 1820), 347; also, review, *Philadelphia Museum*, XXXVI (August, 1839), 454.

[6] Reviews, *Living Age*, XXXI (October, 1851), 138; *North American Review*, LXXXVIII (April, 1859), 463; *North American Review*, XL (January, 1835), 100.

[7] This is based on the 439 textbooks, 625 works by leading historians, and 147 best sellers discussed above. Multivolume studies are counted as a single work.

United States History

United States history comprised only about one-third of American general interest in the past, probably a smaller proportion than it does today. Stimulated by the nationalism following the Revolution, interest in American history developed earliest among the historians themselves, who were anxious to know and proclaim the historic mission of America. The reading public, perhaps dutifully at first, seized upon the first accounts because they were new and flattering. The historians who endeavored to write about the vast and undeveloped subject of the new country were few in number, considerably fewer than those who wrote about a local subject, but they were an able and ambitious group. The five best general histories—written by Abiel Holmes, David Ramsay, George Bancroft, Richard Hildreth, and George Tucker—were all serious multivolume works, based on some degree of original scholarship and occupying a large portion of the author's life.[8] There were, of course, many less ambitious works on general American history, notably the histories of the Revolution by Ramsay, Mercy Otis Warren, Timothy Pitkin, and Benson John Lossing.[9] Except for the Revolution, however, early nineteenth-century historians generally avoided monographic studies of periods, issues, or institutions, for these were

[8] Abiel Holmes, *The Annals of America, From the Discovery by Columbus in the Year 1492, to the Year 1826* (2 vols.; Cambridge, Mass., 1805); David Ramsay, *History of the United States From Their First Settlement as English Colonies in 1607, to the Year 1808* . . . (3 vols.; Philadelphia, 1816–17); George Bancroft, *History of the United States of America From the Discovery of the Continent to 1789* (10 vols.; Boston, 1834–75); Richard Hildreth, *The History of the United States of America* (6 vols.; New York, 1856); George Tucker, *The History of the United States, From their Colonization to 1841* (4 vols.; Philadelphia, 1856–57). For a discussion of these works, see Michael Kraus, *The Writing of American History* (Norman, Okla., 1953); and John Spencer Bassett, *The Middle Group of American Historians* (New York, 1917).

[9] David Ramsay, *The History of the American Revolution* (2 vols.; London, 1793); Mercy Otis Warren, *History of the Rise, Progress and Termination of the American Revolution* . . . (3 vols.; Boston, 1805); Timothy Pitkin, *A Political and Civil History of the United States of America From the Year 1763 to the Close of the Administration of President Washington,* . . . (2 vols.; New Haven, 1828); Benson John Lossing, *The Pictorial Field-Book of the Revolution* (2 vols.; New York, 1851–52).

incomplete and unsatisfying subjects. Instead, if they had to restrict themselves, they usually dealt with biography or with a complete story of some particular locality.

A much larger number of historians were attracted to regional, state, and local history. The more localized, the greater was the interest; indeed, the historians' pre-Civil War concern with local history has never since been equaled. As is often the case, however, the more geographically limited the interest of historians were, the more modest their accomplishments. While American history was characterized by a few important works, regional and state history was characterized by a reasonable number of moderately good works, and town history by a large mass of generally poor histories.

The five-volume *History of New England* by John Gorham Palfrey was the most ambitious and famous of the regional works.[10] Able works on the Mississippi Valley by Timothy Flint, Henry Howe, and John Wesley Monette also appeared.[11] By 1860, every one of the original states and many of the new western ones boasted long, thorough volumes about their past, but they were more likely to be amateurish compilations than the flowing narratives commonly associated with Romantic historians. Among the best were the volumes of Jeremy Belknap, John Daly Burk, David Ramsay, Benjamin Trumbull, and Charles Etienne Gayarré.[12] The vast number of town chronicles were

---

[10] (Boston, 1850–90).

[11] Timothy Flint, *The History and Geography of the Mississippi Valley* (2 vols.; Boston, 1833); Henry Howe, *Historical Collections of the Great West* . . . (2 vols.; Cincinnati, 1852); John Wesley Monette, *History of the Discovery and Settlement of the Valley of the Mississippi* . . . (2 vols.; New York, 1846).

[12] Typical, and among the best state histories before 1860 were: Thomas Hutchinson, *The History of the Colony and Province of Massachusetts Bay* (3 vols.; London, 1764–1828); Alexander Hewat, *An Historical Account of the Rise and Progress of the Colonies of South Carolina and Georgia* . . . (2 vols.; London, 1779); Jeremy Belknap, *The History of New Hampshire* (3 vols.; Philadelphia and Boston, 1784–92); Robert Proud, *The History of Pennsylvania* . . . (2 vols.; Philadelphia, 1797–98); John Daly Burk, *The History of Virginia, From Its First Settlement to the Present Day* (4 vols.; Petersburg, Va., 1804–8); David Ramsay, *The History of South Carolina From Its First Settlement in 1670 to the Year 1808* (2 vols.; Charleston, 1809); John Leeds Bozman, *A Sketch of the History of Maryland during the First Three*

generally detailed, highly factual, liberally sprinkled with genealogy, and frequently 700 pages or more in length.[13] New England
produced the best and most numerous of these chronicles; the
South tended to excel in state histories, and the West boasted the
best regional ones.

The schools lagged behind the public in concern for American
history. Rather than the subject evolving easily from the old classical curriculum, it entered the classroom as a result of the
demands of statesmen, legislators, and the press. Not until the
establishment of public schools in the 1820's, did American history begin to assume an important place. Six states required by
law that American history be taught in the public schools, while
ancient history, which was far more popular in the private
academies, was not required by a single one. The teaching of
American history seemed to be an ideal way of inspiring patriotism and good citizenship, practical results of education that the
public believed it could justifiably expect from the public schools.

The first textbook of American history was the long-anony-
mous *Introduction to the History of America* written by John
McCulloch, a Philadelphia publisher, in 1778.[14] During the next
thirty years only four other texts appeared, but a deluge began

---

Years After Its Settlement (Baltimore, 1811); Benjamin Trumbull, *A Complete
History of Connecticut . . . to the Year 1764* (2 vols.; New Haven, 1818); John
Haywood, *The Civil and Political History of the State of Tennessee* (Knox-
ville, 1823); Humphrey Marshall, *The History of Kentucky* (2 vols.; Frankfort,
1824); William D. Williamson, *The History of the State of Maine . . .* (Hal-
lowell, Me., 1839); William Bacon Stevens, *A History of Georgia* (2 vols.; New
York, 1847–59); Charles Etienne Gayarré, *Louisiana: Its Colonial History and
Romance* (3 vols.; New York, 1851–54); Henderson Yoakum, *History of
Texas from Its First Settlement in 1685 to Its Annexation to the United
States in 1846* (2 vols.; New York, 1856); Francis Lister Hawks, *History of
North Carolina . . .* (2 vols.; Fayetteville, N.C., 1857–58); Edward Duffield
Neill, *The History of Minnesota . . .* (Philadelphia, 1858); Samuel Green
Arnold, *History of the State of Rhode Island and Providence Plantations* (2
vols.; New York, 1859).

[13] Typical of these histories were William Read Staples, *Annals of the
Town of Providence* (Providence, R.I., 1843); Henry R. Stiles. *The History
of Ancient Windsor, Connecticut . . .* (New York, 1859); Daniel Pierce
Thompson, *History of the Town of Montpelier . . .* (Montpelier, Vt., 1860).

[14] See Alice Winifred Spieseke, *The First Textbooks in American History
and Their Compiler John McCulloch* (New York, 1938).

in the 1820's. Out of the more than one hundred American histories that appeared there were about eight which set the pattern and largely dominated the schools. The most prominent author was Samuel Griswold Goodrich, who wrote under the name of Peter Parley. A professional textbook author on every conceivable subject, he claimed to have written 170 volumes, which sold 7,000,000 copies. The most popular of his books was *A Pictorial History of the United States* . . . . Goodrich's chief competitor may have been his brother, Charles Augustus Goodrich, who gave up the profession of clergyman to devote his full time to writing and revising children's texts. Emma Hart Willard, a crusader for female education, was said to have sold a million copies of her textbooks, of which her *History of the United States* . . . was the most successful. Almost as popular were the books of John Frost, Marcius Willson, Jesse Olney, Salma Hale, and William Grimshaw. Of these eight most prominent authors, all but Grimshaw, an Irishman who migrated to Pennsylvania, were from New England; the region most conscious of education and tradition led the way in the study of American history. Seldom professional educators, the textbook authors were men of the world who found this kind of writing needed and profitable. Of the eight, five were at some time public officeholders; however, with the exception of Mrs. Willard, a school principal, all dropped their former professions to devote full time to textbook writing.[15]

The study of United States history was concentrated at the primary level in the schools, while ancient and world history

[15] Samuel Griswold Goodrich, *A Pictorial History of the United States* . . . (Philadelphia, 1845); Charles Augustus Goodrich, *History of the United States of America* (Hartford 1823); Emma Hart Willard, *History of the United States* . . . (New York, 1828); John Frost, *The Pictorial History of the United States* . . . (Philadelphia, 1843); Marcius Willson, *American History* . . . (New York, 1847); Jesse Olney, *A History of the United States for the Use of Academies* (New Haven, 1851); Salma Hale, *History of the United States* . . . (New York, 1825); William Grimshaw, *History of the United States* . . . (Philadelphia, 1822). See Clifton Johnson, *Old Time Schools and School Books* (New York, 1904), p. 372 and *passim;* Alfred Goldberg, "School Histories of the Middle Period," Eric Frederick Goldman, ed., *Historiography and Urbanization, Essays in Honor of W. Stull Holt* (Baltimore, 1941), pp. 171–88.

appeared most often in the upper levels. In part this stemmed from the greater public control over the lower grades, and in part from the assumption that American history was less a difficult subject requiring mature thinking than an easy subject requiring malleable emotions.[16]

There was little state or regional history in the schools in spite of the intense regional feeling and the interest of historians and readers in the subject. Only seventeen textbooks appeared (seven on New England, one on the South, three on South Carolina, three on New York, two on Vermont, and one on New Hampshire), and all were apparently published from a sense of service rather than for expected profits. The subject of local history was never really popular in the schools despite state loyalty and even state laws.[17] The secessionist-minded South seemed particularly uninterested in its distinctiveness as a region, both in studying its history in school and in writing about it.

Universal History

Universal history, the term for both world history and western civilization in the early nineteenth century, was generally a subject for schoolboys, European philosophers, and American journalists who wrote articles but did not have time to write a book. The only significant American contribution in the area was David Ramsay's twelve-volume *Universal History Americanized* . . . , an uninteresting summary of facts compiled in the manner of the eighteenth-century encyclopedists, which was little noticed excepted for its bulk.[18] In Europe, universal history generally meant theories about the stages of civilizations, usually written by philosophers rather than historians. Hundreds of works poured fourth, particularly from Germany and France, including major ones by such important thinkers as Karl von Schlegel,

[16] Agnew O. Roorbach, *The Development of the Social Studies in American Secondary Education Before 1861* (Philadelphia, 1937), pp. 103, 144.

[17] *Ibid.*, pp. 246–78.

[18] David Ramsay, *Universal History Americanized; or, An Historical View of the World From the Earliest Records to the Year 1808* (12 vols.; Philadelphia, 1819).

Georg W. F. Hegel, Johann Gottfried Fichte, Charles C. F. Krause, Victor Cousin, Theodore Jouffroy, Edgar Quinet, François Laurent, and Auguste Comte. Many of these studies were widely read and even more widely discussed in America.

Although these theories remained foreign to the concerns of American historians, dilettantes delighted in sweeping explanations of man's experience on the planet. American magazine editors deluged their readers with summaries and commentaries about the European philosopher-historians, and orators referred glibly to the cycles, stages, streams, and directions of history which they gleaned from others or invented for themselves. It was an age of historical theorizing. Approximately one-third of the historical articles from 1800 to 1860 indexed in *Poole's Index to Periodical Literature* dealt with this mélange of philosophy and universal history. Significantly, most of the authors of these articles were notably undistinguished, and almost none were historians. Although American philosophers like Ralph Waldo Emerson and historians like Bancroft and Prescott wrote extensively about historical theory, their concern was not with explaining universal history but with the methods, the appropriate interpretive themes, and the purpose of historical writing.[19]

World history also had an important place in the schools. The first texts that appeared were in the eighteenth-century classical tradition, emphasizing philosophy and Greek and Roman antiquities more than history. Gradually, world history gained independence from the classics and began to be studied for its own sake, for it had lessons to teach and morals to impart. World history, said a textbook author, was "a source of *practical* wisdom to legislators and rulers, and of *profitable* reflection to private persons."[20] The rise and fall of nations possessed dramatic grandeur, and details of the history of obscure nations served a

[19] Ralph Waldo Emerson, "History," *The Essays of Ralph Waldo Emerson* (Modern Library edition, New York, 1944; originally published 1841); George Bancroft, *Literary and Historical Miscellanies* (New York, 1855); William Hickling Prescott, *Biographical Miscellanies* (New York, 1865).

[20] Royal Robbins, *Outlines of Ancient and Modern History on a New Plan* (Hartford, 1839), p. 7.

passion for the exotic. By 1860, at least 113 textbooks of world history were in use in the United States. The subject was fairly evenly distributed at different grade levels and in the colleges.

The material covered in world history courses was similar to that studied in schools today. The following table shows the average amount of space devoted to different periods by seven of the most widely used world history textbooks before 1860 compared with four of the most popular modern texts:

SUBJECTS COVERED IN WORLD HISTORY TEXTBOOKS [21]

	Percentage of Space in Textbooks, 1800–1860	Percentage of Space in Modern Textbooks
Pre-Greek	9	11
Greece and Rome	26	22
476–1400	15	26
1400–1800	34	26
United States	10	3
Non-Western	5	12

The relatively minor differences indicate that the texts of the early nineteenth century tended to emphasize the classical, the American, and the modern periods; by present standards they somewhat de-emphasized the pre-Greek, the medieval, and the non-European aspects of history. On the one hand writers were doubtless influenced by the prevailing emphasis on the classics, and on the other hand they were influenced by the Romantic desire to delve into exotic topics as only universal history could do. The emphasis on American history reflected the all-pervad-

[21] Early nineteenth-century texts by John Frost (1848), Samuel G. Goodrich (1837), Royal Robbins (1839), Alexander Frazer Tytler (1825), Emma Willard (1858), Samuel Whelpley (1808), and Joseph Emerson Worcester (1840). Texts in use today: Carleton J. H. Hayes et al., World History (New York, 1950); Frederick C. Lane et al., The World's History (New York, 1950); Arthur E. R. Boak et al., World History (New York, 1947); Walter Wallbank and Alastair M. Taylor, Civilization Past and Present (Chicago, 1952); Crane Brinton et al., A History of Civilization (2 vols.; Englewood Cliffs, N.J., 1967). Percentages of all books are based only on material covering the years to 1860.

ing nationalism of the period, for the infant country seemed relatively more important to American educators in the early nineteenth century than it seemed to educators a century later.

No world history textbook stood significantly above its competitors. Some of the more successful authors like Emma Willard, Samuel Griswold Goodrich, and John Frost were professionals, better known for their American history texts; Alexander Frazer Tytler, who wrote under the name of Lord Woodleehouse, was a widely used English author; Royal Robbins and Samuel Whelpley were New England preachers whose college-level texts stressed a theological point of view; Joseph Emerson Worcester was a New England teacher who sold over 100,000 copies of his elementary text by 1860.

Ancient, Medieval, and Modern History

The subject which received what modern readers would consider most extraordinary emphasis in the early nineteenth century was ancient history, the ages of Greece and Rome. Appreciation of the classical world was old, of course, having gradually increased almost without interruption from the time of the Renaissance. Early-nineteenth-century historians made a great contribution by adding to this an appreciation of other periods; but they never rebelled against the classical world. For American artists, architects, and orators it remained the golden age of the past. In popular literature, the love of classical subject matter, though slowly declining throughout the nineteenth century, appeared in such best sellers as Bulwer-Lytton's *The Last Days of Pompeii*.[22] In scholarship Americans expressed interest in the classical world in such works as Thomas Bulfinch's popular mythology, Samuel Eliot's four-volume history of liberty in the ancient world, and Charles Anthon's erudite works on Greek and Roman civilization.[23] In the schools this emphasis was still more apparent, for more courses were taught in ancient history,

---

[22] (London, 1834).

[23] Thomas Bulfinch, *The Age of Fable* (Boston, 1855); Samuel Eliot, *History of Liberty* (4 vols.; Boston, 1853); Charles Anthon, *A Manual of Greek and Roman Antiquities* (2 vols.; New York, 1851–52).

especially in the early decades of the nineteenth century, than in any other single field.

The first history courses taught in the schools were about Greece and Rome, and they were important in preparing the way for the study of other areas. Classical languages had long been a major part of the curriculum, so that when classical history appeared in the nineteenth century, it merged easily with the old educational approach of the eighteenth century. Although ancient history increasingly gained recognition as a separate subject, it tended to remain a part of the conservative concept of education, providing the wisdom of the ancients for gentlemen. It retained its place in the classically oriented academies and colleges; however, the new public schools, with their democratic view of education, found American, modern, and world history better suited to their aims. There was no state requirement for ancient history. As American history was concentrated in the lower grade levels where public control of education was most firmly established, ancient history, along with Latin and Greek, was concentrated in the upper levels and in the colleges.[24] The textbooks of Oliver Goldsmith, a luminary of the English Enlightenment, dominated the field.[25] At least sixty editions of his Greek and Roman histories appeared in various revised forms in America, though by the 1850's there was increasing competition on the elementary and secondary levels from the books of Samuel Griswold Goodrich, and on the college level by the detailed texts of Charles Anthon, William Cooke Taylor, and Samuel Whelpley.[26]

Although European historians were enthusiastically discovering the Middle Ages in the early nineteenth century, this discovery never displaced interest in other periods. To most Americans

[24] Roorbach, *Development of Social Studies,* pp. 103, 144.

[25] Oliver Goldsmith, *The Grecian History, from the Earliest State to the Death of Alexander the Great* (London, 1774); Oliver Goldsmith, *The Roman History from the Founding of the City of Rome to the Destruction of the Western Empire* (London, 1770).

[26] Anthon, *Manual of Antiquities;* William Cooke Taylor, *A Manual of Ancient History . . .* (New York, 1855); Samuel Whelpley, *Lectures on Ancient History . . .* (New York, 1816).

the subject of the Middle Ages was a fanciful one, for entertainment rather than for serious study. It was like the history of pre-classical times, distant Asia, or aboriginal America—fine subjects for historical fiction but hardly for the serious writer and certainly not for the schools. No American produced significant work in these areas, and the first medieval history textbook did not appear until 1854. American readers were dependent upon European novelists, especially Sir Walter Scott, who reached unparalleled popularity in the United States with *Ivanhoe, Kenilworth,* and *The Talisman.*[27] Almost everyone read Alexandre Dumas' *The Three Musketeers,* Victor Hugo's *The Hunchback of Notre Dame,* Charles Reade's *The Cloister and the Hearth,* and Boccaccio's newly translated *Decameron.*[28] American historians produced such popular works as Thomas Bulfinch's *The Age of Chivalry,* Francis Liston Hawks's *The Monuments of Egypt,* and Samuel Gardiner Drake's *Biography and History of the Indians of North America.*[29] Critics found a book on fourth-century Constantinople "a fascinating subject," and the Assyrian Empire provided such a "brilliant chapter of history" that it could only be compared to the story of the Arabian Nights.[30]

The four or five centuries since the Renaissance seemed almost as important in the early nineteenth century as the five or six centuries of modern history seem now. Although the books Americans wrote on modern European history were not great in

[27] (London, 1820); (London, 1821); (London, 1825).

[28] (New York edition, 1844); (Philadelphia edition, 1834); (London, 1855); (Philadelphia edition, 1850).

[29] (Boston, 1859); (New York, 1850); (Cincinnati, 1851).

[30] Reviews in *Eclectic Magazine,* X (January, 1847), 19; *North American Review,* XC (January, 1860), 23. Many scholars have commented on the Romantic love of the exotic. See, for example, Harry Elmer Barnes, *A History of Historical Writing,* (Norman, Okla., 1937) pp. 178–79, and George Peabody Gooch, "The Growth of Historical Science," Aldophus William Ward *et al.,* eds., *The Cambridge Modern History* (New York, 1910), XII, 816–50. Professor Gooch considers the "passionate love for the past, for the exotic, for the marvelous and picturesque, for distant lands and literatures" as the first stimulus to the modern interest in and study of history. (See especially pp. 818–19.) He also sees other stimuli to the study of history—nationalism, the study of institutions, and the beginning of serious criticism of sources.

number, they were among the best-written books of the period. Ambition and ability were needed to compete with foreign authors, and the field particularly attracted those Boston Brahmins —Prescott, Motley, Ticknor, and Eliot—who could afford to travel in Europe, gather expensive collections of materials, and trace a subject for its own sake.

While the schools emphasized ancient history and the public liked to read of the medieval, the outstanding writers concentrated on Spain and her colonies. The Spanish emphasis was not entirely coincidental. Spain itself was appropriately exotic, and its conquest of the noble savage seemed especially rich in heroes and adventure. Prescott led the group with seven beautifully written and scholarly volumes on Spain, three on Mexico, and two on Peru.[31] Motley wrote nine volumes on the Dutch revolt from Spain, Ticknor produced a three-volume history of Spanish literature, and Washington Irving wrote six popular books on Spain.[32] No other works by Americans in the field of modern history could approach these in excellence; perhaps the next best was a single-volume history of Austria by John S. C. Abbott.[33]

In the schools, most courses in modern history were a continuation of ancient history, the second semester of a world survey. Popular texts by William Cooke Taylor and Samuel Griswold

[31] William Hickling Prescott, *History of the Reign of Ferdinand and Isabella, the Catholic* (3 vols.; Boston, 1838); *History of the Reign of Philip the Second, King of Spain* (3 vols.; Boston, 1855-59); *The Life of Charles the Fifth After His Abdication* (Boston, 1857); *History of the Conquest of Mexico with a Preliminary View of the Ancient Mexican Civilization* (3 vols.; Boston, 1843); *History of the Conquest of Peru, With a Preliminary View of the Civilization of the Incas* (2 vols.; New York, 1847).

[32] John Lothrop Motley, *The Rise of the Dutch Republic* (3 vols.; New York, 1856); *History of the United Netherlands, From the Death of William the Silent to the Twelve Years Truce—1609* (4 vols.; New York, 1861-68); *The Life and Death of John of Barneveld, Advocate of Holland . . .* (2 vols.; New York, 1874). George Ticknor, *History of Spanish Literature* (3 vols.; New York, 1849). Washington Irving, *A History of the Life and Voyages of Christopher Columbus . . .* (3 vols.; New York, 1828); *The Alhambra: A Series of Tales and Sketches of the Moors and Spaniards* (Philadelphia, 1832); *Chronicle of the Conquest of Granada . . .* (2 vols.; Philadelphia, 1829).

[33] Abbott, *Empire of Austria.*

Goodrich were designed to follow their texts in ancient history.[34] English history was more important in the schools than general modern history. Despite American nationalism, English history often seemed a necessary introduction to American history, for Americans still looked proudly to the English past for the roots of their institutions. As in ancient history, one textbook was overwhelmingly predominant, and again it was written by Oliver Goldsmith.[35] The eminence in this field of an eighteenth-century English writer gave to English history, as it did to ancient history, an old-fashioned, eighteenth-century approach. France was the only other foreign country whose history was taught separately in the United States. While it was less important than English history, many Francophiles remembered America's Revolutionary ally.

Biography

Biography was an approach to history, perhaps even an independent field, that gained great popularity in the early nineteenth century. Biographical writing has a distinct American heritage in the Puritan concern for the inner man, a concern that had been evident in historical writing from William Bradford to Cotton Mather and perhaps even to the autobiography of Benjamin Franklin. Another heritage of biographical writing came from authors like Voltaire who used biography as a vehicle for history, selecting prominent individuals from the past to epitomize the essence of a period. For nineteenth-century historians, biography became not so much the essence as the ultimate statement of what was unique, particular, and real in history. It appealed to readers, who gained a sense of identification with men of the past; it gave authors a sense of community service as they memorialized the worthy and held up exemplars of the well-spent life; and it appealed to educators who were seeking examples of virtuous behavior for their pupils. "The

[34] William Cooke Taylor, *Student's Manual of Modern History* (New York, 1845); Samuel Griswold Goodrich, *Second Book in History* (New York, 1832).
[35] Oliver Goldsmith, *An Abridgement of the History of England From the Earliest Times to the Death of George II* (London, 1774).

eagerness with which every species of biography is read in the
present day has led to the adoption of this phrase, biography-
mania," wrote a reviewer in 1830, and late in the 1850's the
"Biography Mania" was still the subject of comment.[36] Long
before Thomas Carlyle developed the great man thesis readers
had learned to love the hero, and authors had learned that there
was no surer way of pleasing the public than by catering to its
sense of self-identification with a colorful personality.[37]

Wide sales caused biography to attract the professional author
who was interested in an exciting, flowing narration, a very different kind of man from the devoted antiquarian or gentleman-
scholar in other historical fields. Mason Locke Weems, the biographer of Washington, Marion, Franklin, and Penn, was the
first American to exploit fully the rich field of historical biography. An itinerant clergyman and bookseller, he discovered
fame and fortune could be more easily made by supplying the
masses, and especially children, with inspiring, exciting moral
tales of the past. Although never pretending to be a scholar,
perhaps no Tacitus, Gibbon, or Bancroft has recreated the past
for so large an audience.[38]

Other successful and prolific writers such as Joel Tyler Headley and James Parton followed Weems into the field of biography.
Headley, like Weems, was a preacher who turned to writing pro-
fessionally, and his lives of Napoleon, Washington, and Cromwell
were among the most popular books of the day.[39] Parton, a

[36] Review, *New York Mirror*, VII (May 15, 1830), 359; anon., "The Biographical Mania," *Saturday Evening Gazette* (July 4, 1857), 4. For similar
comment, anon., "The Art of History Writing," *Littell's Living Age*, XLVIII
(January, 1856), 243; reviews, *Christian Examiner*, XXIV (July, 1838), 354;
North American Review, XCIII (July, 1861), 266.

[37] See Edward H. O'Neill, *A History of American Biography, 1800–1935*
(Philadelphia, 1935); Barnes, *History of Historical Writing*, p. 179.

[38] O'Neill, *History of American Biography*, pp. 20–24. The first of many
editions of Weems's *Life of Washington* appeared in 1800. For a complete
bibliography, see Paul Leicester Ford and Emily Ellsworth Ford Skeel,
Mason Locke Weems, His Works and Ways (3 vols.; New York, 1929), I,
1–337.

[39] Joel Tyler Headley, *Napoleon and His Marshals* (2 vols.; New York,
1847); *Washington and His Generals* (2 vols.; New York, 1848); *The Life of
Oliver Cromwell* (New York, 1848).

newspaper man, produced similar works about Aaron Burr, Andrew Jackson, and Horace Greeley.[40] Novelists and writers like Washington Irving, James Kirke Paulding, Benson John Lossing, and John S. C. Abbott joined the historical biographers with lives of Columbus, Mohammed, Washington, and Napoleon.[41] Jared Sparks was quick to see a profitable side to his interest in the past. Besides his lives of Washington, Franklin, and Morris, he undertook the first important series in American historical writing with the editing of the twenty-five volume *The Library of American Biography*, containing the lives of forty American statesmen.[42]

In addition to the fine popular lives of well-known heroes by professional writers, a far greater number of biographers produced life-and-letters biographies to memorialize beloved and recently deceased local worthies. Often "authorized" and written by a kinsman or local clergyman, they tended to be tedious panegyrics, less concerned with recreating the subject than with didactic sermonizing and flights of eloquence.[43] Out of the mass appeared a few moderately able and scholarly biographies such as William Tudor's life of James Otis, Henry Stevens Randall on Jefferson, and Josiah Quincy on John Quincy Adams.[44] Finally, a significant number of campaign biographies, written by such

[40] James Parton, *The Life of Aaron Burr* (New York, 1858); *Life of Andrew Jackson* (3 vols.; New York, 1860); *The Life of Horace Greeley* . . . (New York, 1855).

[41] Washington Irving, *Life and Voyages of Christopher Columbus; Mahomet and His Successors* (2 vols.; New York, 1850); *Life of George Washington* (5 vols.; New York, 1856–59); James Kirke Paulding, *A Life of Washington* (2 vols.; New York, 1836); Benson John Lossing, *Life of Washington* (3 vols.; New York, 1830); John Stevens Cabot Abbott, *The History of Napoleon Bonaparte* (2 vols.; New York, 1855–56).

[42] Jared Sparks, *The Writings of George Washington . . . With a Life of the Author* . . . (12 vols.; Boston, 1834–37); *The Works of Benjamin Franklin . . . With Notes and a Life of the Author* (10 vols.; Boston, 1836–40); *The Life of Gouverneur Morris* . . . (3 vols.; Boston, 1832); *The Library of American Biography* (25 vols.; New York, 1834–49).

[43] O'Neill, *History of American Biography*, pp. 18–22, 30–37.

[44] William Tudor, *Life of James Otis of Massachusetts* . . . (Boston, 1823); Henry Stevens Randall, *The Life of Thomas Jefferson* (3 vols.; New York, 1858); Josiah Quincy, *Memoir of the Life of John Quincy Adams* (Boston, 1856).

men as Nathaniel Hawthorne, James Parton, and even, allegedly, Davy Crockett, served obvious ends.[45]

By far the most popular subject of biography was George Washington.[46] As an inspirational ideal, Washington epitomized what similar biographies of Franklin, Penn, and scores of memorialized local figures also represented.[47] Even more, Washington was the American military hero, and his was the exciting story of the Revolution and of America's greatness. Biographies of such men as Patrick Henry, Lafayette, and Nathanael Greene reflected this as well.[48] In addition to these familiar biographical subjects, tales of the Romantic hero whose life was an adventure remote from the experience of the hearthside reader appeared. Typical of these were the biographies of Napoleon, Columbus, Mohammed, Black Hawk, Pontiac, the Empress Josephine, and Mary Queen of Scots.[49]

The emphasis on great men was much greater in the schools

[45] Nathaniel Hawthorne, *Life of Franklin Pierce* (Boston, 1852); James Parton, *The Life of Horace Greeley* . . . (New York, 1855); David Crockett, *The Life of Martin Van Buren* (Philadelphia, 1835). Crockett's name appears on the title page, but his authorship has recently been questioned.

[46] In addition to the popular lives by professional writers—Weems, Headley, Lossing, Paulding, and Irving—there was the serious one by Jared Sparks and a five-volume work by John Marshall, *The Life of George Washington* . . . (5 vols.; Philadelphia, 1852).

[47] For example, Mason Locke Weems, *The Life of Benjamin Franklin, With Many Choice Anecdotes and Admirable Sayings of the Great Man* . . . (Baltimore, 1820); Samuel Macpherson Janney, *The Life of William Penn* . . . (Philadelphia, 1852).

[48] For example, William Wirt, *Sketches of the Life and Character of Patrick Henry* (Philadelphia, 1817); Phineas Camp Headley, *The Life of General Lafayette, Marquis of France, General in the United States Army* (Auburn, N.Y., 1851); William Johnson, *Sketches of the Life and Correspondence of Nathanael Greene* (2 vols.; Charleston, 1822).

[49] John Stevens Cabot Abbott, *The History of Napoleon Bonaparte* (2 vols.; New York, 1855–56); Headley, *Napoleon and His Marshals;* Irving, *Life and Voyages of Christopher Columbus;* Irving, *Mahomet and His Successors;* Benjamin Drake, *The Life and Adventures of Black Hawk: With Sketches of Keokuk, the Soc and Fox Indians, and the Late Black Hawk War* (Cincinnati, 1851); Francis Parkman, Jr., *History of the Conspiracy of Pontiac* (Boston, 1851); Phineas Camp Headley, *The Life of the Empress Josephine, First Wife of Napoleon Bonaparte* (New York, 1850); *The Life of Mary Queen of Scots* (New York, 1857).

than the number of separate texts would indicate, for much biography was combined with other subjects. Frequently history texts contained appended sections which provided biographical sketches of the "distinguished characters who have been mentioned." [50] By far the most frequently used biography was Mason Locke Weems's famous cherry-tree-embellished life of Washington. Designed to be used in the elementary grades, the book went through more than seventy editions and ranks as one of the most successful books in publishing history. In many ways it epitomized the aims and approach of history in the schools, with every fact deliberately chosen or, if necessary, invented, to add dramatic interest and impart a moral.

Political, Military, and Social History

In 1912 James Harvey Robinson became the spokesman for an advanced idea when he proclaimed the "New History" as "everything that man has ever done, or thought, or hoped or felt";[51] however, the very phrase could have been borrowed from an American philosopher of 1854, who said, "Its subject matter is all that man has thought, felt, and done." [52] The dictum that history was past politics was a product of the late nineteenth century and was as frightening to men of the early nineteenth century as it is today. Endlessly authors and critics proclaimed their dedication to a broad view of history: "The history that is hereafter to be written is not to be merely the history of government and of politics, but of the history of man in all his relations and interests, the history of science, of art, of religion, of social and domestic life." [53] Critics spoke with disgust of history that consisted only of "kings and soldiers"; this was

[50] For example, William Grimshaw, *History of the United States . . . Comprising Biographies of the Most Remarkable Colonists, Writers and Philosophers, Warriors and Statesmen* (Philadelphia, 1822); Robbins, *Outlines of History*.

[51] James Harvey Robinson, *The New History* (New York, 1913), p. 1.

[52] William Greenough Thayer Shedd, "The Nature and Influence of the Historic Spirit," *Bibliotheca Sacra*, XI (April, 1854), 345.

[53] *Proceedings of the American Antiquarian Society, 1812–1849* (Worcester, Mass., 1912), p. 557.

"the mere skeleton of history." [54] "No one department of human research confines our system," they boasted; writers must "embrace the whole field of history, science and the arts." [55] Historical societies were as eager for materials relating to the development of philosophy, art, science, literature, and education as they were for official government documents. The "kind of history written today," said a critic in 1842, is superior to that written by past generations for the reason that now we take "a more enlarged view of the sources . . . depending not alone on books and documents" but on such things as art and architectural remains, literature, pictures, and language development to understand a past era.[56]

The emphasis on political, military, social, and intellectual history was apparent in the school textbooks used by Americans from 1800 to 1860. Comparing a sample of seventeen of the most popular textbooks of that era with twelve of the most widely used ones today shows the percentage of space allotted to each field.

TYPES OF HISTORY IN UNITED STATES HISTORY TEXTBOOKS [57]

	Percentage of Space in Textbooks, 1800–1860	Percentage of Space in Modern Textbooks
Political	46	43
Military	36	12
Social	9	23
Intellectual	8	21

[54] Review, *Southern Quarterly Review*, IX (April, 1846), 361; Samuel Griswold Goodrich, *Pictorial History of Ancient Rome . . .* (New York, 1850), p. vi.

[55] *Transactions at the First Meeting of the Alabama Historical Society* (Tuscaloosa, 1852), p. 5; *Collections of the Virginia Historical and Philosophical Society* (Richmond, 1833), p. 33.

[56] Anon., "The Modern Art and Science of History," *Westminster Review*, XXXVIII (October, 1842), 358.

[57] World history texts by John Frost (1848); Samuel G. Goodrich (1837); Royal Robbins (1839); Alexander Frazer Tytler (1825); Emma Willard (1858); Joseph Emerson Worcester (1840); Samuel Whelpley (1808); Carlton J. H. Hayes *et al.* (1950); Frederick C. Lane *et al.* (1950); Author E. R. Boak *et al.*

By modern standards military history has by far the most striking and disproportionate emphasis in the Romantic period. In
school textbooks, from the most elementary to the most advanced, authors dealt in painful detail with such things as size
of armies, the leaders, strategy, tactics, losses, and military consequences. "The greatest part of history," said one educator, is
"made up of wars and conquests." [58] The emphasis was not limited to textbooks, for it was also evident in such popular books
as Edward S. Creasey's *Fifteen Decisive Battles of the World*,[59]
in countless biographies of Washington and Napoleon, in the
battle-filled narratives of Bancroft and Prescott, in Cooper's fine
history of the American navy,[60] and in the drum and trumpet
novels of Cooper and Scott.

United States and modern history had the greatest amount of
space devoted to military events. The 41 pages devoted to military history before 1815 in a modern college textbook by John
D. Hicks do not approach the detail of the 175 pages on warfare
in Salma Hale's ante-bellum high school text, for example, or
the 165 pages in Charles A. Goodrich, the 160 pages in Emma
Willard, or the 188 pages in John Frost.[61] This emphasis on battles caused the space granted to periods of time in which there
were wars to be swollen out of proportion to the space given
periods of peace. The events of the Revolution and the War of

(1947); Walter Wallbank and Alstair M. Taylor (1952). United States texts
by John Frost (1856); Charles A. Goodrich (1831); Samuel G. Goodrich (1845);
William Grimshaw (1822); Emma Willard (1845); Marcius Willson (1847);
John D. Hicks (1952); Eugene C. Barker and Henry Steele Commager (1950);
David S. Muzzy (1950); Ralph V. Harlow (1953). Ancient history texts by A.
H. L. Heeren (1828); William Cooke Taylor (1855); William Pinnoch (1835);
Oliver Goldsmith (1825); Oliver Goldsmith (1817); Samuel G. Goodrich
(1845); John Frost (1846); William E. Caldwell (1937); Robert K. Speer *et al.*
(1946); Ralph Van Deman Magoffin and Frederic Duncalf (1939).

[58] Eliza Robbins, *English History* (New York, 1839), p. 9.

[59] (London, 1851).

[60] James Fenimore Cooper, *The History of the Navy of the United States
of America* (2 vols.; Philadelphia, 1839).

[61] John D. Hicks, *The Federal Union, A History of the United States to
1865* (Boston, 1952). This includes only the material prior to 1815. Hale,
History of the United States (1825); C. A. Goodrich, *History of the United
States* (1823); Willard, *History of the United States* (1828); Frost, *A History
of the United States* (Philadelphia, 1856).

1812 received almost double the space they do in modern texts, while the eras of discovery and of the writing of the Constitution received about half of present-day emphasis. Alexander's conquests, the Punic Wars, and the Wars of the Roses often required more space than the Age of Pericles, the peaceful era of Augustus, or the constitutional reforms of the Tudors.

Battlefield events offered much that people of the period loved most in history. Men believed that nations in combat for their existence made exciting narrative, full of drama and emotion. War was a time for heroics, and military history offered a limitless display of noble deeds from which could be drawn lessons on bravery and cowardice, patriotism and treason, industry and indolence, pride and humility, honor and disgrace. The very fact of victory tends to make the victor right and the ideals of the vanquished wrong and evil, so that historians could show the triumph of good, with moral lessons of divine retribution for the vanquished and moral superiority of the victor. Finally, military history was essentially factual and relatively memorable, a splendid subject on which to exercise and "improve" the memory. It was entertaining and dramatic; it would inspire virtue and the emulation of noble deeds; it would instill patriotism; it would reveal God's plan and man's truths in its outcome; and it was good for the student and would improve his mind: these things were exactly what men wanted from history.[62]

Critics appear to be forever calling for social history, historians appear to be forever promising to supply it, and no one is ever quite satisfied. Men of the early nineteenth century were neither the first nor the last to want more than they had. "History is learning . . . to condescend to men of low estate"; it has recently become not only "the transactions of the *governments* of a country, but the doings, the progress, the character, of its people"; "every class of society, from the highest to the lowest [at last has found] a place upon the pages of the historian." [63] The

[62] See, for example, Samuel Whelpley, *A Compend of History, From the Earliest Times* . . . (2 vols.; Burlington, Vt., 1808), I, 160.

[63] Anon., "Modern Art and Science of History," p. 366; "Report of the Virginia Historical and Philosophical Society," *Virginia Historical Register,*

historian must picture "domestic society in all its variety," said the critics; he must "devote himself particularly to the study . . . of individuals and of social institutions"; he must write of "the manners and customs," "the domestic life" of a people.[64]

Cultural and intellectual history was as important as social. One observer praised his own generation as the first to attach "supreme and central importance to popular ideas and beliefs, and their changes." [65] A history of the United States with no reference to art, science, religion, and philosophy seemed incomplete, and a history of Spain ought to "treat fully of its thought" and give "a complete account of Spanish literature." [66] School textbook authors often promised more social and intellectual history than they produced; but certainly it was point of pride to claim an abundance, and the texts that offered it were the most popular. "Intellectual history" was a favorite term, and to many it seemed the highest form of history.[67]

Social, cultural, and intellectual history attracted every kind of historian. Works by professional writers included James Peller Malcolm's four-volume social history of London, Thomas Bulfinch's famous works on mythology, and histories of the American arts by William Dunlap and Benson John Lossing.[68] Wealthy hobbyists produced such works as George Ticknor's history of

---

[64] II (October, 1849), 210; review, *Southern Quarterly Review*, XV (August, 1842), 74-76.

[64] Anon., "The Philosophy of History," *North American Review*, XXXIX (July, 1834), 43; anon., "History," *American Quarterly Review*, V (March, 1829), 95; Giles F. Yates, "Ancient History," *American Literary Magazine*, I (December, 1847), 367; anon., "The Study of History," *Southern Quarterly Review*, X (July, 1846), 129.

[65] Anon., "Modern Art and Science of History," p. 366.

[66] Reviews, *North American Review*, XLVI (January, 1838), 277; *North American Review*, XXX (January, 1830), 1.

[67] Reviews, *North American Review*, XCI (October, 1860), 302; *Living Age*, XXIV (February, 1850), 202; anon., "Study of History," p. 129.

[68] James Peller Malcolm, *Anecdotes of the Manners and Customs of London From the Roman Invasion to the Year 1700* (2 vols.; London, 1811); *Anecdotes of the Manners and Customs of London during the Eighteenth Century* . . . (2 vols.; London, 1810); Bulfinch, *Age of Fable; The Age of Chivalry* (Boston, 1855); William Dunlap, *History of the Rise and Progress of the Arts of Design in the United States* (2 vols.; New York, 1834); Benson John Lossing, *Outline History of the Fine Arts* (New York, 1840).

Spanish literature, Samuel Eliot's history of liberty, Isaiah Thomas' history of printing in America, and Josiah Quincy's history of Harvard University.[69] Many American antiquarians, usually clergymen, produced a mass of religious history. Among the most ambitious works were John Gorham Palfrey's four volumes on the Jewish religion and William Buell Sprague's nine volumes of biographies of American preachers. More typical were works by David Benedict, Abel Stevens, Francis Lister Hawks, and Thomas Robbins on the Baptists, Methodists, Episcopalians, and on foreign religions.[70]

One reason why men of the early nineteenth century liked social and intellectual history was that it was more interesting to read than dry accounts of government. Textbooks offered it to lure the student on to more substantial fare. "Intimate social history" allowed readers to identify with men of the past, and critics complained that "mere collections of dates and places, mere rolls of dynasties" were as dull "as the figures of a superannuated almanac." [71] When a reader felt that he could identify with the life of ordinary people of the past and be moved by their ideas, he became a part of the drama of history. Another reason for emphasis on social and intellectual affairs was that they seemed to provide special insight into the very basis of things; they pro-

[69] Ticknor, *History of Spanish Literature* (3 vols.); Samuel Eliot, *History of Liberty* (4 vols.); Isaiah Thomas, *The History of Printing in America* . . . (2 vols.; Worcester, Mass., 1870); Josiah Quincy, *The History of Harvard University* (2 vols.; Cambridge, Mass., 1840).

[70] John Gorham Palfrey, *Academical Lectures on the Jewish Scriptures and Antiquities* (4 vols.; Boston, 1838–52); William Buell Sprague, *Annals of the American Pulpit; or Commemorative Notices of Distinguished American Clergymen of Various Denominations* . . . (9 vols.; New York, 1857–69); David Benedict, *A General History of the Baptist Denomination in America, and Other Parts of the World* (2 vols.; Boston, 1813); Abel Stevens, *The History of the Religious Movement of the Eighteenth Century, Called Methodism* . . . (3 vols.; New York, 1858–61); Francis Lister Hawks, *Contributions to the Ecclesiastical History of the United States of America* (2 vols.; New York, 1836–9); Thomas Robbins, *A View of All Religions; and the Religious Ceremonies of All Nations at the Present Day* (Hartford, 1824).

[71] Reviews, *North American Review*, LXI (July, 1845), 245; *North American Review*, LXXXI (July, 1855), 113; also, anon., "Guizot and the Philosophy of History," *Eclectic Magazine*, IV (February, 1845), 182; anon., "History," pp. 89, 95.

vided the key to the *Zeitgeist,* the core of understanding. Daily life and thought "alone could furnish a true picture of an age"; here was the "reality" of a people.[72] Not only reality, but also the bases of historical change seemed to lie here. Social history explained "the movements of societies"; "ideas make worlds, and . . . changes of ideas make revolutions." [73]

In sum, then, Americans of the early nineteenth century loved their own history as new and exciting, especially the drama of the Revolutionary period. The schools emphasized classical history, scholars turned to Spain, readers often looked to the medieval period for entertainment, and orators and journalists preferred the philosophy of history. Perhaps the American concern with the present and future promoted an attention to the past, even the selection of a mythological heritage, in a spirit of eclecticism. The American heritage was the Revolution, Greece and Rome, Columbus and Cortez. Americans loved the intimate biographical approach to history, the drama of military clashes, and the depth of understanding which social and intellectual history always promised and never quite provided. There was also a place for the antiquarian who was primarily concerned about the history of the city of Houston.

[72] Anon., "A Course of Historical Reading," *Universalist Quarterly and General Review,* VII (January, 1850), 6; reviews, *North American Review,* XCI (October, 1860), 301–2; also, *North American Review,* XLVI (January, 1838), 237; *Living Age,* XXIV (February, 1850), 202–12.
[73] S. G. Goodrich, *Pictorial History of Ancient Rome,* p. iv; anon., "Modern Art and Science of History," p. 366.

VI

Antiquarianism in the Age of Literary History

Although the period from 1800 to 1860 is remembered primarily for the stirring narratives of men like Scott and Bancroft, it was also an age of the antiquarian. Romanticism included love of the specific as well as the grand, of minutiae as well as rhetoric. Men avidly compiled details and perused documents; their enthusiasm for the particular was as great as it was for epics.

Minutiae appealed not only to the odd recluse but to the same general public that acclaimed historical novels and epic pageantry. Magazine editors deluged their readers with "Olden Time Miscellaney" and "Antiquities," "so that the reader might share with us a delight in the unadorned facts." [1] Editors of popular magazines explained that their readers had "a fondness for . . . details" because trivialities "are of personal interest and come home to the bosom of every individual." [2] The *North American Review* devoted at least 10 per cent of its total

[1] *DeBow's Review*, III (April, 1847), 293; *Portfolio*, IV (October, 1813), 14; *American Museum*, V (January, 1789), 94.

[2] Preface, *Collections Topographical, Historical, and Biographical, Relating Principally to New Hampshire*, I (1822), 3; reviews, *North American Review*, XXXIX (July, 1834), 32; also, *American Quarterly Review*, XV (June, 1834), 276; *American Quarterly Observer*, III (July, 1834), 121.

space to reprints and reviews of historical documents.[3] In 1782 an editor noted that "a spirit of collecting and publishing historical documents begins at length to discover itself in the united states [sic]"; by 1838 a writer boasted that "New England people . . . have always been a documentary people"; and on the eve of the Civil War observers were still acclaiming "the tendency in our time, daily on the ascendant," to collect, publish, and enjoy "all original correspondences and documents." [4] A recent scholar, David Van Tassel, has spoken of the "documania" of the period as "a national obsession." [5]

Reviewers who were often hard to please with narrative histories could be relied upon to welcome almost anything that quoted sufficiently from original sources. "The reviewers began to talk of a documentary history as the only real way in which history was to be written," John Spencer Bassett observed, "having in mind that posterity, if not themselves, would wile away its hours of ease pouring over collections of laws, state papers and political correspondence." [6] Many reviewers seemed to find plenty of time. "For several years," one wrote, "we have found pleasant material for filling in the gaps between intervals of sterner study in reading from week to week . . . the exact details gathered from the newly opened treasures of the English State Paper Office," and another declared that for pure amusement "the best history . . . in Virginia is to be found in

[3] Sampling every five years of the *North American Review* from 1815 to 1860, I count 9,952 pages in total, of which 2,401 pages or 24 per cent deal with history, plus 1,052 pages or 11 per cent that deals with documentary or source material of history. Articles and reviews of secondary works build to a peak in 1850 and decline; primary materials are scattered evenly throughout the period.

[4] Editorial, *Universal Asylum and Columbian Magazine*, VII (February, 1782), III; review, *North American Review*, XXXXVI (April, 1838), 476; "Recent Historical Revelations," *Eclectic Magazine*, XXXIV (July, 1858), 347; also William Leete Stone, *Life of Joseph Brant* . . . (2 vols.; New York, 1838), I, xxvi–xxvii.

[5] David D. Van Tassel, *Recording America's Past: An Interpretation of the Development of Historical Studies in America, 1607–1884* (Chicago, 1960), pp. 103–10.

[6] John Spencer Bassett, *The Middle Group of American Historians* (New York, 1917), p. 88.

'Hennig's Statutes at Large.' " [7] Scores of magazine articles proclaimed that reading source materials was the "most delightful
of intellectual recreations," and "cannot fail to afford high gratification." [8] "For a public desirous only of entertainment," said
one writer, "nothing can be more satisfactory than original documents." [9] "Exciting," "interesting," "tantalizing," they chorused,
"one of the most disinterested pleasures" and "prolific of interest
. . . for the casual reader." [10] One editor, acquiring the Jonathan Trumbull papers for publication, rejoiced that "we shall
be able to give the public a rich repast," and reviewers thanked
publishers of such documents "for the pleasure . . . afforded
us." [11]

Public delight in source materials found expression in the
activities of historical societies, in historical journals which
devoted as much as half of their space to documents, in con-
gressional and local appropriations for documentary publications, and in the remarkable sales which many compilations
enjoyed. By 1852 Jared Sparks had sold 7,000 sets of his twelve-
volume *Writings of Washington,* while in 1889 Worthington
Chauncey Ford could sell but 750 sets of a much finer edition
to a nation more than twice as large.[12] The first two volumes
of the Massachusetts Historical Society *Collections* went through
three editions; the Wisconsin society published its *Collections*
in English, German, and Norwegian in order to meet public
demand; Francis P. Blair's seven-volume *Diplomatic Correspondence* and Thomas B. Wait's eight-volume *State Papers*

[7] "History and Biography," *Christian Examiner,* LXX (March, 1861), 314;
Jonathan Peter Cushing, "Address Before the First Annual Meeting . . . ,"
Virginia Historical and Philosophical Society, *Collections,* I (1833), 20.
[8] Reviews, *North American Review,* LXXX (April, 1855), 390; *Portfolio,*
V (May, 1815), 468.
[9] Review, *North American Review,* XCI (October, 1860), 354; "Recent
Historical Revelations," p. 347.
[10] Reviews, *Christian Examiner,* LXX (May, 1861), 399; *North American
Review,* XCI (October, 1860), 354, and *Southern Literary Messenger,* XVIII
(May, 1852), 311.
[11] Jeremy Belknap to Ebenezer Hazard, February 19, 1791, in Massachusetts
Historical Society, *Collections,* 5th series, III (1897), 356; review, *DeBow's
Review,* III (April, 1847), 293.
[12] Bassett, *Middle Group of American Historians,* p. 88.

and Publick Documents both had three editions by 1861; and
Jonathan Elliot's *Debates . . . on . . . the Adoption of the
Federal Constitution* went through four editions. Although
American material predominated, editors and publishers could
also count on brisk sales for such works as Charles Anthon's
Oration of Cicero or John S. C. Abbott's *Confidential Corre-
spondence of Napoleon*.

Documania appeared most clearly, perhaps, in the attitudes
of hundreds of antiquarians who would never have presumed to
call themselves historians. For every Bancroft writing a dozen
volumes there was a Jared Sparks or a Peter Force compiling forty or more; for every Prescott or Parkman there were
scores of nearly anonymous men quietly collecting the annals of
a local township. Probably the most frequent historical cliché
of the period was "to rescue from oblivion." "If I shall succeed
in rescuing . . . from the obliterating hand of time, one event
elevating to our State character," said one writer, "my end will
be accomplished." [13] Washington Irving poked fun at the antiquarian, but the antiquarian did not apologize for his activity.
"We permit the entomologist to chase butterflies interminably,"
said Abiel Holmes, "let us be permitted quietly to spell out inscriptions in old grave yards, to pour over musty books . . . to
ransack the records of the days of other years, to be transported
at the discovery of an ancient manuscript. . . ." [14]

Men understood that the words "historian" and "compiler"
denoted altogether separate occupations, a distinction that was

[13] John Hill Wheeler, *Historical Sketches of North Carolina from 1584 to
1851* (2 vols.; Philadelphia, 1851), I, xix; also Francis Parkman, *History of
the Conspiracy of Pontiac . . .* (Boston, 1851), p. viii; Nathaniel Bradstreet
Shurtleff, ed., *Records of the Colony of New Plymouth in England* (8 vols.;
Boston, 1855–57), I, iii; Josiah Quincy, *The History of Harvard University*
(2 vols.; Cambridge, Mass., 1840), I, ix; Samuel Prescott Hildreth, *Pioneer
History: Being an Account of the First Examination of the Ohio Valley, and
the Early Settlement of the Northwest Territory* (Cincinnati, 1856), p. iii;
Timothy Alden, *A Collection of American Epitaphs* (5 vols.; New York,
1841), I, 5–6.

[14] Abiel Holmes, "American Antiquarian Society," *Portfolio*, V (May, 1815),
470.

subsequently to be lost. The common title "Historical and Antiquarian Society" was not redundant.[15] "The study of antiquities
is an auxiliary to history," explained one writer. "The one
furnishes a few of the valuable materials, with which the other
constructs her superb edifice." [16] In a day when literary etiquette
required self-effacement, writers were generally modest about pretending to the dignity that the word historian implied. Writers
confessed readily that they "were aspiring not to the dignified
title of history"; that they "aspire here to no more than the
humble office of a compiler"; and that they "could not claim to
the position of a historian, for that niche in the temple of face
must be occupied by some more worthy person." [17] They acknowledged "the future historians" and "the abler hands" who
would transform and elevate annals into history through "the
trappings of art." [18]

Well might writers be careful of their claims, for the pretentious were likely to be rudely put down. Reviewers generally
received the works of Abiel Holmes, Timothy Pitkin, and Richard Hildreth with great coolness because of the indeterminate
status of their works, halfway between flowing narrative and
unadorned fact. Holmes's modest title, *The Annals of America,*

[15] At least nine organizations used both words in their name. Appleton
P. C. Griffin, *Bibliography of American Historical Societies* (2 vols.; Washington, 1907).

[16] Holmes, "Antiquarian Society," p. 471; reviews, *Museum of Foreign
Literature,* XXII (February, 1833), 230; *American Review,* LXXIII (October,
1851), 447.

[17] James Thatcher, *A Military Journal during the American Revolutionary
War* . . . (Boston, 1823), p. v; Francis Lister Hawks, *The Monuments of
Egypt* . . . (New York, 1850), p. 13; Wheeler, *Historical Sketches of North
Carolina,* p. xix; also Joel Munsell, *The Typographical Miscellany* (Albany,
1850), p. iii; and Henry Onderdonk, Jr., *Documents and Letters Intended
to Illustrate the Revolutionary Incidents of Queens County* . . . (New
York, 1846), p. 7.

[18] Wheeler, *Historical Sketches of North Carolina,* p. xvii; David Benedict,
*A General History of the Baptist Denomination in America and Others of
the World* (2 vols.; Boston, 1813), I, 5; also, Preface, *Collections Relating to
New Hampshire,* p. 5; Abiel Holmes, *The Annals of America* . . . (2 vols.;
Cambridge, Mass., 1829), I, iii; John Haywood, *The Civil and Political His-
tory of the State of Tennessee* . . . (2 vols.; Knoxville, 1823), I, iii.

was brushed aside. "As History . . . in the full import" of the word it was "meagre and miserably imperfect." [19] Pitkins' *Political and Civil History of the United States* was "imperfect," merely "the raw materials out of which history is made." [20] Hildreth's ambitious but colorless *History of the United States* was "a fine chronicle, but not history," since the true historian "must not only chronicle the occurrences, but decipher their meaning." [21]

If the task of the pure antiquarian was humble, he seemed all the more worthy of gratitude. "We hardly know of a more important service that can be rendered to the cause of useful Knowledge," wrote a reviewer, "than the collecting and reprinting of scarce documents." [22] Men like Jared Sparks were almost universally acclaimed: "No one in the wide circle of literature . . . has rendered greater benefits" to mankind; "the American press has produced no work of higher value." [23] The compiler worked for service and for love and allowed others to enjoy fame. "He labors for posterity, and, like David, gathers together the gold and silver, the brass and iron, the timber and stone, while another erects the Temple and calls it by his name." [24]

There were precise reasons why antiquarianism appealed to men of the early nineteenth century. For one thing, the very newness of history, particularly American history, imbued the sources with an excitement which was largely lost in later generations. The basic facts about the past were not as close as the nearest textbook, and history was more a matter of discovery

[19] Reviews, *North American Review*, XXIX (October, 1829), 429; also *Quarterly Review*, II (November, 1809), 319; for a digest of contemporary reviews, see S. Austin Allibone, *A Critical Dictionary of English Literature and English and American Authors* . . . (3 vols.; Philadelphia, 1899); also Michael Kraus, *The Writing of American History* (Norman, Okla., 1953).

[20] Reviews, *North American Review*, XXX (January, 1830), 2; and XXXXII (April, 1836), 452.

[21] Reviews, *Living Age*, XXIII (November, 1849), 365; *North American Review*, LXXIII (October, 1851), 412; and *DeBow's Review*, XI (September, 1851), 344.

[22] Reviews, *North American Review*, XXXXIII (July, 1836), 274; and LXXI (July, 1850), 34.

[23] Review, *North American Review*, XXXXVII (October, 1838), 318.

[24] Review, *Southern Quarterly Review*, III (January, 1843), 43.

than of recalling childhood school lessons. The facts, untarnished by commentary and interpretation, had a freshness that later generations would find in facts about conditions on the moon. Every man *was* his own historian, searching for himself in the old manuscripts and colonial records, enjoying the mysterious lure of the unknown, standing at the frontier of knowledge. The experience of Benjamin L. C. Wailes, a Mississippi planter, was typical. Accidentally stumbling across lost and important facts in forgotten files, he developed a lifelong passion for history and founded the Mississippi Historical Society as a sort of treasure-hunters' club.[25] The explorers were searching "especially those minor points . . . which have escaped the notice of historians." [26] A reviewer of the *Public Records of Connecticut* found them interesting "for the very reason that they relate chiefly to minute and insignificant events," and a reviewer of the *American Archives* noted how Force's "collection of these small things . . . constitutes . . . their chief historic attraction." [27] The fascination and joy of first discovery made men eager to find more.

Details often provided an intimacy to history that momentous movements somehow lacked. Readers could identify with the story of an individual soldier when the strategy of armies was cold and distant. Skillful authors knew that "it is this minuteness of detail which forms one of the principal charms in books of fiction," and they promised to provide "the smaller matters of individual experience," which more pretentious history "in its stately march could not step aside to notice." [28] "A great variety of details" gave "color and interest to the narrative"; it

[25] Charles Sydnor, *Gentleman of the Old Natchez Region; Benjamin L. C. Wailes* (Durham, N.C., 1938), pp. 236–39.

[26] Frederick A. Porcher, "Address . . . ," *South Carolina Historical Society, Collections*, I (1857), 10; also George Rainsford Fairbanks, *Early History of Florida . . .* (St. Augustine, 1857), p. 24.

[27] Reviews, *North American Review*, LXXI (July, 1850), 36; XXXXVI (April, 1838), 486.

[28] Lambert Lilly [Francis Lister Hawks], *History of the Western States, Illustrated by Tales, Sketches and Anecdotes* (Boston, 1835), p. 4; Henry Howe, *Historical Collections of Ohio . . .* (Cincinnati, 1848), p. 3.

was "the magic by which we make the dry bones live again." [29]

Minutiae provided not only interest but also insight, for often the obscure detail seemed to capture the spirit of the past, to give atmosphere, and to point up the significant in history as no narrative could do. The history of a town was a microcosm of the entire country; in the letters of Napoleon lay an understanding of the French nation; in the papers of a Revolutionary diplomat lay an understanding of mankind.[30] Sometimes the unimportant document that "had no claim to being copied" was just the one "to illustrate the manners and spirit of the times." [31] This "minuteness of detail is indispensable," historians said, for there was more truth in the "impression" conveyed by a well-chosen detail than in the finest generalized analysis.[32]

Historical data was still scarce enough that new material, no matter how obscure, was welcomed as adding to the picture rather than confusing it. Instead of discouraging men with the apparent impossibility of comprehending all, the uncovering of new facts encouraged them to seek further. Detail seemed essential to thoroughness, to ascertaining the authentic truth about the past; and men were not afraid of the entire truth. Compiling the story of the past for the first time, historians were inclined to suppose that by including all facts they could tell the story for all time. "If one would study history thoroughly he must not despise small things, but condescend to the minutest details

[29] John Lothrop Motley, *The Rise of the Dutch Republic*, I (New York, 1856), viii; Shurtleff, *Colony of New Plymouth*, p. viii; Washington Irving, *A History of the Life and Voyages of Christopher Columbus* . . . (3 vols.; New York, 1828), I, 20; Stone, *Life of Joseph Brant*, p. xxvi; reviews, *North American Review*, XXXIX (October, 1834), 467; and *American Quarterly Review*, XV (June, 1834), 276.

[30] "Recent Historical Revelations," p. 374; reviews, *North American Review*, XLII (April, 1836), 453; XLIII (July, 1836), 276; *Christian Examiner*, XL (March, 1856), 248; Ralph Waldo Emerson, "History," *Essays of Ralph Waldo Emerson* (Modern Library edition, New York, 1944).

[31] Hugh Williamson, *The History of North Carolina* (Philadelphia, 1812), I, viii; and John Marshall, *The Life of George Washington* . . . (5 vols.; Philadelphia, 1804), I, xv.

[32] James Thatcher, *History of the Town of Plymouth* . . . (Boston, 1832), p. iv; Joel Tyler Headley, *Washington and His Generals* (2 vols.; New York, 1848), I, ix.

. . . the bottom facts." [33] One writer admitted that some of his material was "quite minute and trifling" but insisted that he would "omit nothing," and another believed that any facts at all, if authentic, were "too deply interesting to be consigned to oblivion." [34]

Eagerness to perform useful service to society—a motive for many historians of the period—especially motivated antiquarian compilers in their humble and congenial labors. Men truly believed, then, that "man subserves the purpose of moral existence when he does what is a real benefit to his Country," and compilation seemed to be such a benefit.[35] "I looked around in search of some object, in pursuit of which I could benefit my fellow-citizens," explained one annalist; "*Public Utility* has been the predominant object of my labour," said another; and a third implied that he was not really fond of his task at all but worked "for the pleasure of contributing his mite to the service of the community." [36] Documentary collections provided "a store-house of new materials . . . to facilitate the future labors of the historian." [37] Collectors hoped that properly preserved documents would inspire latent scholars, that because of available materials there "may arise . . . literary characters who will one day do honour to the land that gave them their birth." [38] Americans

[33] Philip Slaughter, *A History of Bristol Parish, Virginia* . . . (Richmond, 1846), p. xiv.

[34] William Read Staples, *Annals of the Town of Providence* . . . (Providence, 1843), p. v; Thatcher, *Military Journal,* p. vi; also Jared Sparks, ed., *Works of Benjamin Franklin* . . . (10 vols.; Boston, 1844), I, xii.

[35] William Durken Williamson, *The History of the State of Maine* . . . , (2 vols.; Hallowell, Me., 1839), I, iv; Lorenzo Sabine, *American Loyalists or Biographical Sketches of Adherents to the British Crown* (Boston, 1847), p. iv; Samuel Greene Arnold, *The Life of Patrick Henry of Virginia* (Auburn and Buffalo, N.Y., 1854), p. 14.

[36] Albert James Pickett, *A History of Alabama* . . . (Sheffield, Ala., 1851), 10; Humphrey Marshall, *The History of Kentucky* (2 vols.; Frankfort, 1824), I, iii; Benjamin Trumbull, *A Complete History of Connecticut . . . to the Year 1764* (2 vols.; New Haven, 1818), I, 5.

[37] Review, *North American Review,* XXXIII (October, 1831), 449; "Prospectus," *American Pioneer,* I (January, 1842), 3; "Recent Historical Revelations," p. 347.

[38] Historical and Literary Committee of the American Philosophical Society, *Transactions,* I (1819), xvi; also, review, *North American Review,* XLIII (July, 1836), 276.

realized that great histories could not be written until the materials were gathered, and, willingly, they took the first step.

A patriotism which was closely related to the sense of service also stimulated interest in antiquarianism. Collections served as monuments to the great men and deeds of past generations. The new nation, so painfully conscious of cultural immaturity, feared "the discredit brought upon our national reputation" by the neglect of documents.[39] "Why this ransacking of old cupboards for dusty documents? . . . We . . . make but one reply. Because we love our country." [40] A collection of the papers or chronicles of heroic deeds was a memorial to deserving ancestors, "a monument to those whose memory ought to live forever." [41] "If there were no other consideration to recommend it," said one writer, "we owe it to the generation of patriots who achieved our independence, to bring out from the archives in which they are perishing, the monuments of their talent, for their honor and our instruction." [42]

The early nineteenth century seemed to be the focus of some attitudes toward detail that began long before 1800 and of others that lasted long after 1860. Men of the period still shared the Enlightenment's encyclopedic approach to facts, the desire to compile and know everything. They were also beginning to transform this into the late nineteenth-century view of historical facts as pieces in a giant jigsaw puzzle, the solution of which would end dispute and provide a scientific conclusion. "The very highest value" of details, said a reviewer in 1834, is "in settling, or verifying, or rectifying, or reversing judgments upon marked men or marked events." [43] The bridge between the two attitudes, however, seemed to lie primarily in the essentially

[39] C. P. Cooper, "Materials for History," *Museum of Foreign Literature*, XXII (February, 1833), 229.

[40] John Romeyn Brodhead, *Address Delivered before the New York Historical Society, at Its Fortieth Anniversary* (New York, 1844), p. 46.

[41] Review, *North American Review*, LXXI (July, 1850), 34.

[42] Reviews, *North American Review*, XXXIII (October, 1831), 484; also, ibid., XLVI (April, 1838), 486, and LV (July, 1842), 258; and *Christian Examiner*, LX (March, 1856), 266.

[43] "History and Biography," *Christian Examiner*, LXX (March, 1861), 315; and review, *American Quarterly Observer*, III (July, 1834), 121.

Romantic belief that reality existed more in the particular than in the general. Said William Blake:[44]

> To see the world in a grain of sand,
>   And heaven in a wild flower;
> Hold infinity in the palm of your hand,
>   And eternity in an hour.

The entomologists chased butterflies, as Abiel Holmes observed, the historians wrote history, and the antiquarians collected details—and there were more collectors than either entomologists or historians.

[44] "Auguries of Innocence," 1803. In 1869 Alfred Tennyson wrote:
> Flower in the crannied wall,
> I pluck you out of the crannies,
> I hold you here, root and all, in my hand,
> Little flower—but if I could understand
> What you are, root and all, and all in all,
> I should know what God and man is.

VII

Methods of Writing History

HISTORIANS and critics generally agreed on the basic techniques by which the historian appealed to so large an audience. First, after choosing the right topic, scrupulous scholarship was necessary to give a work credibility. Next, literary style was essential to transform facts into a flowing story. Finally the historian had to utilize personal emotion which reached beyond scholarship and style and elevated them into art. Such techniques were really ways of being interesting. "Interest, interest, interest," Prescott exorted himself as he worked, "the great requirement . . . interest!" [1]

Scholarship and Honesty

The principal criticism which men of the early nineteenth century leveled against eighteenth-century historians was their tendency to be grandiloquent without sufficient regard to the facts. The new generation had no quarrel with grand ideas, but one of their major contributions to the development of historical study was an insistence on interpretation based upon accurate, factual scholarship. During the late nineteenth century, scientific historians carried the argument a step further, claiming that any

---

[1] C. Harvey Gardiner, ed., *The Literary Memoranda of William Hickling Prescott* (2 vols.; Norman, Okla., 1961), I, 50–52, 86–117; II, 69.

interpretation rested upon a biased selection of facts and that truth lay only in unadorned research itself. Finally, during the twentieth century, historians found unadorned research both impossible and meaningless, and they tried again, like the Romantic historians, to combine data and interpretation.

Early nineteenth-century writers were excited by what they believed was a new concept, the idea that history could be based on research rather than philosophy. Perhaps each generation of historians begins with an attack on the factual inaccuracy of its predecessors; certainly early nineteenth-century historians considered careful research the primary basis of their own superiority. "As history has developed," said one critic, "it has taught us the extreme value of close, critical, truthful investigation." "Historians are immeasurably more painstaking than they were," said another, "more particular about facts and authorities." Writers spoke of "modern criticism" which had demolished the eighteenth-century approach to the past, and of "the new historical school" which had made history into "an exact science." Accurate research was not everything, but "modern scholars . . . in our time" realized it was the "indispensable preliminary." [2] To be sure, this view was generally unsophisticated, as the very certainty of the statements revealed. Seldom did historians consider what really constituted a fact, or the likelihood of bias in their selection.[3] The German scholars under Leopold von Ranke made their contribution later in the century by calling attention to such questions and demanding a purified methodology. Even if

[2] Review, *North American Review*, LXXX (April, 1855), 483; anon., "The Modern Art and Science of History," *Westminster Review*, XXXVIII (October, 1842), 356, 369; anon., "The Uses of History," *New Englander*, XXII (July, 1863), 429; anon., "Hegel's Philosophy of History," *Eclectic Magazine*, XLV (September, 1858), 1.

[3] David Ramsay, *The History of the Revolution of South Carolina* . . . (2 vols.; Trenton, N.J., 1785), I, ix; Mercy Otis Warren, *History of the Rise, Progress, and Termination of the American Revolution* . . . (3 vols.; Boston, 1805), I, i–v; Abiel Holmes, *The Annals of America* . . . (2 vols.; Cambridge, Mass., 1829), I, iii–iv; George Bancroft, *History of the United States* . . . (10 vols.; Boston, 1834–75), I, v; William Hickling Prescott, *History of the Reign of Ferdinand and Isabella, the Catholic* (3 vols.; Boston, 1838), I, viii–ix; John Gorham Palfrey, *History of New England* (5 vols.; Boston, 1859–90), I, xv; James Parton, *The Life of Horace Greeley* . . . (New York, 1855), p. ix.

the Romantic concepts were naive, however, they were conscious standards by which history had to be measured. "In estimating a new history . . . the first point, of course, to be settled is authenticity." [4]

Critics defined the tedious virtues of the scholar as honesty, accuracy, and thoroughness. First, honesty, "the highest and noblest qualification of an historian"; "the principle of truth is predominant." If it were lacking then history would be perverted into uselessness or even evil. "An historian without fidelity is worse than useless," said one critic. "He is injurious to mankind [for] upon the credit of his narrative the happiness of future generations may rest." [5]

Next, accuracy, "the *sine qua non* of history"; "everything is to be sacrificed for it." "Accuracy, that prime virtue of an historian, distinguishes the narrative and gives us, throughout, the impression of reality." [6] Critics liked to say that a particular book had "the mark of authenticity," or that its excellence depended "mainly on accuracy," or that its virtues stemmed from "exact research." [7] By the 1850's, as Romantic history came under at-

[4] Francis Lister Hawks, *Contributions to the Ecclesiastical History of the United States of America* (2 vols.; New York, 1836–39), I, vii; William Gilmore Simms, *The History of South Carolina* . . . (Charleston, 1840), pp. vi-vii; Philip Schaff, *History of the Apostolic Church* . . . (New York, 1854), p. iii; review, *Living Age*, XXXI (October, 1851), 134; *North American Review*, XLVI (January, 1838), 221; also, anon., "Ancient and Modern History," *North American Review*, XXVIII (April, 1829), 320; Gardiner, *Literary Memoranda of Prescott*, I, 91, 121.

[5] Anon., "The Study of History," *Southern Quarterly Review*, X (July, 1846), 144; review, *Christian Examiner*, LX (March, 1856), 266; also, anon., "History," *American Quarterly Review*, V (March, 1829), 87; John Hill, "An Essay upon the Principles of Historical Composition," *Portfolio*, IX (April, 1820), 342; Preface, *The American Pioneer*, I (January, 1842), 4; also, reviews, *Christian Examiner*, IV (September, 1827), 383; *North American Review*, LXXXI (October, 1855), 350; *North American Review*, XXIX (October, 1829), 293.

[6] Review, *North American Review*, XLII (April, 1836), 449; anon., "The Art of History Writing," *Living Age*, XLVIII (January, 1856), 244; review, *Christian Examiner*, XXIV (March, 1838), 100.

[7] Reviews, *North American Review*, XLVI (January, 1838), 217; *Harper's Magazine*, XVIII (April, 1859), 692; *London Quarterly*, CLXIV (June, 1839), 7; also, *Democratic Review*, II (May, 1838), 162; *Museum of Foreign Literature*, XL (September, 1840), 26; Samuel Green Arnold, *History of the State*

tack for its florid narrative, exact research became not only a means of telling the truth but an end in itself.[8]

Finally, in discussing the requisite qualities of a scholar, critics emphasized thoroughness, even though this was sometimes difficult to combine with imaginative flair. Scholarly research, said the critics, was a matter of "great labor and unwearied toil," "untiring patience and careful discrimination," "indefatigable industry," and "grave and patient research."[9] Thoroughness included "exhaustive use of abundant materials, and a most conscious fidelity in digesting them"; it meant "minute and thorough investigation," "industrious research and . . . critical acumen," "close, critical, truthful investigation," and "profound diligence."[10]

Given these basic scholarly virtues, the historian must then proceed with exhaustive use of original sources. This concern over sources appeared in the zeal for documentary collections. The good historian, said the critics, will "never willfully take a second-hand or second-rate authority as his guide when a primary was accessible," and historians swore then they had relied, whenever possible, on "the original authorities."[11] Historians liked to

---

of Rhode Island and Plymouth Plantations (2 vols.; New York, 1859), I, viii; Edward Duffield Neill, *The History of Minnesota* . . . (Philadelphia, 1858), p. vi; James Fenimore Cooper, *The History of the Navy of the United States of America* (2 vols.; Philadelphia, 1839), I, viii; Benjamin Trumbull, *A Complete History of Connecticut* . . . *to the Year 1764* (2 vols.; New Haven, 1818), I, 7; Palfrey, *History of New England*, I, xvi; anon., "Ancient and Modern History," *North American Review*, XXVIII (April, 1829), 320.

[8] Richard Hildreth, *The History of the United States* . . . (6 vols.; New York, 1856), I, vii; Donald Eugene Emerson, *Richard Hildreth* (Baltimore, 1946), pp. 164–66; John Warner Barber, *Historical Collections of the State of New York* (New York, 1851), p. iv; Arnold, *History of Rhode Island*, I, viii.

[9] Reviews, *Foreign Quarterly Review*, XXVI (October, 1840), 1; *New York Review*, II (April, 1838), 308; *North American Review*, LXXXVIII (April, 1859), 461; *Living Age*, XXXI (October, 1851), 138.

[10] Reviews, *Atlantic Monthly*, VII (April, 1859), 442; *North American Review*, LXXXVIII (April, 1859), 462; *Living Age*, LXII (April, 1859), 392; *North American Review*, LXXX (April, 1855), 483; *Eclectic Magazine*, XLI (May, 1857), 26; *Living Age*, XXXI (October, 1851), 138.

[11] Review, *Living Age*, LXII (August, 1859), 393; Hildreth, *History of the United States*, I, viii; also Bancroft, *History of the United States*, I, v; John

give evidence of their diligent search for materials by lengthy discussions of the "vast labor" that went into the compilation of a book. Somehow, it was not considered immodest to dwell upon the long, lonely searches for materials, the great expense involved in collecting material, and the "endless months" of patient reading.[12]

American writers had a broad view of primary sources. Private papers, government documents, and newspapers were the stand-bys, and historical societies were eager to provide them. The labor of copyists was cheap, and men like William H. Prescott were able to spend many thousands of dollars purchasing distant materials and having them copied. Early-nineteenth-century writers were more aware than many subsequent historians of the value of literature and artifacts as a source of knowledge about the past. Historical societies eagerly transcribed the reminiscences of old men, and many writers went out of their way to emphasize that "drinking in, from aged lips, rich stores of historic lore" was a "favorite source" of information.[13] Historians were aware that the generation preceding them had seen momentous events take place, and they liked the intimate personal flavor that interviews gave to history.

To use the sources was a simple dictum, but to criticize them, weigh their authenticity, and use them discreetly was an art. "It is the duty of the historian first to examine with critical exactness the weight and authenticity of all the sources of information." [14] "He must subject these materials to the ordeal of strictest examination, with the utmost candor and impartiality"; he

Francis Hamtramck Claiborne, *Life and Correspondence of John A. Quitman* . . . (2 vols.; New York, 1860), I, v.

[12] Francis Parkman, Jr., *History of the Conspiracy of Pontiac* . . . (Boston, 1851), pp. viii–x; James Parton, *Life of Andrew Jackson* (3 vols.; New York, 1860), I, vi–x; David Benedict, *A General History of the Baptist Denomination* . . . (2 vols.; Boston, 1813), I, 3; Timothy Flint, *The History and Geography of the Mississippi Valley* (2 vols.; Boston, 1833), I, 9.

[13] Henry Reed Stiles, *The History of Ancient Windsor, Connecticut* . . . (New York, 1859), p. v; Daniel Pierce Thompson, *History of the Town of Montpelier* . . . (Montpelier, Vt., 1860), p. v; Milton Embick Flower, *James Parton: The Father of Modern Biography* (Durham, N.C., 1951), pp. 26–30.

[14] Anon., "History," *American Quarterly Review*, V (March, 1829), 95.

must demonstrate "complete mastery and unchallenged criticism of his authorities." [15] The historian was a lawyer who "rests on such evidence as would be receivable in a court of justice." [16] He was a judge who must "examine the strength of the evidence and the character of the witness. The rules of our courts of jurisprudence are generally applicable here." [17]

This age of literary history emphasized the scholarly trappings of footnotes and bibliography as much as did subsequent scholars. Prescott devoted approximately one-third of the words in his histories of Peru, Mexico, and Spain to footnotes and bibliographical discussion. Only slightly less space was assigned to this sort of matter by George Bancroft, Francis Parkman, John Gorham Palfrey, John Lothrop Motley, and George Ticknor. Reviewers praised these authors for fine research and outstanding notes.[18] Even men like Washington Irving and Benson John Lossing, who wrote history almost solely to entertain, devoted a sizable portion of each page to footnote references. Of the most popular historians, only Sir Walter Scott and Charles Gayarré

[15] Giles F. Yates, "Ancient History," *American Literary Magazine,* I (December, 1847), 367; review, *North American Review,* LXXXVIII (April, 1859), 461; also Timothy Pitkin, *A Political and Civil History of the United States . . .* (2 vols.; New Haven, 1828), I, 4–7; Richard Frothingham, *History of the Siege of Boston . . .* (Boston, 1850), p. iii; Bancroft, *History of the United States,* I, v.

[16] Charles Etienne Gayarré, *Louisiana: Its Colonial History and Romance* (3 vols.; New York, 1851–54), I, xiv.

[17] Anon., "The Philosophy of History," *North American Review,* XXXIX (July, 1834), 45; also, anon., "Ancient and Modern History," p. 322; review, *North American Review,* XCI (July, 1860), 41.

[18] See, for example, the following reviews: on Bancroft, *North American Review,* XL (January, 1835), 99–100; *North American Review,* LII (January, 1840), 101; on Parkman, *Knickerbocker Review,* XXXVIII (July, 1851), 68–69; *Living Age,* XXXI (October, 1851), 138; on Palfrey, *Harper's Magazine,* XLVIII (April, 1859), 692; *Atlantic Monthly,* VII (April, 1859), 442; *North American Review,* LXXXVIII (April, 1859), 461; on Motley, *North American Review,* LXXXIII (July, 1856), 187; on Ticknor, *Living Age,* XXIV (January, 1844), 157; *Christian Examiner,* XXVI (March, 1844), 266; *Atlantic Monthly,* III (January, 1859), 127; *Democratic Review,* II (May, 1838), 162; Samuel Austin Allibone, *A Critical Dictionary of English Literature, and British and American Authors* (3 vols.; Philadelphia, 1899), *passim.*

wrote without evidence of their research, and both were chastised by critics for the presumption.[19]

Readers were not intimidated by footnotes; citation of sources did not imply a distinction between good writing and bad. On the contrary, the presence of footnotes imparted a comfortable sense of authenticity to the narrative. Readers felt reassured to find "copious notes . . . authorities carefully noted, and full references given"; here was "the stamp of guarantee." [20] For leisurely reading, where the unfolding of the story itself mattered most, notes offered stimulating suggestions for additional reading, "a mine of ample and varied wealth for the historical student." [21] Notes often provided a pleasing cache of amusing and irrelevant anecdotes "like flowers along the wayside" to enliven and amuse the reader.[22] Only occasionally did a critic disagree with the use of footnotes, observing that they did not "prove anything" and only served as a showcase for the author's egotism.[23]

Historians and critics liked to remind themselves that the purpose of careful scholarship was to give their works the mark of authenticity and thus provide whatever advantage history had over fiction. While novelists struggled to make imaginary situations seem real, the historian began with reality. He was considered the perfect artist when he recounted the absolute truth

[19] For example, the following reviews: on Scott, *Christian Examiner,* IV (September, 1827), 382; *Christian Examiner,* XXIV (July, 1838), 345; on Gayarré, *Southern Literary Messenger,* XVIII (May, 1852), 311; *DeBow's Review,* XI (July, 1851), 7; *Southern Quarterly Review,* XX (July, 1851), 69; also Allibone, *British and American Authors, passim.*

[20] Reviews, *North American Review,* LXXXVIII (April, 1859), 463; *London Quarterly,* CLXIV (June, 1839); *North American Review,* XLVI (January, 1838), 281.

[21] Review, *North American Review,* XCI (October, 1860), 421.

[22] Reviews, *North American Review,* XLVI (January, 1838), 281; also, *North American Review,* LXXX (April, 1855), 488; *Christian Examiner,* XLIII (September, 1847), 262; *Southern Literary Messenger,* XVIII (May, 1852), 312; anon., "Art of History Writing," p. 244.

[23] Review, *North American Review,* LXXX (April, 1855), 390–91; William Read Staples, *Annals of the Town of Providence . . .* (Providence, R.I., 1843), p. vi.

about the past.[24] Not only was truth as interesting as fiction; it was far more valuable as insight into the eternal questions of life. "History is progress toward . . . true unity and universality . . . not in the neglect of details but in the more perfect verification, the more careful mastery." [25] The best history was the truest:

> If a historian alters his facts, he . . . destroys his peculiar advantage as a historian. If he mutilates, glosses over, colors . . . in any way tampers with the materials with which human nature has furnished him, the portraits he portrays will be correspondingly false—false not alone to fact, but false to the 'conditions of humanity,' false to nature itself.[26]

Scholarship and the Quotation Mark

Despite their emphasis on honest scholarship, the Romantic historians have suffered grievously at the hands of subsequent scholars, for they have been accused of dishonesty, of altering direct quotations, and of using each other's material without the scrupulous use of quotation marks. One by one, the early nineteenth-century historians have fallen under attack—Jared Sparks, George Bancroft, John Marshall, David Ramsay, Washington Irving, and Francis Parkman—branded as plagiarists, inaccurate ones at that.[27] Their outraged critics have been justified in con-

---

[24] James Anthony Froude, "The Science of History," *Hours at Home,* II (February, 1866), 328.

[25] Anon., "Art and Science of History," p. 369; also, review, *Christian Examiner,* XXIV (March, 1838), 100; anon., "Thoughts on the Manner of Writing History," *Southern Literary Messenger,* III (February, 1837), 156.

[26] G. H. E., "Hildreth's History of the United States," *Universalist Quarterly and General Review,* XII (October, 1855), 349.

[27] For some attacks on early nineteenth-century plagiarism, see Orin Grant Libby, "Some Pseudo Histories of the American Revolution," *Transactions of the Wisconsin Academy of Sciences, Arts, and Letters,* XIII (1901), 419–25; Orin Grant Libby, "Ramsay as a Plagiarist," *American Historical Review,* VII (July, 1902), 697–703; William A. Foran, "John Marshall as a Plagiarist," *American Historical Review,* XLIII (October, 1937), 51–64; R. Kent Newmeyer, "Charles Stedman's History of the American War," *American Historical Review,* LXIII (July, 1958), 924–34; Michael Kraus, *The Writing of American History* (Norman, Okla., 1953), pp. 72–73, 78, 86, and *passim;* John Spencer Bassett, *The Middle Group of American Historians* (New York, 1917), pp. 100–110, and *passim.*

demning a practice of which they disapproved, and, indeed, the aims of modern scholarship have made the methods of the early nineteenth century obsolete. However, accusations of dishonesty were unjust, for the historians were never secretive about their practices, and they must be judged by their own standards. It had never occurred to many that accurate quoting was desirable. Others had carefully weighed the problem, explicitly stated their intentions, and thoughtfully defended their positions.

Jared Sparks has borne the brunt of the charges for altering the spelling and grammar of direct quotations in his twelve-volume edition of Washington's writings, but Sparks was utterly frank about his policy. In the first volume he devoted five pages of the introduction to an explanation of how and why he had altered quotations: "I have of course considered it a duty, appertaining to the function of a faithful editor, to hazard such corrections as the construction of a sentence manifestly warranted, or a cool judgement dictated." [28] In the last volume, three years later, he again presented his justification of revisions.[29]

Before undertaking this project, Sparks had agonized over the question of alterations. Carefully he canvassed the opinion of statesmen and historians, even obtaining an interview on the subject with the president of the United States. In his journal he noted that John Adams "thought it best to correct freely all blunders in orthography and grammar which appeared in Washington's letters." He consulted the Massachusetts Historical Society; John Marshall, Edward Everett, and Noah Webster were interviewed; all advised Sparks to correct and revise.[30] When the work appeared, reviewers unstintingly praised it, noted the avowed practice of revision as being "ex-

[28] Jared Sparks, ed., *The Writings of George Washington* . . . (12 vols.; Boston, 1834–37), II, xv. Volume II, beginning the correspondence of Washington, was the first to be published, and volume I, the biography, was the last to appear.

[29] *Ibid.*, I, viii.

[30] Sparks's Journal, January 15, 1828, Herbert Baxter Adams, *The Life and Writings of Jared Sparks, Comprising Selections from His Journals and Correspondence* (2 vols.; Boston, 1893), I, 46; II, 269–72, 501–32.

tremely judicious," and praised the editor for his "extraordinary diligence." [31]

Seventeen years after the publication of Sparks's series on Washington, in 1854, an English historian—a fervid advocate of the coming school of scientific history—launched the first assault on Sparks's methods. Even so, this attack concerned only the degree of revision that was desirable, for the Englishman still admitted that "trifling inaccuracies of grammar and spelling" should be corrected.[32] Contemporaries, however, immediately saw in these strictures an attack upon a whole school of history, and the pamphlet war and literary debate which followed had grave implications for the future of the entire Romantic approach to the past. John Gorham Palfrey, Washington Irving, Edward Everett, and Peter Force came vigorously to Sparks's defense.[33] Sparks, more hurt than outraged, explained that during his preparation of the Washington volumes "no critic, friendly or hostile, no individual within my knowledge,

[31] John Gorham Palfrey, "The Washington Papers," *North American Review*, XXXIX (October, 1834), 468–71; reviews, *American Quarterly Review*, XV (June, 1834), 275–310; *American Quarterly Observer*, III (July, 1834), 120–35; *North American Review*, LXXV (July, 1852), 185–208. For a digest of contemporary reviews, see Allibone, *British and American Authors*, II, 2191–93.

[32] The attack was launched by Lord Mahon [Philip Henry Stanhope], *History of England from the Peace of Utrecht to the Peace of Versailles, 1713–1783* (7 vols.; London, 1836–54), VI, appendix. The following were prominent pamphlets in the controversy: Jared Sparks, *A Reply to the Strictures of Lord Mahon* . . . (Cambridge, Mass., 1852); Lord Mahon, *Letter to Jared Sparks, Esq.; Being a Rejoinder to his "Reply to the Strictures . . . "* (Boston, 1852); William Bradford Reed, *Reprint of the Original Letters from Washington to Joseph Reed, during the American Revolution, Referred to in the Pamphlets of Lord Mahon and Jared Sparks* (Philadelphia, 1852); Jared Sparks, *Remarks on a "Reprint of the Original Letters from Washington to Joseph Reed* . . . (Boston, 1853).

[33] John Gorham Palfrey, "Lord Mahon's History of England," *North American Review*, LXXV (July, 1852), 185–208; Pierre Munroe Irving, *The Life and Letters of Washington Irving* (4 vols.; New York, 1864), IV, 146; Washington Irving, *Life of George Washington* (5 vols.; New York, 1856–59), I, vi–vii; Edward Everett, *The Life of George Washington* (New York, 1860), pp. vi, 27, 273; Peter Force, *The Declaration of Independence, or Notes on Lord Mahon's History of the Declaration of Independence* (London, 1855), p. 5 and ff.

ever hinted that the plan, or the rules of executing it were founded on erroneous principles or were perverted in their application." [34] Even in 1860, when scientific methods were gaining approval, men like Richard Hildreth and John Lothrop Motley, who had become increasingly critical of revising quotations, never implied that it was dishonest and acknowledged that it was the recognized practice of the day.[35]

In a period when documentary collections were designed for and read by the general public for pleasure, many other editors followed Sparks's practice in order to attract readers. The editor of the Rhode Island colonial records, for example, lamented that many writers "were evidently not familiar with the pen, and not well versed in the rules of grammar and punctuation," and he promised obligingly to clear up these matters.[36] Another editor assured his readers that "it has not been deemed necessary to adhere closely" to such matters as punctuation and capitalization; still another boasted at length of his extensive and careful corrections, promising the public that all necessary changes "have been employed in the manner most in accordance with the best modern printing." [37]

Editors of documentary works were not alone in admitting their alteration of quotations. George Bancroft "felt free to change tenses or moods, to transpose parts of quotations, to simplify language, and to give free rendition." His biographer notes that he had "no compunction at blending material from several quotations to form a single uninterrupted speech. . . ." [38]

[34] Sparks, *Reply to Lord Mahon*, p. 18.

[35] Hildreth, *History of the United States*, I, 10; John Lothrop Motley, *History of the United Netherlands: From the Death of William the Silent to the Synod of Dort* (3 vols.; New York, 1861–67), I, v; William Hickling Prescott, *History of the Conquest of Mexico* . . . (3 vols.; Boston, 1843), I, x.

[36] John Russell Bartlett, ed., *Records of the Colony of Rhode Island, and Providence Plantations in New England* (10 vols.; Providence, R.I., 1856–65), I, ix.

[37] James Hammond Trumbull, ed., *The Public Records of the Colony of Connecticut, Prior to the Union with the New Haven Colony, May 1665* (3 vols.; Hartford, 1850–59), I, v; Nathaniel Bradstreet Shurtleff, ed., *Records of the Colony of New Plymouth in England* (8 vols.; Boston, 1855–57), I, x.

[38] Russel B. Nye, *George Bancroft: Brahmin Rebel* (New York, 1944), p. 193.

William Gordon boasted of altering sources to prove that he was a thorough and conscientious historian.[39] Popular writers assured their readers that they had carefully "modernized the spelling," made quotations "more intelligible," and altered grammar to conform "to that in general use at the present time." [40]

Historians did not revise indiscriminately. They approved only those minor changes which they felt did not alter the strict meaning—or even the flavor—of the original. Writers were aware that the value of quotations depended upon general, if not literal, accuracy, and that "changes must not deprive them of one innate mark of authenticity," [41] Alteration extended "only to verbal and grammatical mistakes" or to orthography, "scrupulous care" being taken that the precise connotation "thereby in no degree be changed or affected." "Quaintness" of expression which would impart the flavor and feeling of the original had to be preserved.[42] It was the historians' trust to combine authenticity with the benefits of readability.[43]

More important than the fact that historians revised quotations were their reasons for doing so. First, they thought that altering quotations would make history more lucid and pleasing to readers without damaging the essential truth of the original. One author revised "when assistance could thereby be afforded the reader." Another explained that he revised quotations in order to "render them more easily read and understood." [44] To

[39] Gordon to Washington, February 16, 1789, William Gordon, "Letters of the Reverend William Gordon, Historian of the American Revolution, 1770–1799," *Proceedings of the Massachusetts Historical Society,* LXIII (June, 1930), 553.

[40] Joel Tyler Headley, *The Life of Oliver Cromwell* (New York, 1848), pp. xi–xiii; Samuel Gardner Drake, *Biography and History of the Indians of North America* (Boston, 1827), p. viii; William Read Staples, *Town of Providence,* p. vi.

[41] Trumbull, *Records of Connecticut,* I, iii; Staples, *Town of Providence,* p. vi.

[42] Sparks, *Writings of Washington,* II, xv; John Warner Barber, *Interesting Events in the History of the United States* (New Haven, 1829), p. iv.

[43] Shurtleff, *Records of New Plymouth,* I, x; also Drake, *Indians of North America,* p. viii.

[44] Shurtleff, *Records of New Plymouth,* I, x; Staples, *Town of Providence,* p. vi.

follow the original exactly would have "increased the difficulties of perusal and materially detracted from the interest of the volume to the general reader." [45] Here was the major basis of misunderstanding by the critics who so bitterly attacked the alteration of quotations, for early-nineteenth-century history was directed toward the general public rather than toward the professional scholar. Even documentary history was compiled for the leisure reading of people who insisted upon entertainment as well as honesty and truth. Men assumed that if the historian were honest, alterations did not affect the truth and did contribute to the pleasure of reading.

Editors further argued that it was indecent to publish private correspondence without putting it into the form which the writer himself might have demanded before allowing publication. Sparks argued that since Washington had corrected and revised much of his correspondence, good taste necessitated the revision of whatever else was used from his private files. "It would be an act of unpardonable injustice to any author, after his death," wrote Sparks, "to bring forth compositions, and particularly letters written with no design to their publication and commit them to the press without previously subjecting them to a careful revision." [46] It was an editor's "solemn duty to correct obvious slips of the pen . . . which the writer himself, if he could have revised his own manuscripts, would never for a moment have allowed to appear in print." [47] Often papers of prominent men were copied by secretaries rather than by the authors themselves, and a conscientious editor was only being as careful as a secretary.[48]

The rationale for revising quotations which most shocked later historians, however, was the early nineteenth-century belief that a few careful alterations would actually come closer to what a writer had intended originally; a few discreet omissions and corrections would give a more faithful picture of a man or

[45] Trumbull, *Records of Connecticut*, I, v.
[46] Sparks, *Writings of Washington*, II, xv.
[47] Sparks, *Reply to Lord Mahon*, p. 6.
[48] Sparks, *Writings of Washington*, I, viii–ix; also, Bartlett, *Records of Rhode Island*, I, ix.

event than the original words themselves. Bitterly critical of an English historian who had reprinted Washington's mistakes, John Gorham Palfrey demanded "Is the reader better instructed? Is Washington better understood? Is fidelity to history usefully subserved?" The qualified historian knows, argued Palfrey, that these shortcomings of the first president "are not illustrations of the man." [49] A difficulty arose, however, when historians differed among themselves as to what comprised a true illustration of the man; these disagreements eventually destroyed the Romantic approach to history and led to an insistence upon rigid accuracy and new scientific methods. Until about the time of the Civil War there were fewer contradictions in interpretation, and people trusted that a careful editing not only made documents more interesting to the reader and fairer to the original author but also more accurate in recreating the past.

Similar to the problem of altering quotations was the matter of selecting documents to be published. Later historians had great difficulty in deciding to omit anything; the frustration of their inability to print all of the written matter that existed about a given period or man partly explains the decline of documentary history in the late nineteenth century. The early nineteenth-century historians, however, admitting that selection was a difficult task requiring conscientious care, never doubted the propriety of the practice or the ability of the careful editor to perform the task.[50]

The second major asault by modern scholars on the historians of the early nineteenth century centered about plagiarism, the practice of using in their own works the same phraseology as someone else had used. The early nineteenth-century historian would have been dismayed by the attack, would have pleaded *nolo contendere,* and would simply have pointed out that he had never pretended to be original when he could find someone else who had satisfactorily said what he had in mind.

One of the first to be attacked was William Gordon for using material from the *Annual Register* without quotation marks.

---

[49] Palfrey, "Lord Mahon's History of England," p. 200.
[50] See, for example, Sparks, *Writings of Washington,* II, xiii–xiv.

Again, disagreement with his approach was justified, but the implication of dishonesty was not, for Gordon, after discussing in his introduction his use of various sources, carefully explained that he had "frequently quoted from them without varying the language, except for method and conciseness." With pride rather than apology he explained to Washington the sources he had used and that he had "at times inserted them as though they were originally my own." [51] Gordon believed that the people wanted the story of the Revolution. The only available account was in the *Annual Register,* which was hard for Americans to obtain. Moreover, by making some corrections and some additions to this account, he could retell, or reprint, the story in a more convenient, more easily available, and corrected form. He consistently referred to himself as "a compiler" of the account and would probably have called himself an editor if he had known that it would have pleased his later critics.[52]

A similar attack was made on John Marshall, but his statement of intention, prominently displayed in the introduction of his book on Washington, could hardly have been more explicit:

> The very language has sometimes been employed without distinguishing the passages, especially when intermingled with others, by marks of quotation, and the author persuades himself that this public declaration will rescue him from the imputation of receiving aids he is unwilling to acknowledge, or of wishing, by a concealed plagiarism, to usher to the world, as his own, the labours of others.[53]

Countless lesser historians were as frank. After citing his sources, a typical writer stated that he "would here publically acknowledge that he has often copied their language as well as their facts, and has not been particular to disfigure his page with quotation marks." Another glibly explained that his "first five chapters . . . are from the admirably written historical sketch

---

[51] William Gordon, *The History of the Rise, Progress, and Establishment of the Independence of the United States of America* . . . (4 vols.; London, 1788), I, vii; Gordon to Washington, February 16, 1789, Gordon, "Letters," p. 553.

[52] Gorden, *Establishment of Independence,* I, vi–vii.

[53] John Marshall, *The Life of George Washington* . . . (5 vols.; Philadelphia, 1804–07), I, x.

in Martin's Gazetteer." [54] Others openly stated that they "had not scrupled" to copy a well-written previous study; that they "used substantially another's language"; that they utilized the work of others "without introducing my authorities"; that if a good source was found they had "adopted the phraseology of the author entire"; and that they had "made use of them as public property." [55]

The early nineteenth-century historian felt no need to argue for originality, and he would not have understood why he should make a fetish of reworking material when what he wanted to say already had been better said by another. Before the Civil War, there was little sense of competition among historians; it appeared entirely proper to borrow literally as well as factually. The unfolding of the story was more important than the fear that the author would receive undeserved credit for eloquence. There was ample new material for all, and whether a writer chose to relate a new subject or popularize an old one, he usually believed that he was presenting it in his particular way for the first time. A historian need not be jealous of his work; neither should he be any more original than was absolutely necessary.

Historians usually felt flattered rather than insulted when their words were used by another. The period is remarkable for the lack of scholarly rivalry, and writers who borrowed from each other remained on the warmest terms. One man, discussing his fellow historians, noted that he had "availed myself of their labours with the same freedom which I would myself allow in like circumstance." [56] When phrases from David Ramsay's history were incorporated, with slight improvements (but without

[54] Zadock Thompson, *History of Vermont, Natural, Civil, and Statistical* (Burlington, Vt., 1842), p. iv; Henry Howe, *Historical Collections of Virginia* (Charleston, S.C., 1852), p. iii.

[55] Simms, *South Carolina*, vi–vii; William Buell Sprague, *Annals of the American Pulpit; or Commemorative Notices of Distinguished American Clergymen of Various Denominations* (9 vols.; New York, 1857–69), I, vii; Ramsay, *Revolution of South-Carolina*, I, ix; Flint, *The Mississippi Valley*, I, 10–13; Drake, *Indians of North America*, p. viii.

[56] Stiles, *Ancient Windsor, Connecticut*, p. vi.

quotation marks), in his friend William Gordon's work, Ramsay accepted the improved version of his own words when he had occasion to make use of the material again.[57]

As contemporary critics understood the altering of quotations, they also understood and approved what the plagiarizers were doing. Critics were aware of having seen the same words before and frequently compared the later account with its source, remarking on the improvement that had been made over the earlier account but seldom considering it a matter of dishonesty in the use of phraseology.[58] A twentieth-century scholar attacking Ramsay as a plagiarist expressed surprise that in this "generation of successfully plagiarized histories . . . all of them were more or less well received by an uncritical public." [59] In fact, one contemporary review had criticized Ramsay's "plagiarism" not on the basis of honesty but because he felt Ramsay's literary skill was greater than that of his sources.[60]

When critics did speak out on plagiarism it was frequently in actual defense of the practice. One article, for example, condemned at length narrow-minded authors who hampered their own work by a stubborn determination to be original when rewriting merely meant being inferior.[61] Another article entitled "An Apology For The Late Comer" urged writers to keep in

[57] Ramsay, *Revolution of South-Carolina,* II, 153; Gordon, *Establishment of Independence,* III, 448; David Ramsay, *The History of the American Revolution* (2 vols.; Philadelphia, 1789), I, iv. See Elmer Douglass Johnson, "David Ramsay: Historian or Plagiarist?" *South Carolina Historical Magazine,* LVII (October, 1956), 195.

[58] For comparisons of works which borowed from each other, see William Smyth, *Lectures on Modern History, from the Irruption of the Northern Nations to the Close of the American Revolution* (Boston, 1851), pp. 550–53, 591–608; reviews, *Monthly Review* (London), LXXX (May, 1789), 441–42; *Edinburgh Review,* XIII (October, 1808), 151; *Blackwood's Monthly Journal,* XVII (February, 1825), 200; *North American Review,* LXXXVI (April, 1858), 334–35.

[59] Libby, "Ramsay as a Plagiarist," p. 703.

[60] Review, "Ramsay's History of the United States," *North American Review,* VI (March, 1818), 334–35. This review also pointed to sources Ramsay used of which Libby was apparently unaware.

[61] Anon., "Plagiarism and John Bunyan," *Catholic World,* VI (January, 1858), 534–35.

mind the worthy end to be accomplished and not to fear copying another work when it could help achieve that end.[62] "A charge of plagiarism against an author is considered as pretty sure evidence of his superiority as a writer," said still another critic, because it means the author is above the petty fetish of originality. "Charges of this kind most frequently come from young men of small reading and little experience." The historian should make changes only to improve the story. "What are Macaulay's and Bancroft's histories but 'rehashes'?" The man of genius was not afraid to "rehash," because he had no fear of displaying his originality in the form of new ideas rather than as reworked sentences.[63]

The essential difference between early nineteenth-century historians and their modern critics in the matter of altering and copying was that the former assumed their compeers were telling the truth and the latter are unwilling to make this assumption. If a historian had been basically honest and capable in examining a document, veneration of quotation marks was unnecessary. Historians of the early nineteenth century were aware that their whole approach to the past depended upon trustworthiness. "The value which may attach to it must, of course, mainly depend upon the degree of confidence entertained in its accuracy," said one writer; "The value of a work of this kind depends, of course, wholly upon its credibility." [64] All that a man could do to attest to his reliability was to offer his name and swear by it; this was done effusively, with the assertion that no word was written "for which I was not confident there was a credible authority" and promising "in the sincerity of my heart" to have told the truth.[65] The reader was left to believe or not.

[62] Anon., "An Apology For the Late Comer," *American Whig Review*, X (August, 1848), 139–50.
[63] A. Mitchell, "Plagiarism," *Knickerbocker Magazine*, XLIII (April, 1854), 331, 336.
[64] Trumbull, *Records of Connecticut*, I, iii; Parton, *Andrew Jackson*, I, vi.
[65] Sparks, *Writings of Washington*, I, xiii; John Delano Hammond, *The History of Political Parties in the State of New York* . . . (2 vols.; Cooperstown, N.Y., 1844), I, iv.

Style

After a historian had selected his topic and established the facts of his story, the next step was embellishment with a suitable literary style. The critic demanded that the historian utilize all of the devices of the journalist, dramatist, and poet so that history would be "as pleasant reading as the airiest novel," "as entertaining as a nursery tale." [66] Motley observed that stylistic excellence was the historian's most essential tool and "above all other qualities seems to embalm for posterity." [67] Sparks believed that the historian's labor was only "half done" until literary polish made his story entertaining.[68] "*No* work can dispense with excellence of style," said Prescott. "If this be wanting, a work . . . cannot give pleasure or create interest." [69] Almost every major historian had dabbled in literary criticism. Motley and Parkman wrote novels; Bancroft wrote poetry. The historian was a man of letters.

Beyond serving to make a story readable, style seemed to some historians an essential means of approaching truth. Just as Keats depicted a skylark better than an ornithologist, so the historian must convey a more profound reality than lay in the facts alone. A good writer should make the reader experience the past, feel its mood, and become involved in its spirit. Parkman argued for style rather than detail as the noblest means to historical truth; Prescott observed that words sometimes came closer than facts in explaining the past; and Bancroft spoke of the poet as the greatest realist.[70]

[66] Reviews, *Atlantic Monthly,* III (January, 1859), 127; *North American Review,* LXXIII (October, 1851), 495; *North American Review,* LXIX (July, 1849), 177.

[67] John Lothrop Motley, "The Novels of Balzac," *North American Review,* LXV (July, 1847), 108.

[68] Jared Sparks, ed., *The Library of American Biography* (25 vols.; New York, 1834–47), I, iv.

[69] Prescott's Journal, 1844, cited in George Ticknor, *Life of William Hickling Prescott* (Boston, 1864), p. 224; see also, William H. Prescott, *Biographical and Critical Miscellanies* (Philadelphia, 1865), p. 88.

[70] Henry Dwight Sedgwick, *Francis Parkman* (Boston, 1904), pp. 248–249; Prescott, *Miscellanies,* pp. 285–87; Nye, *George Bancroft,* p. 80.

Reviewers found no contradiction between laborious research and beautiful storytelling. "The greater diligence and precision of our more recent historians in the collection and verification of facts, has no sort of affinity to dull and dry 'factology,'" insisted one critic. While the historian "is not allowed to *fabricate,* yet he is required to *embellish.*" A research clerk was no more qualified to write history than a lexicographer to write poetry. One critic denied that meaning could exist without beauty: "Let no writer excuse his inattention to form by supposing the object of a book is to convey meaning, for . . . whatever is deep, or lofty, or beautiful in thought or feeling, refuses to be expressed in a form which is less than beautiful also." [71]

The best historians expressed more concern about style of writing than any other aspect of their work. Although modesty prevented boasting of style as of painstaking research, they labored wearily over words and were inordinately depressed or elated over critical response. When Prescott decided to become a scholar, he began with a systematic survey of the history of English prose, studying "as if he had been a school-boy." Throughout his life he collected examples of good writing, weighed critics' remarks, and filled his journals with hundreds of pages of rules, self-analysis, and arguments about style. Parkman compiled scores of notebooks of words, sentences, and experimental paragraphs. Bancroft began each writing day by reading Gibbon, then laboriously composed four lines to a page, sometimes rewriting each line a half-dozen times and each page up to ten times.[72] Successful journalistic writers like Parton, Weems, Irving, and Paulding never gave up their self-conscious cultivation of style.[73]

[71] Anon., "Art and Science of History," p. 363; Hill, "Historical Composition," p. 339; anon., "History, Biography, Voyages and Travel," *Westminster Review,* LXII (July, 1854), 150; see also, reviews, *North American Review,* LVIII (January, 1844), 157; *North American Review,* LXXX (April, 1855), 391.

[72] Ticknor, *Life of Prescott,* pp. 205–208, 220–224; Gardiner, *Literary Memoranda of Prescott, passim;* Sedgwick, *Francis Parkman,* 9–10; Nye, *George Bancroft,* p. 98.

[73] Flower, *James Parton,* p. 200 and *passim;* Bassett, *Middle Group of American Historians,* p. 19; Stanley T. Williams, *The Life of Washington Irving*

History was storytelling in the early nineteenth century; this required catching the reader up in a personal involvement in the story itself. The favorite word of critics for the style they liked was flowing. Endlessly they spoke of "easy continuity," "spontaneous grace," and "flowing sweetness." [74] History should "win the literary voluptuary to its pages by . . . the flowing ease of its style." It should be "flowing and spirited," avoiding the "unvaried and level," but always "fluent," "clean and clear," "with nothing standing in the way of the narrative." [75]

Critics often defined the flowing style they liked by specifically contrasting it with the historical writing of the eighteenth century. Authors like Voltaire, Gibbon, and Hume were primarily essayists who sought to impress the reader; they had him at a distance while self-consciously displaying their own wit, wisdom, and eloquence. To Romantic tastes, however, history was more closely related to fiction and poetry than to the essay, and the grandiose display of the Enlightenment authors was artificial, lacking in warmth and spontaneity, and an obstacle to the story. Critics vigorously attacked historians who could not resist the eighteenth-century egotism of "philosophical discussions" and "prolix disquisitions." [76] After exposure to such writing, according to Motley, the unhappy readers "imbibe greedily the draught set before them and begin to babble." [77] Similarly, a writer must

---

(2 vols.; New York, 1935), II, 218–38; Amos L. Harold, *James Kirke Paulding: Versatile American* (New York, 1926), p. 118 and *passim*.

[74] Reviews, *Harpers Magazine*, XVIII (January, 1859), 403; *North American Review*, XCI (October, 1860), 421; *North American Review*, LXXXVIII (April, 1859), 461; *Christian Examiner*, XXXVI (March, 1844), 266.

[75] Reviews, *North American Review*, LVIII (January, 1844), 157; LXXXIII (July, 1856), 96; *Edinburgh Review*, LXVIII (January, 1839), 378; *Living Age*, LXII (August, 1859), 393.

[76] Simms, *South Carolina*, p. iii; also Henry Howe, *Historical Collections of Ohio . . .* (Cincinnati, 1848), p. iii; Washington Irving, *A History of the Life and Voyages of Christopher Columbus . . .* (3 vols.; New York, 1828), I, 20–21; Charles Etienne Gayarré, *Romance of the History of Louisiana* (New York, 1848), p. 16.

[77] Chester Penn Higby and Bertram Torrey Schantz, *John Lothrop Motley* (New York, 1939), pp. xxviii–xxix; also Diedrich Knickerbocker [Washington Irving], *A History of New York, from the beginning of the world to the end of the Dutch Dynasty . . . being the only authentic history of the time*

avoid the temptation of displaying his eloquence. "It is an imposition upon his readers, to give reins to his imagination and freedom to his pen." [78] Critics berated writers who were "too ornate," "too sugary," "too oratorical," or guilty of "elaborate and artificial fastidiousness"; good history was "never a collection of phrases" or well known for its "quotability." [79] Reviewers were especially harsh with Bancroft for his oratorial tendencies. "You would say that he could never entirely divest himself of the feeling that he was speaking to the multitude," said one reviewer. "We are too often reminded of the effort by which the sentences were produced, and are seldom allowed to forget the artist in his work." [80]

Sweeping the reader up into the narrative required natural words, simple expression, and concrete images. Critics called for vivid scenes rather than abstract ideas, representative characters rather than generalized sentiments, and action rather than rhetoric. This, in turn, required direct language, strong verbs, and everyday expressions. Noah Webster believed a plain style was not only natural but basically American, an overdue corrective to the decadence of the English aristocracy.[81] "It is best to use simple, *unnoticeable* terms," Prescott admonished himself. " 'To send' is better than 'to transmit' . . . 'guns fired' to 'guns discharged' . . . 'to read' than 'peruse'. . . ." [82] Motley believed German influence was responsible for "the most detestable style"

---

that hath ever been, or ever will be published (2 vols.; New York, 1809), I, 25–26.

[78] William Durken Williamson, *The History of the State of Maine* . . . (2 vols.; Hallowell, Me., 1839), I, iv; Simms, *South Carolina*, p. vii; also Sedgwick, *Francis Parkman*, pp. 133, 222.

[79] Reviews, *Christian Examiner*, XXIV (July, 1838), 345; *Museum of Foreign Literature, Science, and Art*, XL (September, 1840), 26; *North American Review*, LXXXIII (October, 1851), 495. See also Herbert Read, *English Prose Style* (London, 1952), 138 and *passim*; David Levin, *History as Romantic Art: Bancroft, Prescott, Motley, and Parkman* (Stanford, 1959), 182–85, 205–09, 223–27, and *passim*; Ticknor, *Life of Prescott*, 220–23.

[80] Review, *North American Review*, LXXXVI (April, 1858), 353–54; review, *Christian Examiner*, XXIV (July, 1838), 359.

[81] Benjamin T. Spencer, *The Quest for Nationality* (Syracuse, 1957), pp. 53–60.

[82] Gardiner, *Literary Memoranda of Prescott*, II, 35.

in America. By striving for false elegance "the sense is almost strangled in the coils of parentheses and other convolutions." [83]

For all their emphasis of flowing narrative and natural expression, early nineteenth-century style still seems hopelessly discursive to modern ears. The pompous and oratorical style of the eighteenth century had evolved into a lyrical and florid expression. When critics called for a "natural" style, they implied freedom rather than conciseness. Although the Romantic means of expression generally served to promote the story and did not exist to be admired in its own right, still men read at leisure, frequently aloud, enjoying the telling as well as the tale. The story itself was fresh, the sentiments and phrases were not yet clichés, and often the flow of the story was leisurely. The first sentence of Prescott's *Conquest of Mexico* contained 109 words; the first sentence of Irving's *Life and Voyages of Christopher Columbus* wandered for 99 words before the verb; and one of Bancroft's chapters began with 15 dependent clauses. Benson Lossing began his history of the American Revolution with a poem and then a declamation:

> The love of country, springing up from the rich soil of the domestic affections, is a feeling consistent and coextensive with social union itself. Although a dreary climate, barren lands, and unrighteous laws, wickedly administered, may repress the luxuriant growth of this sentiment, it will still maintain firm root in the heart, and bear with patience the most cruel wrongs. Man loves the soil that gave him birth as the child loves the mother, and from the same inherent impulses. When exiled from his father-land he yearns for it as a child yearns for home; and though he may, by legal oath, disclaim allegiance to his own and swear fealty to another government, the invisible links of patriotism which bind him to his country cannot be severed; his lips and hands bear false witness against his truthful heart.
>
> Stronger far is this sentiment in the bosom of him whose country is a pleasant land, where nature in smiling beneficence woos him

[83] Motley to Prescott, 1844, cited in Roger Wolcott, ed., *Correspondence of William Hickling Prescott, 1833–1847* (Boston, 1925), p. 429; also James Peller Malcolm, *Anecdotes of the Manners and Customs of London during the Eighteenth Century* (2 vols.; London, 1810), I, xiii; Drake, *Indians of North America*, p. vii; Sparks, *Library of American Biography*, I, iv; Nye, *George Bancroft*, p. 103.

on every side; where education quickens into refining activity the intellect of society; and where just laws, righteously administered, impress all possession, whether of property or of character, with the broad seal of security . . . .[84]

Writers often copied the stylistic devices of the dramatist as a means of stimulating interest in their stories. Bancroft, Prescott, Motley, and Parkman each utilized the organization of the stage play for at least one of their major works, with a prologue, five acts, and an epilogue. Writers and critics thought in terms of the plot, the scenes, the actors, the alternating confrontations, climaxes, and interludes, and the resolution of the whole composition with regard to the proscribed unities. Later historians were generally skeptical of such writing, feeling that it forced the facts into artificial symmetry. For historians who viewed themselves as storytellers, however, the series of facts which could not be honestly arranged into plot, scenes, and unity were probably not worth the historian's time.[85]

The historian also liked to think of himself as a painter, filling a canvas with color, action, and mood. Pictures were scenes in a drama, bringing the past to life and giving the reader a feeling of participation in the action. Prescott's glittering military processions, Parkman's fragrant and foreboding forests, Irving's medieval courts are among the most vivid scenes in literature. The historian conceived of his subject in pictorial terms, a colorful "series of tableaux" passing before the reader.[86] Carefully, the best writers matched action with the mood of the landscape, alert for the leafless tree against the stormy sky, or the bird's chirp at dawn after the battle, alert for those de-

[84] Benson John Lossing, *The Pictorial Field Book of the Revolution* . . . (2 vols.; New York, 1850–52), I, 33; see also last sentence of the first volume.

[85] Levin, *History as Romantic Art*, 19–21; Nye, *George Bancroft*, p. 310; Higby and Schantz, *John Lothrop Motley*, pp. xxi–xxiv, xciv–cxi; Ticknor, *Life of Prescott*, p. 176; James Kirke Paulding, *A Sketch of Old New England* . . . (2 vols.; New York, 1822), I, 218.

[86] Joel Tyler Headley, *Napoleon and His Marshals* (2 vols.; New York, 1847), I, v–vi; Howe, *Historical Virginia*, p. iv; Williamson, *History of Maine*, I, iii; Harry Elmer Barnes, *A History of Historical Writing* (Norman, Okla. 1937), p. 189.

tails "that escape the ordinary eye." [87] Critics liked the word "picturesque" and compared scenes for their lifelike quality and emotional impact.[88]

One of the most important stylistic devices of the literary historians was the use of historical characters, actors in the drama who developed the story and also supplied a focus for reader identification. A sense of personal uniqueness and a concurrent search for identity in fictional and historical characters permeated all Romantic literature. This dual concept helps to explain the rise of the novel as a major literary form and also the popularity of historical biography. Ralph Waldo Emerson believed the greatest appeal of the past lay in the reader's vicariously becoming a historical hero. The historian, observed Emerson, "describes to each reader his own ideal, describes his unattained but attainable self." [89] Prescott reminded himself of the importance of live characters. "Instead of a mere abstraction, at once we see a being like ourselves," he wrote. "We place ourselves in his position and see the passing current of events through his eyes." [90] Critics delighted in "vivid reproduction of personages" and were appropriately scornful of "unskillful delineation of character." [91]

A literary scholar, Professor David Levin, has recently placed particular emphasis on the historical hero in Bancroft, Prescott, Motley, and Parkman, not only as a literary device for creating interest but also as a stock-type character. Each of these historians accepted the contemporary literary convention of the By-

[87] Hill, "Historical Composition," p. 341.

[88] Reviews, *Christian Examiner*, XXIV (July, 1838), 346; also, *Living Age*, XIV (July, 1847), 122; *North American Review* LXXIII (October, 1851), 495; *Living Age*, I (May, 1844), 10.

[89] Ralph Waldo Emerson, "History," *The Essays of Ralph Waldo Emerson* (Modern Library edition, New York, 1944), p. 5.

[90] Prescott, *Miscellanies*, pp. 107–108; see also Lambert Lilly [Francis Lister Hawks], *The History of the Western States* . . . (Boston, 1835), pp. 3–4; Harold, *James Kirke Paulding*, p. 108.

[91] Reviews, *Methodist Quarterly Review*, XX (January, 1838), 173; *North American Review*, LXXXVIII (April, 1859), 461; *American Quarterly Review*, VI (December, 1829), 408; *North American Review*, XLVI (January, 1838), 282.

ronic hero, a figure of special grandeur and sublimity, "spotless marble against a stormy sky," misunderstood, suffering, and lonely, but nobly enduring despite the odds against him. Queen Isabella, Queen Elizabeth, Cortez, Washington, Jefferson, and LaSalle all became stereotypes, simple, natural, self-reliant, pious, frugal, humble, and impelled by superhuman will. The hero embodied the spirit of the people he led and, in turn, inspired them. The villain was also a stock character, haughty, pompous, wealthy, selfish, and effete. The inner spirit of hero or villain was always evident in the eyes, physical appearance, and manner. These carefully drawn stereotypes, which can be followed for many lesser figures in the drama, characterized all forms of Romantic literature, and, according to Levin, marked the ablest historians as self-conscious parts of the literary tradition.[92]

Historians, like Romantic painters, liked turbulent action scenes as a means of rousing emotions and creating interest, scenes of dramatic crisis, battle, and violence. "The public is hungering and thirsting after food for admiration and abhorrence," said one critic.[93] The appeal of history lay in its blood and thunder, its "stirring incidents and blood-stirring adventure," its "heroic actions and resplendent virtues." [94] "The plurality . . . expect, as a matter of right . . . to be gratified with admiration and horror, with suffering saints and triumphing monsters." [95] The appeal of violence helps explain the popularity of military history.

A good writer knew that style was an individual matter, a

[92] Levin, *History As Romantic Art*, pp. 49–73; Peter L. Thorslev, *The Byronic Hero: Types and Prototypes* (Minneapolis, 1962), pp. 35–64 and *passim*.

[93] Anon., "History," *American Quarterly Review*, V (March, 1829), 89.

[94] Review, *North American Review*, XLVI (January, 1838), 215; John Romeyn Brodhead, *An Address Delivered before the New York Historical Society* (New York, 1844), p. 46; also, reviews, *Museum of Foreign Literature, Science and Art,* XL (September, 1840), 26; *Blackwood's Magazine* LXXIX (April, 1856), 421.

[95] Anon., "History," *American Quarterly Review*, V (March, 1829), 89; also, anon., "Historic Speculations," *Southern Literary Messenger*, VI (September, 1840), 606.

subjective reflection of himself. To most men of the early nine-teenth century, art itself was subjective, an intuitive feeling, an inspiration of the artist reaching out to a corresponding in-spiration in his audience. "A man's style, to be worth anything, should be the natural expression of his moral character," said Prescott. "One man's style will no more fit another, than one man's coat, or hat, or shoe will fit another." [96] The artist must know his own style, be honest to it, even cultivate it, and then match it to a subject appropriate to himself. Style was a matter of genius, but knowledge and use of it remained a matter of deliberation and skill.

Feeling

History had matured into art in early nineteenth-century America because it required one element more than scholarship and style: that element was feeling. To be either true or inter-esting, history required the historian's passion, his subjective insight, his individual genius. This was the essentially "Roman-tic" element in early nineteenth-century historical writing and the element most firmly rejected by later generations. By 1875 critics were baffled or annoyed if a historian dared to speak of intuition, but for almost half a century men like Emerson, Ban-croft, and Prescott spoke of their "intuitive insights" into the past, and critics praised them for their perception.[97]

Just as Transcendentalists found no contradiction between mind and heart, critics found no conflict between objective his-torical truth and passionate, intuitive conviction. A historical "fact" that coincided with deeply held principles was more sig-nificant than a "fact" that did not, and a man of deep convic-tions had a better standard of judgment than a man with none. Passion and subjectivity, "far from proving an obstruction, are, in fact, auxiliary to the surest operations of the judgement. . . . Full scope must be given to the natural, elevated, warm feelings,

---

[96] Prescott, *Conquest of Mexico,* I, 617.
[97] See Nye, *George Bancroft,* p. 286; review, *American Quarterly Review,* III (March, 1828), 174.

and to the vehement, unsubordinated passions of the heart." [98]
"Sufficient passion" and "honest enthusiasm" would actually
"excuse prejudice . . . and general weakness." [99] Good history,
critics observed, was necessarily "an attribute of the heart," while
"fairness and impartiality" are too often "exaggerated into
faults" and become "indifferency." [100] "Is it said that if a historian be in love with his theme, he will run into extravagance?"
asked a Bancroft defender. "Let it be remembered that we would
chasten this love with a sound philosophy, with a spirit of research," he continued, but "fortified with these let the historian
be extravagant; he ought to be extravagant." [101]

Critics accepted subjective dedication to principles in an era
when right principles seemed beyond dispute and based on both
natural law and intuition. Patriotism, for example, or liberty,
morality, or progress were established with more certainty than
historical facts, and these abstracts, in turn, established the
significance of facts. The historian, dedicated to right principles,
did not search for truth so much as illustrate it. As long as no
important disagreement occurred over these principles, there
was no reason to believe that enthusiasm resulted in distortion.
To be sure, the proposition that enthusiasm did not distort was
a defensive argument, even one that betrayed uneasiness. Critics
were more comfortable in discussing the positive advantages
which passion provided in promoting interest and understanding.

Almost everyone agreed that a historian's enthusiasm contributed as much as his scholarship or style to the production
of lively narrative. "History only becomes dramatic on two

[98] "Prospectus," *The American Review of History and Politics,* I (January,
1811), ii.
[99] Review, *North American Review,* XL (January, 1835), 100; anon., "Art of
History Writing," p. 244.
[100] Hill, "Historical Composition," p. 346; review, *Christian Examiner,*
XXX (July, 1841), 314.
[101] Reviews, *North American Review,* XL (January, 1835), 115; also, *North
American Review,* XL (January, 1860), 40; *Christian Examiner,* LX (March,
1856), 248, 266; anon., "History and Its Philosophy," *Putnam's Monthly
Magazine,* XI (April, 1868), 407; anon., "Art and Science of History," p. 363;
anon., "History," *Monthly Anthology,* I (January, 1804), 119.

conditions: it must either have the passion of the politician or the imagination of the poet." [102] Depth of feeling "gives animation and glow to the silent page," for with it "the historian's language acquires energy, his descriptions liveliness." [103] "Ardor . . . infuses a life and vigor into discussions of these topics which . . . having fallen into the hands of mere scholars, are by general readers considered as little better than the offal of literature." [104] Similarly, writers who lacked emotion were berated for "cold and naked recital of facts," for "never rising into anything like fervour," for "frigid, colorless, soulless writing," and for "that callousness which proceeds from want of feelings." [105]

Above all, however, emotion and subjective intuition were necessary for understanding. The historian who surrounded himself with the facts of a past era possessed a feeling for that era dependent upon but more profound than his knowledge of it. The *Zeitgeist*, particularly, would always elude the fact-monger. The historian, like the author of a play, must be able to place himself in the era and mind of his characters in order to think as they did. "He who relates those great transactions in which the passions of men have been interested," explained a critic, "must enter into the scenes which he describes, and must speak the language of those who bore a part in them. A cold narrative that is literally true, would often be a false picture." [106] The historian, like the artist, had to feel the reality of his subject, had to feel the essence of truth and transmit that feeling. With passion and inspiration, with faith in sound principles, "facts are made more pregnant, shadows are deepened, characters are distinguished by a sharpness of outline which does not, in reality, belong to them. . . . A noble imagination is a wiser

[102] Review, *Edinburgh Review,* CV (January, 1857), 23.
[103] Review, *North American Review,* XL (January, 1835), 117.
[104] Reviews, *North American Review,* XCI (October, 1860), 301; also, *Living Age,* XXIII (November, 1849), 365; anon., "History," *American Quarterly Review,* V (March, 1829), 88.
[105] Reviews, *North American Review,* LXXIII (October, 1851), 414; *Athenaeum, Number* 1158 (January, 1850), 13; *Living Age,* XXIII (November, 1849), 365; Hill, "Historical Composition," p. 341; also, reviews, *Living Age,* LXII (August, 1859), 393; *Southern Quarterly Review,* IX (April, 1846), 363.
[106] Hill, "Historical Composition," pp. 242-43.

guide . . . than an ignoble and mean understanding." [107] Occasionally historians were willing even to sacrifice factual accuracy for the sake of accuracy of impression. They altered direct quotations, for example, in the belief that the alteration might come closer than the original to the speaker's true intention. Authors like Nathaniel Hawthorne would invent or tamper with details to capture a deeper reality than lay in perfect accuracy of detail.[108] Subsequent historians were disturbed, of course, at the thought that there could exist an impressionistic truth deeper than the facts. Even by the 1850's men like Richard Hildreth were persuaded that subjectivity, and even writing style, were undesirable when they led the reader beyond the facts alone.[109] For the early nineteenth-century reader who trusted the historian, however, the scholar's impression could be far more interesting and vivid, far more real and true, than the literal details.

Men of the Romantic era never forgot that the method of writing history was a means toward an end and not a sacred thing in itself. After the historian had carefully selected his topic, honestly researched it, polished his writing style, and infused the whole with right feelings, all of these elements should combine into a harmonious whole. "Form and substance" must blend together, said critics, "in the unity and fullness of organic life." [110] If all of the procedures blended smoothly, the product was a composition of "dramatic interest" and "high art." [111] At that point method was complete and men could concentrate on the purpose of history.

[107] Anon., "History, Its Use and Meaning," *Westminster Review,* LXII (October, 1854), 230–31; also William Greenough Thayer Shedd, "The Nature and Influence of the Historic Spirit," *Bibliotheca Sacra,* XI (April, 1854), 345; review, *Living Age,* XXXI (October, 1851), 138.

[108] Nathaniel Hawthorne, *True Stories from History and Biography* (Boston, 1851), p. iv; also Joel Tyler Headley, *The Life of Oliver Cromwell* (New York, 1848), p. vi; Bassett, *Middle Group of American Historians,* pp. 105–6.

[109] Emerson, *Richard Hildreth,* p. 164.

[110] Anon., "Art and Science of History," p. 363; also, reviews, *Atlantic Monthly,* III (January, 1859), 127; *Living Age,* XXXI (October, 1851), 138.

[111] Hill, "Historical Composition," p. 339; reviews, *Christian Examiner,* XXVI (March, 1844), 198; *North American Review,* XLVI (January, 1838), 280–81; *Knickerbocker Review,* XXXVIII (July, 1851), 69.

VIII

Interpreting the Past

CERTAIN basic themes pervade the history written during the early nineteenth century, and these themes reveal many of the fundamental assumptions of that period. At the time men hardly thought of these themes as interpretations, for the word carries an implication of bias or tenuous hypothesis. Often the historian was hardly aware of the themes uniting his work, thinking of them as his techniques for making history interesting, or as incontestable facts. The interpretations which unite a generation of historians are generally more evident to subsequent observers than to the men who make them.

The historians of the early nineteenth century knew, of course, that they began with preconceived ideas; freely they admitted the obvious. "Every man," said one critic, "sits down to study under some mental influence or prepossession which unconsciously directs his attention to those facts, and those relations of facts, that are most in harmony with the idea latent in his mind." "You have but to select such facts as suit you," observed another critic, "and let your theory of history be what it will, you can have no difficulty in providing facts to prove it." The important thing was to begin with "right" assumptions, and since most men could agree on basic principles of morality, progress, patriotism, and the existence of God, these assump-

tions could be generally accepted as desirable unifying themes.[1]
Each person, of course, must "judge for himself, to adopt, dis-
criminate and reject" the historian's assumptions, but this was
hardly difficult. The critic never begrudged the historian the
right to begin with preconceptions, just as he never doubted
his own right to judge them.[2]

Basic assumptions about life seemed not only inevitable but
positively desirable as a means of finding meaning in history.
Although men respected the compiler and were fascinated with
detail, the historian's true occupation was more elevated. He
had to "digest" the facts into "high-toned philosophical narrative." "With the qualifications of an antiquarian . . . the modern
historian must combine those of a philosopher, deducing from
the mass of general theorums." Reviewers observed that "the
most perfect history when separated from its philosophical accomplishments, is, in reality, but a series of anecdotes." [3] One
critic was moved to Old Testament wrath at the idea of facts
alone serving as history:

> Thou hoary bookworm, whose life is almost worn out in the study
> of the past, what has it availed thee in the acquisition of true
> knowledge? Is thy spirit purer, wiser, or happier in the long research?
> . . . History has been to thee no teacher because thou hast dealt
> with the letter and not the spirit of her lessons . . . . Thou hast
> hoarded details. . . . Thou canst rehearse battles and successions,

[1] Anon., "Hegel's Philosophy of History," *Eclectic Magazine*, XLV (September, 1858), 3; James Anthony Froude, "The Science of History," *Hours at
Home*, II (February, 1866), 323; review, *North American Review*, LX (April,
1845), 368–69.

[2] Anon., "The Philosophy of History," *North American Review*, XXXIX
(July, 1834), 40; also John Spencer Bassett, "Later Historians," William P.
Trent *et al.*, eds., *Cambridge, History of American Literature* (4 vols.; New
York, 1912), III, 171–72.

[3] Reviews, *Atlantic Monthly*, VI (April, 1856), 442; *North American Review*,
XXIX (October, 1829), 295; anon., "Thoughts on the Manner of Writing
History," *Southern Literary Messenger*, III (February, 1837), 157; also, anon.,
"Ancient and Modern History," *North American Review*, XXVIII (April,
1829), 334–35; anon., "History of Our Own Times," *Eclectic Review*, IX
(October, 1846), 165; reviews, *North American Review*, LXXIII (October,
1851), 411; *North American Review*, LXXV (July, 1852), 258.

boundary-lines and eras . . . but the subtle electric current that floats on it, and with it, has never made itself known to thy mind.[4]

While critics disliked the interruption in flow that marked eighteenth-century disquisition, they never maintained that the facts spoke for themselves. The historian ought to generalize boldly. All of the "various facts and details" should be gathered, comprehended, and organized toward some elucidation, however modest, of "the general destinies of mankind." History, argued one critic should be "the product of reflection and analysis—in which events and their significance . . . are critically determined, and distinctly and formally interpreted." "Large deductions must be made." "Generalizations . . . alone offer a rich field for moral, political and social studies." A good historian must penetrate the facts "with a burst of interpretive speculation" to discover the truth in history.[5]

Essence and Causation

Interpretation is most necessary when facts alone seem inadequately revealing. In the twentieth century historians have been preoccupied with causation, and interpretation has most often involved emphasis on the facts that reveal the reasons for change. In the early nineteenth century, however, historians were less concerned with cause than with describing the inmost essence of a society in the past, and, as a consequence, interpretation involved particular emphasis on those facts which best captured this elusive entity—for example, those which

---

[4] L. J. B. C., "History," *Universalist Quarterly and General Review*, I (April, 1844), 165.

[5] Anon., "Historical Studies," *Church Review*, IV (April, 1851), 10; anon., "History and Its Philosophy," *Putnam's Monthly Magazine*, XI (April, 1868), 407; anon., "The Aim of History," *Princeton Review*, XXIX (April, 1857), 233; anon., "Recent Historical Revelations," *Eclectic Magazine*, XLIV (July, 1858), 346; anon., "Thoughts on Writing History," pp. 156–57; also, anon., "Hegel's Philosophy of History," p. 2; anon., "Lord Macaulay As An Historian," *North American Review*, XCIII (October, 1861), 455; Willie, "Use of Imagination in the Study of History," *North Carolina University Magazine*, IX (May, 1860), 557.

demonstrated American democracy, or Puritan piety, or Spanish pomp. Understanding essence helped explain how change occurred, but the problem of change remained secondary.

Historians recognized well enough their concern with essence. This mysterious spirit deep within a society was related to what German Romantic historians called the *Zeitgeist,* though the term was not used in English until Matthew Arnold introduced it in 1884.[6] Americans spoke variously of "the spirit of an age," "the real character of a people," "the current . . . of public feeling," "the principle which vibrates through a nation's pulse," and "the informing spirit which gives life to the whole." [7] Using terms that sounded like those of Arnold Toynbee a century later, writers tried to define society's essence: "In the history of every people who have become distinguished in the annals of the earth is found the manifestation of some predominant thought. This gives vitality to a people, stimulates their energies and makes them great." The reviewer instructed historians to "deduce that great sentiment which it is the mission of a people to express and illustrate." [8]

The probing for essence usually led historians to treat each country separately in order to determine their distinguishing characteristics. Historians writing about Europe moved easily from the idea of essence to consideration of national character and race; and historians writing about America stopped barely short of race as they offered full descriptions of the type of people who lived in Massachusetts, New York, or Virginia. Similarly,

---

[6] *The Oxford English Dictionary* (13 vols.; Oxford, 1933), XII, ch. 2, 88.
[7] Anon., "Philosophy of History," p. 55; Humphrey Marshall, *History of Kentucky* (2 vols.; Frankfort, 1824), I, iv; Joel Tyler Headley, *The Second War with England* (2 vols.; New York, 1853), I, iv; F. A. P., "False Views of History," *Southern Quarterly Review,* XXII (July, 1852), 23; William H. Prescott, *Biographical and Critical Miscellanies* (Philadelphia, 1865), p. 88; also Daniel Pierce Thompson, *The Green Mountain Boys* . . . (Boston, 1848), p. vi; John Marshall, *The Life of George Washington* . . . (5 vols.; (Philadelphia, 1804–07), I, xi; anon., "History," *American Quarterly Review,* I (March, 1829), 98; anon., "Philosophy of History," p. 55; George Ticknor to Charles Lyell, 1848, cited in Anna Ticknor, ed., *Life, Letters and Journals of George Ticknor* (2 vols.; Boston, 1877), II, 253.
[8] F. A. P., "False Views of History," p. 24.

writers dwelled on the particular spirit of each period, for example, the spirit of the Roman republic, of early American settlement, or of the Revolution.

Men tended to think of political, economic, ideological, and social factors not as causes of change, but as elements of the ever-flowing *Zeitgeist*. In discussing the movement for American independence, historians found that the facts "explained" the movement fully enough. Oppression, in a word, evident in a multitude of well-described incidents, stimulated a latent American spirit of independence. The historian's interpretive skill was necessary in analyzing that spirit. "The Revolution was in the minds and hearts of the people," wrote John Adams, who was always threatening to become a historian. It was the historian's duty, he believed, to describe the Revolution's essence—its "principles, opinions, sentiments, and affections." [9] Similarly, the fall of Rome, the rise of Spain, or the coming of industrialization were to be described rather than explained; such events were evident in a changing psyche of the people, probably inspired by God, and probably illustrative of progress. The *Zeitgeist* was the cause, and it was tautological to look for the cause of the cause.[10] Although historians spoke of causation, they usually related it to essence. "The historian must give us causes, connections, and consequences of events," said one critic, "by defining the invisible actuating spirit" of the age. The historian "unfolds the causes," said another, when he "collects in one grand coup-d'oeil, all those characteristic qualities, moral, intellectual, and physical, which constitute the national being." [11]

Causation as a key to understanding the past is largely a

[9] Adams to Hezekiah Niles, 13 February 1818, in Charles F. Adams, ed., *The Works of John Adams* . . . (10 vols.; Boston, 1851–56), X, 282–83.

[10] Harry Elmer Barnes, *A History of Historical Writing* (Norman, Okla., 1937), 178–80; John Spencer Bassett, *The Middle Group of American Historians* (New York, 1917), pp. 114–15; Marshall, *Kentucky*, p. iv; Francis Lister Hawks, *History of North Carolina* . . . (2 vols.; Fayetteville, 1857–58), I, vii–viii.

[11] Anon., "History and Its Philosophy," p. 407; review, *North American Review*, XLVI (January, 1838), 277; also anon., "Guizot and the Philosophy of History," *Eclectic Magazine*, IV (February, 1845), 184 and *passim*; anon., "Reading of History," *Princeton Review*, XIX (April, 1847), 214.

post-Darwinism concept. After Saint Augustine, men assumed that God was cause and that what happened in history was the will of God. Medieval and Reformation historians, such men as Cotton Mather in America, related the changes which God had decreed for society but did not consider why they occurred, except within the realm of theology. History was often neglected, therefore, because it could say little that theology could not explain better. The historians of the Renaissance, tentatively, and those of the eighteenth century, more confidently, substituted a combination of fortuity and human reason to explain change. To Voltaire and Gibbon, and to David Ramsay and Thomas Hutchinson in America, changes occurred for the better when men acted rationally and for the worse when they acted irrationally. The Romantic historians shifted the emphasis to morality; change was for the better when men acted morally. Still, they took cause almost for granted, to be observed rather than analyzed. Only in the latter half of the nineteenth century, as men began to disagree over moral interpretations and as Darwinism focused attention on the process of development, did thorough analysis of causative factors become the major task of the historian.

Morality

Early nineteenth-century American historical thought, like most other thought of the era, was permeated with moral consciousness. The Romantic movement in America, for all its insistence upon freedom from restraint, revived and intensified the Puritanical virtues. Transcendentalism emphasized self-control and rectitude; the fundamentalist revival stressed personal ethics; and popular literature was filled with didactic lessons about individual conduct and moral obligation. For the historian, an important means of grasping truth was having the right moral feeling, an important purpose of history was the promotion of morality, and the most pervasive single assumption was the existence of moral law.

Writers and critics of the Romantic period noted that "moral enthusiasm" distinguished the writings of their own generation from the history written before and after. On the one hand the writings of Voltaire and Gibbon were "lacking [in] moral sensitivity," and "nowhere warmed by a generous moral sentiment." On the other hand young writers like Richard Hildreth in the 1850's were condemned for "moral indifferency," and the absence "of an elevated standard of right." [12] Bancroft, Prescott, Sparks, Motley, and Parker all wrote explicitly about the need for ethical standards in historical writing. "The moral character of events," said one reviewer is "the only standard by which the events of history can be judged." [13]

The men of the time defined standards of personal morality as simply "the feelings and opinions which the vast majority . . . hold sacred," the standard written in "the depths" of each man's consciousness.[14] The particular virtues were evident in the stereotypic Romantic hero: he was marked by strength of will and character, self-reliance, integrity, piety, plain living, industry, practicality, temperance, courage, and patriotism. These were virtues of early nineteenth-century America, so taken for granted as to be beyond dispute. The other end of the scale was equally plain: it consisted of pride, pomp, deceit, luxury, materialism, atheism, slothfulness, sensuousness, dissipation, and effeminacy. These characteristics appeared explicitly when men talked of the lessons history was supposed to inculcate.

The emphasis on morality, with the implication of absolute right and wrong, came logically to rest in the concept of history as a court of justice. Here was the final bar on earth where deeds and men received their just reward or condemnation. "The province of history is to establish a tribunal," said a critic, "where princes and private men alike may be tried and judged

[12] William Hickling Prescott, "Historical Composition," *North American Review*, XXIX (October, 1829), 310–13; review, *North American Review*, LXXXVIII (April, 1859), 462; Samuel G. Goodrich, *History of All Nations* . . . (2 vols.; Cincinnati, 1852), I, 10.

[13] See David Levin, *History as Romantic Art: Bancroft, Prescott, Motley, and Parkman* (Stanford, 1959), pp. 24–27 and ff.; Michael Kraus, *The Writing of American History* (Norman, Okla, 1953), pp. 147–48; review, *North American Review*, LXX (January, 1850), 239.

[14] Anon., "Buckle's History of Civilization," *North American Review*, XCIII (October, 1861), 559; Levin, *History as Romantic Art*, p. 29.

after death." "It is her business," said another, "to pass sentence . . . like a merciful, but righteous judge." [15] One writer believed that "Judgement in a historian is better than a facility in aggregating facts." The historian-judge needed a keen moral sense and a rigid impartiality. "His sensibility to every moral sentiment, not only detects what is good or bad in human conduct, but is accompanied with an immediate approbation of the one, and abhorrence of the other." Even if the judge made mistakes, "still it is better [that] the moral nature should act imperfectly than be set aside." [16]

The act of judging forced the historian to interpret in moral terms which gave unity and meaning to his writing. Ralph Waldo Emerson argued that only by measuring deeds against a moral standard did one learn from the past. The historian must "not suffer himself to be bullied by kings and empires," he said, "and not deny his conviction that he is the court. . . . If England or Egypt have anything to say to him he will try the case, if not let them forever be silent." [17] If moral judgment could be perfect, then the historian "would be the truest preacher, and . . . would sound forth with irresistible effect the lessons of duty." [18]

Judging men and events of the past gave men a comforting sense of correcting injustice and provided an important justification for the study of history. It was pleasant to play God and satisfying to believe that justice might finally be done on earth. The historian was "the great earthly judge, reprobating the inequities of the past." The public "eagerly awaited" the his-

[15] Anon., "Philosophy of History," p. 40; review, *North American Review*, XXXIII (October, 1831), 451; also reviews, *London Quarterly*, LXIV (June, 1839), 42; *Christian Examiner*, XXIV (July, 1838), 358; John Hill, "An Essay upon the Principles of Historical Composition," *Portfolio*, IX (April, 1820), 345-47.

[16] Anon., "The Lessons of History," *North American Review*, LXXX (January, 1855), 90; Hill, "Historical Composition," p. 342; reviews, *Christian Examiner*, XXIV (July, 1838), 358; *Living Age*, I (May, 1844), 10.

[17] Ralph Waldo Emerson, *Essays of Ralph Waldo Emerson* (Modern Library edition, New York, 1944), p. 6.

[18] Reviews, *Christian Examiner*, XXIV (July, 1838), 358; *North American Review*, LXX (January, 1850), 238-40.

torian's verdict, "zealous to atone" for past neglect or misjudgment. Presumably, the future historian would also pass judgment, so that any good man could rest assured that posterity if not his contemporaries would cast opprobrium on his enemies and do justice to his memory.[19]

Although historians considered principles absolute for their own time, they generally acknowledged that historical understanding if not simple fairness required the judgment of a past society by its own standards. Critics noted that "the thought of a people or of an age must furnish the standard by which that people or age is to be judged"; "the standard of right in the nineteenth century is very different from what was acknowledged in the twelfth." One reviewer maintained that "the most distinct and impressive teaching of history is, that not every opinion which springs up and has currency in a particular age, is true for all time."[20]

In practice, this moral enthusiasm caused almost every person and deed to undergo the historians' careful evaluation. In schoolbooks, popular literature, and scholarly books, characters and their actions were explicitly judged by an adjective or an essay. For the ablest literary artists, men like Bancroft, Prescott, Motley, and Parkman, the good or evil characters of major protagonists became unifying themes of the entire work. Generally, a man's character was rather definitely fixed according to the cause to which he was committed. For an Indian fighting Europeans, a Spaniard fighting Englishmen or Dutchmen, or an Englishman fighting Americans, extraordinary action was necessary to transform inherent moral defect into a forgivable error

[19] Anon., "Recent Historical Revelations," *Eclectic Magazine*, LXIV (July, 1858), 346; reviews, *North American Review*, XCI (October, 1860), 354; *North American Review*, XL (January, 1835), 120; *North American Review*, XCI (July, 1860), 41; *North American Review*, LXX (January, 1850), 239; anon., "History and Biography," *Christian Examiner*, LXX (March, 1861), 315.

[20] Review, *North American Review*, LXX (January, 1850), 239; F. A. P., "False Views of History," p. 24; William Greenough Thayer Shedd, "The Nature and Influence of the Historic Spirit," *Bibliotheca Sacra*, XI (April, 1854), 359; C. R., "Impostures of History," *Portfolio*, I (May, 1816), 369; review, *North American Review*, XCI (October, 1860), 354.

of judgment. Antiquarians were usually hard pressed to find moral defects in any of the founding fathers.

Progress

Progress was another of the deeply pervasive assumptions of the early nineteenth century, though it too was often confused and even contradicted by its own corollaries. Men were torn between Thoreau's glorification of the simple life and Whitman's glorification of the age of steam, and it was difficult to reconcile the two. Along with progress, new ideas developed about the state of nature, the evolution from savagery to civilization, the guiding hand of God, free will, the nature of evil residing in corrupt institutions, and the greatness of the United States as the capstone of human history.

With regard to progress itself, virtually every historian accepted both the word and the principle as beyond dispute. Based on the eighteenth-century assumption that reason led to social improvement and buttressed by Transcendental faith in human aspiration, progress provided the underlying theme of human development. It was more certain than any series of historical facts; instead of facts establishing the existence of progress, progress established the accuracy of particular facts. "Man was made for progress," said the Transcendentalist philosopher, Orestes Brownson. "The historian should always assume man's progressiveness as his point of departure, and judge all the facts and events he encounters according to their bearing on this great theme." [21] Bancroft, given to analysis of his assumptions, wrote of *The Necessity, the Reality, and the Promise of the Progress of the Human Race,* explaining that the existence of human reason proved its necessity, every page of history proved its reality, and the existence of man's spiritual nature guaranteed its continuance.[22] Motley, Prescott, and Hildreth also wrote

[21] Orestes Augustus Brownson, "Remarks on Universal History," *United States Magazine and Democratic Review,* XII (May, 1843), 458; also, anon., "Buckle's History of Civilization," p. 519.

[22] (New York, 1854); Russel B. Nye, *George Bancroft: Brahmin Rebel* (New York, 1945), pp. 96, 189, 196–98.

explicitly of progress as the central theme of history. Schoolbooks spoke of the "all-embracing" and "basic law" of human progress "from the lowly and desponding vale of struggle and obscurity, to the already lofty heights of wealth, of happiness, and of power." [23]

Men found it easy to define progress simply as the evolution of purer concepts of morality, religion, government, and science. The Greeks conquered barbarism, the Romans developed law, the Christians gave the world true religion, Spain created the modern national state, the German reformation provided moral regeneration, England built civil institutions, and America gave the world democracy. Sometimes historians called this the progress of philosophy from ignorance to truth; sometimes it was called the progress of civilization from barbarism to enlightenment. Within the frame of reference of recent American history, men saw progress in terms of the development of sentiment for independence, the purification of democracy, and, perhaps, the growth of abolitionist sentiment. Men noted that progress moved from east to west. The image of spiral progress provided a ready explanation of the temporary setbacks of righteous and progressive principles.[24]

American historians never accepted the Garden of Eden or the idyllic state of nature as a historical phenomenon. Although schoolbooks usually began dutifully with the biblical account of creation, real history began after the Fall, as men struggled upward from barbarism to civilization. This struggle was most clear in the clash of paganism and Christianity. Although Europeans like Rousseau and Chateaubriand in their glorification of

[23] Motley, "Historic Progress and American Democracy," Chester Penn Higby and Bindford Toney Schantz, eds., *John Lothrop Motley . . .* (New York, 1939), pp. 100–120; Prescott, "Historical Composition," pp. 293–314; Hildreth, *Theory of Politics . . . and Progress . . .* (New York, 1854); Charles Prentiss, *History of the United States . . .* (Keene, N.H., 1820), p. 4; Samuel G. Goodrich, *A Pictorial History of England* (Philadelphia, 1857), p. 12; Lyman Cobb, *Cobb's North American Reader . . .* (New York, 1852), pp. 419–20; J. Merton England, "England and America in the Schoolbooks of the Republic, 1783–1861," *University of Birmingham Historical Journal,* IX (1963), 92–111.

[24] See, Levin, *History as Romantic Art,* pp. 27–36.

the simple life had implied that the pristine German or Indian tribesman was superior to civilized man, Americans were too close to Indian wars for such a view. Americans saw progress from savagery to refinement, from primitive confusion to civilized harmony with nature. "Some traditions begin with a golden age of innocence and happinesss; others with a state of original barbarism and wild disorder," explained a popular American textbook. "It is probable, however," explained the author, "even if we suppose a primeval state of knowledge and refinement, that mankind afterward descended to barbarism, from which they gradually arose to a full development of their faculties." [25]

Progress and morality defined each other, since progress was inevitable and right was eventually triumphant. The historian had only to choose the victor to show what was progressive and good. Parkman pointed out, for example, that while the French may have protracted the Seven Years' War they could not possibly have won it, since the priesthood and absolutism of France were recognized evils; and Prescott proved that the Aztecs must have been immoral and despotic since they lost disasterously. America would have developed democratically no matter what the Mayflower Compact said; Washington would have eventually won no matter what happened at Yorktown. Historians lacking sufficient explanation for events could always rely on "the resistless march of progress," or "the great current of events" as the ultimate and obvious explanation.[26]

Americans easily transferred their own experience as a nation into generalizations about all history. Local antiquarians, far more than literary historians, found the theme of progress self-evident in the growth of struggling settlements into flourishing cities. To them, progress was not only philosophical but concrete and physical. This American experience, evident in every man's memory and confirmed by every local chronicler, provided an ideological base for the more sophisticated thought of historians and for the more virulent evolutionary progress which reached a peak after Darwin.

[25] Goodrich, *History of All Nations*, p. 560.
[26] Levin, *History as Romantic Art*, p. 28.

For most historians the concept of progress rested comfortably on parallel assumptions about God. Religious feeling characterized the American Romantic movement, permeated almost all fields of thought, and seemed especially to mark history. Not a single significant historian of the period professed agnosticism; Prescott, Motley, and Parkman constantly observed "the workings of Providence"; Bancroft, Sparks, and Palfrey, along with a clear majority of the schoolbook authors and local chroniclers, were clergymen. Aware that piety marked their own generation, critics rejoiced that eighteenth-century free thought was "no longer present" in historical writing. With correct attitudes toward religion, "the events more naturally fall into their places." Religion, claimed an observer, guaranteed "a more profound understanding of the hidden links of events." A reviewer noted that "historians have been successful in proportion as they have recognized a providential plan in the career of the world." By the middle of the century critics frowned at the appearance of younger writers led by Professor Ranke, who are "too much occupied with their learned researches to pay much attention to God." [27]

God, in turn, helped explain both morality and progress. The presence of God presupposed right behavior, and piety in any man was an important measure of his morality. God also insured progress, the inevitable natural process of history. According to David Levin in his close analysis of four Romantic historians, progress was a march "toward nineteenth century Unitarianism." [28] The triumph of Christianity over paganism was invariably good, whether in the ancient world against Rome, in Spain against the Moors, or in the New World against the Indians. Almost unanimously American historians approved the Protestant Reformation. For Irving, Motley, and Prescott, the once-pious Spaniards suddenly became priest-ridden and fanatical in contrast with the progressive religionists of England or Hol-

[27] Anon., "Historical Studies," *Church Review*, IV (April, 1851), 21; anon., "History," *American Quarterly Review*, V (March, 1829), 93; Shedd, "Nature and Influence of the Historic Spirit," p. 349; review, *Museum of Foreign Literature, Science and Art*, XL (September, 1840), 29.

[28] Levin, *History as Romantic Art*, p. 32.

land; for Parkman and Bancroft, the formerly brave Jesuits of North America now appeared evil alongside of the Protestant settlers. To Bancroft, Sparks, Palfrey, and Hildreth, Puritan piety was at first inspiring and beautiful, but was then perverted by witch trials and rationalist agnosticism. Piety and enlightenment combined during the early nineteenth century, especially in New England. A few Southern historians like Charles Etienne Gayarré and George Tucker modified God's plan for the world as sectionalism required.

Preconceptions about morality, progress, and God led historians to polar preconceptions about immorality, decay, and evil. As men struggled to live a moral life, they were tempted. As societies carried forward the banner of progress, they grew old and decadent. As God was a force, so was Satan. The clearest signs of decay were wealth and tyranny. With increasing wealth, plain living gave way to self-indulgence, dissipation, and torpor. The people, or at any rate the upper classes, became tyrannical, arrogant, and cruel. Ignorance and superstition spread; the society collapsed from within.

Decay could occur wherever great wealth or tyranny appeared. Most primitive societies, Prescott's Aztecs and Incas, for example, or Parkman's Iroquois, revealed this evil. Almost every schoolbook found luxury, immorality, and despotism in the late Roman empire. These were the characteristics of the Spanish Habsburgs, the Roman Catholic priesthood, the French Bourbons, and, increasingly, of the English monarchy. "It is difficult," confessed one writer, "for the mind to conceive of characters more selfish, profligate and vile, than the line of English kings, with two or three doubtful exceptions, have uniformly exhibited from the earliest periods to the present day." Historians thus discovered a law of aristocratic degeneracy. "It is so, and always has been so, with every aristocracy that the world has produced." [29] Wealth was acceptable, of course, if it was well dis-

---

[29] Jacob Abbott, *Narration of the General Course of History* . . . (New York, 1856), pp. 218–19; England, "England and America in the Schoolbooks of the Republic," pp. 96–104.

tributed and if it did not breed indolence. To historians writing about the United States or their own local areas, however, improving economic statistics were a sign of progress, not decadence.

Simple, democratic people like the American pioneers regularly infused a moral regeneration into the stream of history. Benefiting from the previous progress of civilization but escaping from degeneracy in the world around them, vigorous men carried the torch forward. The early Christians, the early Renaissance Spaniards, the northern Europeans of the Reformation, the English yeomanry, and, finally, the Americans each in turn served mankind by their renewed sense of morality, their simple innocence, and their youthful vigor. For many of the literary historians, including Bancroft, Prescott, Motley, and Parkman, the great drama of history was the clash of the simple and vigorous with the old and decayed, always with predictable result. For the historian, as for the theologian, immorality and decay were instruments for regeneration and further progress.

The assumption of progress led historians to think of origins, to look for the earliest seeds of national institutions. Often institutions and ideas seemed to grow from primitive origins, from the inspiration of vigorous new people. The concept of liberty, for example, appeared to have come into the modern world from the German forests, to have evolved through the British parliamentary system, and to have been reinvigorated in the American colonies where it reached its culmination. The American spirit seemed evident at Jamestown and Plymouth. Bancroft observed, typically, that "The maturity of the nation is but the continuation of its youth," and he promised to dwell "at considerable length on this first period, because it is the germ of our institutions." Hildreth likewise promised "to trace our institutions, religious, social, and political, from their embryo state"; and local writers volunteered to emphasize "the seeds of things, watch their first germinations, observe their gradual growth, and witness their flowering and fruit." [30]

[30] George Bancroft, *History of the United States* . . . (10 vols.; Boston, 1834–75), I, vii; Richard Hildreth, *The History of the United States of*

Progress became easily entwined not only with morality but also with assumptions about American character and democracy. If mankind had evolved toward New England Unitarianism, it had also evolved toward the American system of government. A verbose Boston historian, Samuel Eliot, began a twelve-volume *History of Liberty*, of which he completed four volumes, tracing the evolution of government upward from the Greeks to the Americans. "The history of Liberty," said Edward Everett in a typical Fourth of July oration, "is the real history of man." [31] Bulfinch writing on Charlemagne, Irving on Christopher Columbus, Motley on the Dutch, and almost every state and town chronicler established his topic as an episode in the development of American democracy. "We are here to work out, not alone our destiny, but that of the whole world," said a popular schoolbook. "Here, for the first time in human history, man will be *truly* man. . . . Here shall be realized the long-prophesied, long-expected *Golden Age*." [32]

National Character

The early nineteenth-century approach to history pointed to nationalism and, ultimately, racism. Emphasis on the "essence" of a people prepared the way for evaluation of national traits; conscious dramatization and shading of characters invited the use of national types as a leitmotiv; assumptions of progress implied that each nation or race provided a step upward; and, most of all, the Americans' conviction of separateness and superiority contributed to the impression that the genes some-

---

America . . . (6 vols.; New York, 1849–56), I, vii–viii; Mercy Otis Warren, *History of the Rise, Progress and Termination of the American Revolution* . . . (3 vols.; Boston, 1805), I, 5–20; Philip Slaughter, *A History of Bristol Parish, Virginia* . . . (Richmond, 1849), p. xiv.

[31] Edward Everett, *An Oration Delivered before the Citizens* . . . (Charleston, Mass., 1828), pp. 5–6; also J. L. Reynolds, *The Man of Letters* (Richmond, 1849), p. 18.

[32] Jesse Olney, *A History of the United States* (New Haven, 1851), pp. v–vi; also J. Merton England, "The Democratic Faith in American Schoolbooks," *American Quarterly*, XV (summer, 1963), 191–99.

how dictated national character. Although few American historians of the early nineteenth century were prepared to offer a coherent theory of racial traits, they had more than they realized come to depend upon preconceptions about national traits to dramatize and even to explain the course of history.

Americans arrived at their assumptions about national character earlier than most people in western society. Gibbon and Hume had specifically ridiculed the concept, and during the early decades of the nineteenth century all leading English historians avoided the pitfall. In America, however, soon after the Revolution the early geography textbooks of Noah Webster and Jedidiah Morse introduced generalizations about national manners and morals which suggested racial traits. Scholars like David Ramsay and Timothy Pitkin accepted racial characteristics to explain the Negroes and Indians who lived among them. Theodore Parker and Ralph Waldo Emerson infused the concept into the Unitarianism and Transcendentalism which influenced so many historians. German education and German Romantic nationalism influenced Bancroft and Motley directly, and filtered indirectly into the thinking of Sparks, Prescott, Parkman, and Hildreth. By the 1830's, in any case, most of America's best historians assumed the existence of national character as a racial trait. Rapidly, it seeped from scholars into schoolbooks and popular thought.[33]

At the bottom of the racial scale but often omitted altogether from mention was the Negro "savage" of Africa. Historians commonly believed that all black Africans were "of the same species," that they had always existed in a "rude and barbarous state," that they were "lacking in vigor of mind," were "despotic and warlike," but were also "gentle, faithful and affectionate." Although ferocity and docility appear contradictory, both were based on evidence and the contradiction had to stand. North-

[33] Winthrop D. Jordan, *White over Black: American Attitudes toward the Negro, 1550–1812* (Chapel Hill, 1968), pp. 331–41, 482–502, and *passim;* Thomas F. Gossett, *Race: The History of An Idea in America* (Dallas, 1963), pp. 84–88 ff.

erners and southerners found little to quarrel about in this characterization, for even outspoken abolitionists like Richard Hildreth thought of the African as "a most objectionable species of population." Since most national historians were northerners, however, they found it easiest to avoid discussion of the Negro himself and focus instead on the evils of slavery. Although they spoke as publicists rather than historians on the issue, few scholars or textbook authors could refrain from at least a veiled attack on the institution. George Bancroft, combining racism with hatred of slavery, suggested that slavery had elevated the Negro and then become obsolete. "But for the slave-trade," he observed, "the African race would have had no inheritance in the New World." [34]

Romanticists both in Europe and America were fascinated with the American Indian as the complete barbarian and the uncorrupted child of nature. First, he was a barbarian, above the Negro and above savagery, but unalterably primitive. He was baffled by abstractions and unable to grasp concepts of morality. A slave to his impulses rather than their master, he was a sensualist with no concept of propriety, a liar, a thief, and a murderer. Although admirably democratic in the United States, the more advanced Indians of Mexico quickly became materialistic, inclined to luxury, and, consequently, inclined to despotism. The Indians always were noted for dishonesty and treachery. Americans emphasized their "sanguinary character," their bloody raids on unsuspecting families, their legendary tortures, and their human sacrifices. Ultimate proof of Indian depravity appeared in their apparent inability to accept a superior civilization, particularly the concepts of Protestant Christianity. One critic has observed that careful literary historians like Prescott and Parkman utilized the Indian to fit the Romantic convention of Gothic villainy, of dark, shadowy,

---

[34] Goodrich, *History of All Nations*, I, 49; II, 640–41; Joseph Emerson Worcester, *Elements of Geography* . . . (Boston, 1844), p. 197; Hildreth, *History of the United States*, I, 119, 523–24; Bancroft, *History of the United States*, I, 173.

diabolical terror. To almost every historian, at the very least the Indian stood in the way of mankind's progress.[35]

The inevitability of Indian defeat, however, made him into a sympathetic figure also. Indians were children of nature, in perfect harmony with the forest, simple and unspoiled, but destined to destruction by the march of civilization. Their defense of home and freedom was in accord with natural law, and in this cause even their ferocity "invests their character with a kind of moral grandeur." Historians found the essence of tragedy in the clash of two laws of nature, the one which guaranteed the Indian his land and the apparently stronger law of progress. The Indian gave way to the settler as the forest gave way to the farm. Prescott and Parkman created their major works on this theme of the Indian's tragic fate. "Shall we not drop a tear?" asked Bancroft, indulging himself in the sweet sadness of the Indians' doom. Local historians, especially in the West, generally managed to counter their hatred of the Indian with a sad awareness of his fate. By the 1850's, however a few critical historians like Hildreth had rejected sentiment to embrace a much harsher racism.[36]

Somewhere above the Indian, though probably related, were the infidel oriental "nationalities," variously including the Moors, Turks, Jews, Chinese, and Malayans. Although American historians dealt little with these exotic peoples, schoolbooks clearly defined their traits, and they frequently appeared on the scene in minor roles. Orientals, unlike American Indians, were generally marked by over-refinement, decadence, and torpor.

[35] Goodrich, *History of All Nations*, I, 48; II, 1156–62; William Grimshaw, *History of the United States . . . With a Progressive View of the Aborigines* . . . (Philadelphia, 1857), pp. 45–51; David Ramsay, *History of the United States . . .* (3 vols.; Philadelphia, 1816), I, 9–14; Levin, *History as Romantic Art*, pp. 126–159.

[36] Worcester, *Elements of Geography*, p. 12; Bancroft, *History of the United States*, II, 266–69; Samuel Gardner Drake, *Biography and History of the Indians of North America* (Boston, 1837); Henry Howe, *Historical Collections of the Great West . . .* (2 vols.; Cincinnati, 1851); Hildreth, *History of the United States*, pp. 50–70; see also Henry Nash Smith, *Virgin Land, The American West As Symbol and Myth* (Cambridge, Mass., 1950), *passim*.

Love of vast riches, immorality, and cruel despotism marked their character. They were more civilized than the Indian but "less active and enterprizing; more effeminate in their character and habits." Prescott and Irving, unable to hide admiration for Moorish Spain, employed the theme used for Indians, the tragic and inevitable fall of inferior peoples. For most Americans, however, this failed to diminish the simpler images of "Oriental despotism" and the sensualism of the harem.[37]

National stereotypes almost faded before religious emotions when American historians considered the Spaniards, Italians, French, and Irish. Running through the works of virtually all of the great literary historians, through those of hundreds of local chroniclers, blatant in popular magazines, and in almost every schoolbook, the hatred of Roman Catholicism colored the sweep of history. Sophisticated writers like Prescott and Parkman dramatized the theme of the sympathetic Indian against civilization, and the countertheme of savagery against fanatical Catholicism. "Popery" seemed both unreasonable and unnatural to most Americans, a relic of the past, epitomized by the sallow, effete, thin-lipped Jesuit. The Church remained, however, not so much a corrupt institution which fostered authoritarianism as a refuge for decadent, superstitious, authoritarian, morally lax peoples. Without the Church such people would have hardly been different. Racially they were Latin or Celts, characterized by emotional instability, indolence, and greed. Specific traits marked each one—Spanish pride, Italian affability, French refinement, and Irish passion.[38]

The Germans, Dutch, and English represented vigor and a striving for liberty. Romantic historians looked to the ancient forests of northern Europe for the men who carried civilization to

---

[37] Worcester, *Elements of Geography*, pp. 164–65; Emma Willard, *Universal History in Perspective* (New York, 1851), p. 280; Goodrich, *History of All Nations*, II, 824–25; Levin, *History as Romantic Art*, pp. 142–48.

[38] See any geography textbook; for example, Jesse Olney, *A Practical System of Geography* (Hartford, 1828), pp. 154–65; John Lothrop Motley, *The Rise of the Dutch Republic* (3 vols.; New York, 1859), I, 1–11; Marie Leonore Fell, *Foundations of Nativism in American Textbooks, 1783–1860* (Washington, 1941), p. 224 and *passim*.

new heights. Spontaneous folk, free from artificiality and corrupting institutions, they provided the primitive vigor for progress. Their simple instincts led them to piety, aspiration, self-reliance, and industry. Their special gift, however, was independence, a love of liberty, a determination to protect liberty through democratic institutions. Historians seeking the origins of tolerance, democracy, or the various institutions of representative government assumed that they must look for the Teutonic embryos. Rising German nationalism of the early nineteenth century emphasized the *Volk* virtues and the forest origins of institutions. Americans like Emerson and Bancroft easily absorbed the German theories. Toward the middle of the century, as race became increasingly basic to these traits, Americans assumed that the German–English racial heritage was also their own.[39]

Assumptions about Teutonic traits provided a distinctly post-Gibbon explanation of the fall of Rome. "The corrupted Roman world," observed a popular textbook of the 1830's, "could not but fall before such a people." German piety explained the strength of medieval Christianity. The Reformation was a reassertion of that piety but, far more, was a reassertion of the German spirit of liberty. Prescott suggested that a Visigothic heritage and possibly the Magna Carta invigorated fifteenth-century Spain and inspired Ferdinand and Isabella to become liberated from the Moors. Motley observed that the history of liberty was "essentially the same, whether in Friesland, England, or Massachusetts"; Bancroft promised to trace liberty from "that Germanic race most famed for love of personal independence"; and Parkman gloried in the "ancient energy, that wild and daring spirit, that force and hardihood of mind, which marked our barbarous ancestors of Germany." The differences between the nationalities were less important—German idealism and seriousness, Dutch industry and frugality, and English intelligence and enterprise.[40]

[39] See Gossett, *Race*, pp. 84–122; Levin, *History as Romantic Art*, pp. 74–92; Ralph Waldo Emerson, *English Traits* (Boston, 1856).
[40] Royal Robbins, *The World Displayed in Its History and Geography* (2 vols.; New York, 1833), II, 361; Alexander Fraser Tytler, *Elements of*

Finally, of course, the chosen people, the Americans, entered. The glorification of American character stemmed from all the assumptions about morality, God's guidance, progress, and the existence of national traits. Further stimulus came from the natural filial piety of the young nation and from the exuberant nationalism which flowered after the war of 1812. For textbook authors, American superiority was not only an interpretive assumption, but also a major lesson for history to reveal. For popular writers—such as Weems, Irving, Barber, Headley, Lossing, and Parton—revelation of American traits allowed both reverent display of honest emotion and deliberate appeal for sales. Assumption of the superior traits of Americans supplied Prescott and Motley with a standard by which to measure other peoples; it provided inspiration for compilers and local chroniclers; it was a motivation for such national historians as Holmes, Pitkin, Sparks, and Bancroft. The cynical Hildreth, who ostentatiously condemned "centennial sermons and Fourth-of-July orations," came closest of all to a frankly racial explanation of American character.

Historians generally assumed that the religious basis of settlement, the simple pioneer life, and the widespread landholdings all reinvigorated the virtues once ascribed to the Northern Europeans. Above all, Americans loved liberty, hated oppression and aristocracy, were democratic and willing to sacrifice personal gain for the common good. Their plain life promoted moral strength—the qualities of industry, temperance, and self-reliance that historians celebrated in defining moral virtue.[41] Most writers found a distinctly conservative tendency in the American character. Even devoted Jacksonians like George Bancroft emphasized the nonradical, nonviolent stance of Americans, and viewed the

---

General History . . . (Concord, N.H., 1830), p. 110; Goodrich, *History of All Nations,* II, 971, 1008; Prescott, *History of the Reign of Ferdinand and Isabella, the Catholic* (3 vols.; Boston, 1837), I, xxxii–xxxiii; Motley, *Rise of the Dutch Republic,* p. iii; Bancroft, *History of the United States,* II, 454; Parkman, *History of the Conspiracy of Pontiac* . . . (2 vols.; Boston, 1880), I, 158.

[41] See England, "Democratic Faith in American Schoolbooks," pp. 191–99.

American Revolution as a defense of ancient liberties, property, and the status quo. Although Bancroft praised Bacon's Rebellion as a harbinger of independence, he joined the majority of his contemporaries in condemning Shays' Rebellion and the Whiskey Rebellion as dangerously subversive. Northern and southern historians, as they gradually began using history to attack each other, compared northern traits of piety and industry with southern traits of honor and graciousness. Such concepts could be made laudatory or pejorative as necessary.

The Romantic approach to history ended, however, when historians ceased to share assumptions and began to prove their own theses. Readers were eager for their historians to interpret the past as long as they agreed with the basic interpretations. An era of historical writing was marked by general consensus about essence, morality, progress, and national character. When men began to disagree about these things, a different approach to historical scholarship and a different kind of history were required.

IX

The Social Uses of History

THE most essential characteristic of the idea of history in the early nineteenth century was its clear projection toward definite ends. While German Romantic philosophers struggled to define the meaning and patterns of history, Americans were primarily concerned with the matter of utility. They knew exactly why they were interested in the past and were eager to explain what those reasons were.

The sense of purpose gave unity to the concept of history. The importance of the past, selection of subject matter, methods and interpretation all pointed toward specific ends. Historians and critics believed that the study of history was successful to the extent to which it possessed and achieved a purpose. "Any consideration of the past," said one, "must begin with some notion of the practical use to which the teachings of history are to be applied." [1] Again and again critics posed and answered the question, "What avails us to know all this?" "What is the use of it?" [2]

[1] T. B. T., "A Course of Historical Reading," *Universalist Quarterly and General Review*, VII (January, 1850), 9.

[2] Anon., "History, Its Use and Meaning," *Westminster Review*, LXII (October, 1854), 223; L. J. B. C., "History," *Universalist Quarterly and General Review*, I (April, 1844), 167; anon., "The Dignity of History," *Nation*, IV (May, 1867), 417; anon., "The Modern Art and Science of His-

Americans are proverbially concerned with utility, and they seemed especially concerned with it during the early nineteenth century. Eighteenth-century thinkers like Vico and Hume had been primarily concerned with the epistemological question of history as a legitimate form of knowledge; Romantic philosophers in Germany and France debated content and pattern; after the Civil War in the United States the central issue was method; and in the twentieth century, as history and philosophy diverged, historians became concerned with the past itself and its interpretation, leaving to a handful of philosophers such problems as definition, cause, content, and value judgment.[3]

Some early nineteenth-century observers believed that the chief distinction between their history and that of an earlier day lay in the consciousness of purpose. "History today," said one, "has far higher ends and purposes" than ever before.[4] "The new historical school," said another, "is characterized by greater earnestness and energy and sense of direction."[5] "Its lessons have been advanced in dignity and increased in value. Its scope is wider, its fathomings are more profound."[6] "History today," said one observer, is "very different from that which would formally have satisfied us [because] history is becoming moral. . . . The ethical sciences are emerging to replace the physical."[7]

---

tory," *Westminster Review,* XXXVIII (October, 1842), 337; anon., "The Philosophy of History," *North American Review,* XXXIX (July, 1834), 36; anon., "Lectures on the History of France," *North American Review,* LXXV (July, 1852), 259; anon., "Leading Theories on the Philosophy of History," *North American Review,* XCIII (July, 1862), 163; Eliza Robbins, *English History* (New York, 1839), p. 7; anon., "The Reading of History," *Princeton Review,* XIX (April, 1847), 211; anon., "The Importance of Historical Knowledge," *North Carolina Historical Magazine,* IX (September, 1859), 98; anon., "The Aim of History," *Princeton Review,* XXIX (April, 1857), 212; C. R., "Impostures of History," *Portfolio,* I (May, 1816), 369.

[3] See, R. G. Collingwood, *The Idea of History* (Oxford, 1946), pp. 63–122.

[4] Henry L. Pinckney, *The Spirit of the Age* (Raleigh, N.C., 1836), p. 20.

[5] P., "Modern Art and Science of History," p. 369.

[6] Anon., "Historical Studies," *Church Review,* IV (April, 1851), 10.

[7] Review, *Southern Quarterly Review,* V (April, 1844), 266–67; also John Hill, "An Essay upon the Principles of Historical Composition," *Portfolio,* IX (April, 1820), 340; Giles F. Yates, "Ancient History," *American Literary Magazine,* I (December, 1847), 366.

In Support of Principles

The primary use of history was social: it was the purpose of history to strengthen society by supporting the basic principles in which men believed—society's concepts of morality, religion, and nationalism. To men of the Romantic era it was not falsifying the past to select those facts which illustrated a particular principle, for principles were certain and the facts of history were not. The facts which supported absolute principles were the relevant facts, the ones worth using, and the facts which did not support them were misunderstood, irrelevant, and, in all probability, simply untrue.

The belief that history ought to support social values originated in part in the eighteenth-century concept of historical knowledge as a means of broadening man's understanding of behavior. Enlightenment thinkers sometimes claimed that knowledge of past experience helped to fill John Locke's blank slate, adding to one's own experience that of the past. Viscount Bolingbroke made of this the famous homily that history was "philosophy teaching by examples." This, he explained, meant that history revealed "certain general principles, and rules of life and conduct, which must always be true, because they are comfortable to the invariable nature of things." [8] Men continued to quote Bolingbroke approvingly during the early nineteenth century, but they made his statement much more pointed. The statement came to mean that philosophy furnished true principles—such as the importance of moral conduct or patriotism—and history proved them.

As nineteenth-century antiquarians uncovered ever vaster quantities of details, and as Romantic philosophers like Herder and Emerson mobilized intuition as well as reason in pursuit of truth, fundamental assumptions about society became increasingly important as a starting point for comprehending the past. History, in other words, was not so much the search for social truths, because truths came first and were already known; its

[8] Cited in Trygve R. Tholfsen, *Historical Thinking: An Introduction* (New York, 1967), p. 85.

purpose was to illustrate the truths on which men had agreed. Not only reason and intuition but history as well would strengthen men's convictions and, consequently, strengthen the fabric of society.

Critics emphasized that a reliable and true history must be preceded by right principles. "It is useless," said one, "to know any fact if it does not illustrate some truth." [9] If the historian's principles were unsound, then "his facts will be torn from their proper surroundings in order to deceive the reader." [10] Critics warned historians to keep Bolingbroke's injunction before them. "The only useful purpose to which history . . . has been susceptible of application, has been simply as a code of morals teaching by example." [11] History "must exist as an object lesson"; it must "always teach a valuable lesson"; "the object is to instruct." [12]

Important educational philosophers laid a broad theoretical base for the study of history as a support for social values. While these theorists probably embraced history because it had already assumed social functions, they understood the implications of using the past better than most historians, and their

[9] Anon., "Lectures on the History of France," *North American Review,* LXXV (July, 1852), 250; also, anon., "Reading of History," p. 211; anon., "The Uses of History to the Preacher," *New Englander,* XXII (July, 1863), 423–424; C. R., "Impostures of History," p. 370; anon., "History," *American Quarterly Review,* V (March, 1829), 95; anon., "Lessons from History," *Aurora,* I (October 29, 1834), 123.

[10] James Anthony Froude, "The Science of History," *Hours at Home,* II (February, 1866), 323; also, anon., "Importance of Historical Knowledge," p. 99; anon., "History," *Monthly Anthology,* I (January, 1804), 119.

[11] C. C. S. Farrar, "The Science of History," *DeBow's Review,* V (January, 1848), 60; also, review, *North American Review,* LXX (January, 1850), pp. 339–40; anon., "Aim of History," p. 234; "Introduction," *The Historical Family Library,* I (June, 1835), 1; review, *North American Review,* XL (January, 1834), 117–120; Samuel Griswold Goodrich, *Pictorial History of England* (Philadelphia, 1857), p. v; Samuel Whelpley, *A Compend of History From the Earliest Times* . . . (2 vols.; Burlington, Vt., 1808), I, 162.

[12] Reviews, *North American Review,* LXXXIII (October, 1851), 411; XLVI (January, 1838), 235; Giles F. Yates, "Ancient History," *American Literary Magazine,* p. 366; also, anon., "The Historical Romance," *Blackwood's Magazine,* LVIII (September, 1845), 343; Dr. Aikin, "On the Comparative Value of Different Studies," *New England Quarterly,* I (May, 1802), 156.

arguments for its utility facilitated its emergence into the school curriculum. Following in the path of Rousseau, the Swiss educator Johann Heinrich Pestalozzi argued that education must abandon its aristocratic aim of leading a few gentlemen into the paths of truth and assume the responsibility for elevating society as a whole. Since the masses did not have the time to gain a complete store of knowledge on which to build their principles, education should aim at immediate instillation of principles, inculcating students with the known truths which society accepted. In other words, education should develop character rather than intellect. It would thus reach everyone, strengthening social ideals and elevating all society.[13]

The German educator Johann Herbart and his American counterparts Henry Barnard and Horace Mann argued that this social utility was best served by two subjects—history and literature. Teachers would use these basic stores of information to draw moral lessons, to imbue students with correct principles of morality and life. To Herbart the past was especially filled with moral lessons; historian, textbook, and teacher must extract and illuminate them. The purpose of education in general and of history in particular was virtue not knowledge. Its purpose was to impart principles and right ideals.[14]

Textbook writers were often ahead of the theorists, for inculcation of principles was the primary justification for the books that began to appear after the Revolution and reached flood proportions after the War of 1812. Noah Webster in 1887 proclaimed that the purpose of his textbook was "to impress . . . truths upon our minds." [15] A few years later Samuel Whelpley

[13] Eva Channing, ed. and trans., Pestalozzi's "Leonard and Gertrude," (Boston, 1885), pp. 129-31 and passim; Will Seymour Monroe, History of the Pestalozzian Movement in the United States (Syracuse, 1907); Richard Hofstadter and C. DeWitt Hardy, Development and Scope of Higher Education in the United States (New York, 1952), especially pp. 13-15.

[14] Johann Friedrich Herbart, Outlines of Educational Doctrine, trans. Alexis F. Lange (New York, 1901), pp. 7, 24, 97, 223-40; Dorothy McMurray, Herbartian Contributions to History Instruction in American Elementary Schools (New York, 1946).

[15] Noah Webster, An American Selection of Lessons in Reading and Speaking (Philadelphia, 1787), p. vi.

justified his popular text on the grounds that "knowledge of history strongly inculcates truth." [16] "The reason for studying history," said others, "is to store the mind with principles"; "the object is to instruct"; history "is instrumental in cultivating truth"; "an apt vehicle of political and moral lessons." [17]

Although didacticism was strongest in the schools, popular historians also considered it their duty to instruct the public. Abiel Holmes hoped that history would "serve to strengthen, illustrate and adorn" those principles men held dear, and George Bancroft sought to produce a historical "understanding" of the truth men felt.[18] Critics found ample praise for the books which were most successful in illustrating principles.

Morality, Religion, and Patriotism

The specific principles which history had to support were remarkably few—personal morality, the existence of God, the greatness of America. During the eighteenth century, writers used history to support a multitude of conflicting ideas, perhaps because they were often attacking the status quo or perhaps because reason led to diverse principles. In the early nineteenth century, however, principles were few, perhaps because men saw the danger in using history for partisan purposes, perhaps because historians were generally supporting the status quo, or perhaps because reason, plus intuition, plus Rousseau's general will led to consensus on major principles. History as support for social principles lasted only as long as did consensus. When men began to disagree over the principles which history proved, new methods of writing history and new justifications for the past were needed.

[16] Samuel Whelpley, *Compend of History*, p. 160.

[17] William Cooke Taylor, *A Manual of Ancient History* (New York, 1855), p. v; Lambert Lilly [Francis Lister Hawks], *The History of New England* (Boston, 1831); Salma Hale, *History of the United States* (New York, 1825), p. iv; Samuel G. Goodrich, *A Pictorial History of the United States . . .* (Philadelphia, 1825), p. iv.

[18] Abiel Holmes, "The American Antiquarian Society," *Portfolio*, V (May, 1815), 471; George Bancroft, *History of the United States . . .* (10 vols.; Boston, 1834–75), I, vii; also, anon., "On History," *Evening Fireside*, II (April 19, 1806), 123.

Personal morality was the primary truth for history to uphold. "The most important advantage of the study of history," said a popular textbook, "is improvement in individual virtue." One after another the textbooks promised "to subserve the cause of morality," "to strengthen the sentiments of virtue," "to furnish rules for conduct," "to restrain some of the common vices of our country." [19] Critics agreed: history "must be regarded as a moral science"; its "only useful purpose" was "to strengthen the love of virtue, and create an abhorrence of vice." [20] Clergymen turned to history as a means of promoting morality, and such clergymen as Charles A. Goodrich, Samuel Whelpley, and Royal Robbins became full-time textbook authors. When Mason Locke Weems left the ministry to write cherry tree fables, he was convinced that he was "still doing God's work, having merely transferred his activities from the pulpit to a wider mission field." [21]

History taught ethical conduct chiefly by inspiring emulation. "One lesson, and only one, history may be said to repeat with distinctness," said one historian, "that in the long run it is well with the good, and ill with the wicked." [22] Writers promised to make morality so attractive that "the youthful heart shall kindle into desires of imitation"; "History sets before us striking incidents of virtue . . . and by a natural principle of emulation, excites us to copy such noble examples." [23] "It is by

[19] Emma Willard, *History of the United States* (New York, 1845), p. v; Royal Robbins, *Outlines of Ancient and Modern History* (Hartford, 1839), p. 7; Taylor, *Manual of Ancient History*, p. v; Noah Webster, *History of the United States* (New Haven, 1832), p. iii; also, anon., *Tales from American History* (3 vols.; New York, 1844), I, 5; Whelpley, *Compend of History*, p. 159; Joseph Emerson Worcester, *Elements of History* (Boston, 1848), p. 3.

[20] William Harper, *The South Carolina Society for the Advancement of Learning* (Washington, 1836), p. 3; Farrar, "Science of History," p. 60; anon., "Philosophy of History," p. 47; also, anon., "History," p. 95; Constantine François Volney, *Lectures of History Delivered in the Normal School of Paris* (Philadelphia, 1801), pp. 68–76.

[21] Emily Elsworth Ford Skeel, "Mason Locke Weems," Allen Johnson and Dumas Malone, eds., *Dictionary of American Biography* (22 vols.; New York, 1928–44), XIX, 604–5.

[22] Froude, "Science of History," p. 323; also, anon., "Importance of Historical Knowledge," p. 98.

[23] Willard, *History of the United States,* p. v; Charles A. Goodrich, *A*

reading the history of generous and noble actions, that sympathetic emotions are kindled in the heart . . . and habits of
virtue are generated and confirmed." [24]

If examples were not enough, history could offer rewards and
punishments as well as any Puritan preacher. Virtuous men lived
happy lives, but the immoral were invariably defeated and led
to suffering. History, when properly recounted, "always presents
us with a picture of the vicious overtaken with misery and
shame, and thus solemnly warns us against vice"; "it uniformly
corroborates the idea, that sin and misery are connected." [25]
The moralists were sure of their case; virtue paid off in cash.
Francis Wayland, the preacher-president of Brown University
and author of one of the first textbooks on political science,
noted that "moral and religious nations grow wealthy much
more rapidly than vicious or irreligious nations." [26]

Especially in textbooks, historians came close to willing distortion of the past to point out to the student that virtue leads
to happiness. Far from apologizing, they boasted that unsavory
episodes were minimized and questionable consequences of
evil omitted. "With regard to bad actions, we have, as far as
possible, given the results, rather than the detail." [27] In fine
Romantic rhetoric one of the most popular textbooks explained
its reorganization of facts:

> A large part of the actions of men, as related by the historian, are
> evil. . . . To reveal these dark pictures to youth, and yet prevent

History of the United States . . . (Hartford, 1831), p. 5; also, anon., *Tales from American History,* p. 5; Willard, *History of the United States,* p. v; James Kirke Paulding, *A Life of Washington* (2 vols.; New York, 1836), I, vi; John Haywood, *The Civil and Aboriginal History of Tennessee* (Knoxville, 1823), p. iii; James Parton, *Life of Andrew Jackson* (3 vols.; New York, 1860), I, xi; Francis Lister Hawks, *A Tale of the Huguenots* (New York, 1838), p. vi.

[24] Anon., "Classical and Moral Education," *Portfolio,* VI (October, 1815), 417.

[25] C. A. Goodrich, *History of the United States,* p. 5; Whelpley, *Compend of History,* p. 163; also Worcester, *Elements of History,* p. 3.

[26] Francis Wayland, *Elements of Political Economy* (Boston, 1837), p. 32; also, anon., "Importance of Historical Knowledge," p. 98; review, *North American Review,* LXX (January, 1850), 239.

[27] Willard, *History of the United States,* p. vi.

the bright and sunny landscape of the heart from being permanently
sullied or shadowed by the acquisition of such knowledge, demands
great care. . . . I have taken advantage of every convenient occasion
to excite hatred of injustice, violence, and falsehood, and to promote
a love of truth, equity, and benevolence.[28]

When educators discussed the purpose of history they spoke
in general terms of virtue, but in practice they had to offer a
specific moral code; this code was closer to what is thought of
as Victorian than to what is generally considered typical of the
Romantic. Virtue meant personal rectitude, honesty, earnestness,
simplicity, industry, and piety—rural as opposed to urban virtues, Washington instead of Hamilton, Cromwell instead of
Napoleon, George Apley or James Forsyte instead of Don Juan.
This middle-class code probably came to England near the middle of the century, but semed to be firmly established in America
by the 1820's. Probably the distinctive American morality was
related to Puritanism and the frontier; perhaps it was shaped as
well as symbolized by the mythology of Franklin, Washington,
and Jackson. The moral code was evident in most history textbooks, in historians' selections of subject matter, and in their
interpretations and assumptions. The code was still more explicit
in primers, sermons, and books of ethics. Actually, later generations probably agree more than they realize with the idea of
history instilling morality and have only substituted new values.
Twentieth-century historians would generally concur that history "proves" the horror of war, poverty, and prejudice, and that
it "teaches" rational behavior and tolerance.

Another absolute principle for history to sustain was the
power of God. The existence of God was a certainty and it was
a matter of selecting only the true and important facts that revealed His presence. Probably half of the history textbooks in
use from 1800 to 1860 explicitly mentioned God in the preface.
"To show that one supreme, eternal God . . . controls all events
is the great design of this work," said a typical author. "With a
steady eye to the special designs of God . . . I have . . . prose-

[28] Samuel Griswold Goodrich, *Peter Parley's Universal History* (Boston,
1837), p. vi.

cuted my work with an unbiased inquiry after truth." [29] A steady
eye on his thesis did not violate unbiased inquiry. If anything,
critics and historians seemed more eager than schoolbook authors to see God in history. "Historians have been successful in
solving the problems of history in proportion as they have recognized a providential plan in the career of the world." [30] A man
could deny God just as he could deny the existence of the stars,
said an observer; but he could no more deny that history was
a study of God than he could deny that astronomy was a study
of the stars. "To write history without correct views on that
subject is like playing Hamlet without the Prince of Den-
mark." [31]

The definition of God was generally broad rather than sectar-
ian, so that Unitarians and fundamentalists usually agreed that
their own era was characterized by correct views of history, unlike
the agnostic history which came before and after them. Teaching
about God meant teaching the prevailing views, the views
generally agreed upon by early nineteenth-century Americans.
Critics noted that eighteenth-century historians "supposed and
hoped that they had made discoveries . . . destructive of inspired
history. But these fond hopes were soon disappointed. When the
path of inquiry was pressed further . . . it was found to terminate
in evidence of a directly contrary kind." [32] "We think it but too

[29] Frederick Butler, *A Complete History of the United States* . . . (3 vols.;
Hartford, 1821), I, iii; also Taylor, *Manual of Ancient History*, p. vi; anon.,
Tales from American History, pp. 6, 226; C. A. Goodrich, *History of the
United States*, p. 6; Marcius Willson, *History of the United States* . . . (New
York, 1847), p. 358; Hosea Hildreth, *A View of the United States* (Boston,
1831), p. iv.

[30] William Greenough Thayer Shedd, "The Nature and Influence of the
Historic Spirit," *Bibliotheca Sacra*, XI (April, 1854), 349; also, anon., "History," p. 93; anon., "Historical Studies," p. 21.

[31] Anon., "Guizot and the Philosophy of History," *Eclectic Magazine*, IV
(February, 1845), 179; also, "Introduction," *Historical Family Library*, I (June,
1835), 1; anon., "Philosophy of History," p. 51; anon., "The Mutual Relation
of History and Religion," *Eclectic Magazine*, XLI (June, 1857), 167; anon.,
"Lectures on the History of France," *North American Review*, LXXV (July,
1852), 250; anon., "Uses of History to the Preacher," p. 424.

[32] Samuel Miller, *A Brief Retrospect of the Eighteenth Century* (New York,
1803), p. 148.

plain that the irreligious spirit of Voltaire, Hume, and Gibbon, had fatally confounded their sentiments of morality." [33] Likewise critics condemned post-Romantic history which seemed to ignore piety. "Men like Professor Ranke . . . are too much preoccupied with their learned researches to pay much attention to the word of God." [34]

On a superficial level, supporting the existence of God meant revealing God's intervention in the affairs of men. George Bancroft showed explicitly that German rulers who sent Hessians to fight America had been destroyed. "Every dynasty which furnished troops to England has ceased to reign. . . . On the other hand, the three Saxon families remain, and in their states local self-government has continually increased. . . . It is useless to ask what would have happened if the eternal Providence had for the moment suspended its rule." [35] Other historians were equally blunt. They would "show the triumph of good over evil"; "illustrate the Holy Writ"; "show the Hand of God directing all"; "exhibit the conduct of Divine Providence"; or "display the dealings of God with Mankind." [36]

More systematic thinkers preferred to see God more indirectly. Even Bancroft admitted that one best saw God in the grandeur of the past rather than in specific interventions. To see direct intervention at every hand was "a violation of common sense and history"; "men are apt to lend to Providence their own schemes of a saisfactory government of the universe." [37] Instead of teaching God's ways in the past, the cautious historian pre-

[33] Review, *Living Age*, XII (March 13, 1847), 525; also, anon., "The Philosophy of History," *American Magazine of Knowledge*, III (October, 1836), 14; also, review, *Analectic Magazine*, VI (August, 1815), 89–112.

[34] Review, *Museum of Foreign Literature, Science and Art*, XL (September, 1840), 29.

[35] Bancroft, *History of the United States*, VI, 109, 115.

[36] C. A. Goodrich, *History of the United States*, p. 6; David Ramsay, *Universal History Americanized* (12 vols.; Philadelphia, 1819), I, iv; Taylor, *Manual of Ancient History*, p. vi; Worcester, *Elements of History*, p. 3; Whelpley, *Compend of History*, pp. 162–63; also Joel Tyler Headley, *Washington and His Generals* (2 vols.; New York, 1848), I, x.

[37] Anon., "Providential and Prophetical Histories," *Edinburgh Review*, L (January, 1830), 293; anon., "History," p. 93; also anon., "History, Its Use and Meaning," p. 230.

ferred simply to adore God. Writing history was an act of worship. History supported the existence of God in the sense that "the pious man views a divine hand conducting the whole, gives thanks, adores and loves." [38]

History also upheld the virtue of patriotism. It was the purpose of history to prove the greatness of the nation, to demonstrate the blessings of American liberty, and to impart a love of country. While teachers tended to emphasize virtue as the most important principle and critics often emphasized religion, historians generally believed that instilling patriotism was their most important social function. Teaching love of country fit the assumption of progress and was a specific way of demonstrating divine guidance. When the historian selected facts and their explanations to honor the nation he was only glorifying illustrious things. He was using an absolute standard to guarantee that his facts were relevant and true, and he was performing the public service of strengthening society.

Teaching patriotism was largely a matter of making American history known so that its greatness would be apparent. "Doubtless there were bad men in America, and those of great virtue in England," noted one historian frankly, "yet, as nations, how great is the disparity in the characters deliniated." [39] "A more intimate knowledge" of American history, said Timothy Pitkin, "would tend to increase the veneration of the citizens of the United States for their institutions, and induce them, with firmer purpose, to adhere to the great charter of the union." [40] Men of all sections of the country agreed that "there is a certain grandeur about everything American," and that knowledge of it caused men "to do and suffer whatever their Country's good may require." [41] One historian, a biographer of Napoleon, recognized

[38] Benjamin Trumbull, *A Complete History of Connecticut . . . to the Year 1764* (2 vols.; New Haven, 1818), I, 5; also, Hawks, *Tale of the Huguenots,* p. vi.

[39] Willard, *History of the United States,* p. vi.

[40] Timothy Pitkin, *A Political and Civil History of the United States* (2 vols.; New Haven, 1828), I, 3.

[41] Review, *Southern Quarterly Review,* IX (April, 1846), 362; David Ramsay, *Life of George Washington* (Baltimore, 1814), p. iii; also Hale, *History of the*

that nationalism often led to militarism, but he embraced that also. "I *desire* to foster that spirit," he said. War stimulated "the most glorious genius and deeds of man" and was a balance to materialism. "We need not fear stimulating too much the love of glory in this age of dollars and cents." [42]

Although patriotism was supposed to strengthen society, it was not the purpose of history to teach citizenship. History inspired love of the nation, but it did not serve as a guide to the voter or statesman except insofar as patriotism and virtue were guides.[43] The good historian restricted himself to general principles; he taught love of God but not theology, virtue but not how to serve on a jury, patriotism but not how to vote. History supported philosophical principles but did not teach the rights and duties of citizens in a republic. Here was where a later age sought to be more practical by transforming history into civics and social studies.

Most historians agreed that the one distinctive element in America's greatness was liberty. This was considered almost important enough to be studied as a separate principle. George Bancroft believed that love of liberty and love of nation were inseparable and that his purpose was to glorify the two together.[44] Samuel Eliot felt that his four-volume *History of Liberty*, which did not get beyond the Middle Ages, was the first chapter of

United States, p. 5; Whelpley, *Compend of History*, p. viii; Jesse Olney and John Warner Barber, *The Family Book of History* (Philadelphia, 1839), p. 5; Tytler, *Elements of General History*, p. 11; S. G. Goodrich, *Pictorial History of the United States*, p. iv; Willard, *History of the United States*, p. v; Michigan, *Report of the Superintendent of Public Instruction* (Detroit, 1837), pp. 16–17; Haywood, *Tennessee*, p. iii; John Van Lean McMahon, *An Historical View of the Government of Maryland* (Baltimore, 1831), p. v.

[42] Joel Tyler Headley, *Life of Oliver Cromwell* (New York, 1848), p. xii; Joel Tyler Headley, *Napoleon and His Marshals* (2 vols.; New York, 1847), I, iv–vi.

[43] See, Olney and Barber, *Family Book of History*, p. 5; Whelpley, *Compend of History*, pp. 161–63; Willard, *History of the United States*, p. v; Tytler, *Elements of General History*, p. 11; David S. Bozart, "The Importance and Utility of History," *American Museum*, II (February, 1792), 45.

[44] Bancroft, *History of the United States*, I, vii; Russel B. Nye, *George Bancroft: Brahmin Rebel* (New York, 1945), p. 99.

American history and was designed to teach patriotism.[45] Similarly, John Lothrop Motley declared that a major purpose of his history of the Netherlands was teaching Americans to love liberty. "If two people in the world," he said, "hate despotism a little more and love civil and religious liberty a little better in consequence of what I have written, I shall be satisfied." [46] Abolitionists and secessionists could both agree.

Occasionally men proclaimed that the purpose of history was to propagate the cause of liberty in the world beyond the United States. "Our fine institutions, by having their foundations laid open to the world," said Peter Force, "will recommend themselves, more and more . . . to the affection and imitation of mankind." [47] George Ticknor proclaimed his purpose "to enable the people of the world to decide on the competency of the American people for self-government, and on the merits of their confederate republic." [48]

The early nineteenth-century faith in history as support for social values lasted as long as men were in basic agreement about what those values were. This faith collapsed when history seemed to support contradictory truths. Critics knew that the use of history to support partisan political principles threatened the credibility of all history, and they were unfriendly toward historians who ventured beyond consensus values. History proved principles, not arguments. Unless a principle was already certain the facts did not illustrate it; the facts themselves became suspect. Most historians were reasonably successful in keeping their politics out of their history. Not until the 1850's did Bancroft,

---

[45] Samuel Eliot, *History of Liberty* (4 vols.; Boston, 1853), I, v.

[46] John Lothrop Motley, *The Rise of the Dutch Republic* (3 vols.; New York, 1856), I, vi; also William Charvat and Michael Kraus, *William Hickling Prescott* (New York, 1943), pp. xlvi–xlvii; Jabez Delano Hammond, *The History of Political Parties in the State of New York* (2 vols.; Cooperstown, N.Y., 1884), I, v; reviews, *North American Review*, LXXXVIII (April, 1859), 474; LXXIII (October, 1851), 446; XXXIX (July, 1834), 50; Willard, *Universal History*, 6; Hale, *History of the United States*, p. 5; C. A. Goodrich, *History of the United States*, p. 6; Tytler, *Elements of General History*, p. 11.

[47] Peter Force, *American Archives* (9 vols.; Washington, 1837–53), I, xv.

[48] George Tucker, *History of the United States* (4 vols.; Philadelphia, 1856–57), I, iii.

Tucker, and Hildreth allow personal opinions to color their writing conspicuously. When principles and arguments became confused, history could no longer claim to be philosophy teaching by example.

Memorializing the Worthy

Local antiquarians liked to justify history as a memorial to departed worthies. In one sense this was a way of saying that history supported principles, for the worthy were by definition men of virtue, religion, and patriotism. This sort of justification underlined the perils of using history for purposes external to itself, for these memorials were usually panegyrics that were seldom entirely true.

Compilers and historians may have been seeking their own immortality by demanding that history venerate their progenitors. Antiquarians sometimes maintained that it was their duty to preserve every deed of every man for future reverence. Valiantly they promised "to rescue from oblivion," "to deliver from the dust of the ages," "to rescue from the obliteration of time." [49] The facts, then, would "serve as a proud monument," would "gain the gratitude of the rising generations," and bygone heroism would be "embalmed in the memory of children." [50] Peter Force dedicated his twelve-volume *American Archives* to the founding fathers and declared that his purpose was to make "a tribute of gratitude to their memory." [51] The eulogizers were doubtless sincere when they boasted that their work was "a labor of love."

[49] Henry Onderdonk, *Documents and Letters . . . of Queens County* (New York, 1846), p. 5; Isaac William Stuart, *The Life of Jonathan Trumbull . . .* (Boston, 1859), p. iii; Haywood, *Tennessee*, p. iii.

[50] James Thatcher, *A Military Journal during the American Revolutionary War* (Boston, 1823), pp. iii–iv; Josiah Quincy, *The History of Harvard University* (2 vols.; Cambridge, Mass., 1840), I, ix; Richard Frothingham, *History of the Siege of Boston . . .* (Boston, 1850), p. iv; John Wesley Monette, *History of the . . . Valley of the Mississippi* (2 vols., New York, 1846), I. v; Haywood, *Tennessee*, p. iii; Robert Mills, *Statistics of South Carolina* (Charleston, 1826), p. 262; Washington Irving, *Works of Washington Irving* (27 vols.; Geoffrey Crayon edition; New York, 1880–82), IX, 7–8; Sprague, *Annals of the American Pulpit*, I, vi.

[51] Force, *American Archives*, I, xiv.

Whether or not they admitted to a desire to be so remembered themselves, they could agree that veneration of ancestors was, in Romantic terminology, "one of the universal human emotions." [52] Although commemorating ancestors was avowedly a service to society, it seemed to satisfy personal needs as well.

Memorializers frequently admitted that they exaggerated the qualities of their subjects in order to promote virtue and inspire emulation. History had more elevated aims than telling the truth. The author of a nine-volume set of biographical sketches boasted that he had scrupulously suppressed defects and built only upon the morality of his subjects so that they might inspire virtue.[53] Others noted that the purpose of such works was to memorialize that which was worthy. Mason Locke Weems defended the cherry tree myth by stating that he was first of all a teacher, that he was seeking the essence rather than the details of truth, and that the facts had to adjust themselves to the lessons he wished to teach.[54]

As panegyrics grew in number and hyperbole, Americans became increasingly skeptical of memorial volumes. "Indiscriminate eulogy," said Jared Sparks, "is seldom sincere, never true, contributing little to accurate history, or to the stock of valuable knowledge either of men or things." [55] Richard Hildreth observed that exaggeration bred skepticism and believed that the best memorial to men was "to tell their story exactly as it

[52] Humphrey Marshall, *History of Kentucky* (2 vols.; Frankfort, 1824), I, vii; James McSherry, *History of Maryland* (Baltimore, 1849), p. v; Alexander Young, *Chronicles of the Pilgrim Fathers* (Boston, 1841), p. x.

[53] Sprague, *Annals of American Pulpit*, I, vi.

[54] See, Edward Hayes O'Neill, *A History of American Biography, 1800–1935* (Philadelphia, 1935), pp. 20–24; Hugh Blair Grigsby, *Discourse on . . . Littleton Waller Tazewell* (Norfolk, 1860), p. 100; Headley, *Napoleon*, I, i–ii; Mills, *Statistics of South Carolina*, p. i; Quincy, *Harvard*, I, ix; McSherry, *Maryland*, p. v; John Russell Bartlett, *Records of the Colony of Rhode Island . . .* (10 vols.; Providence, 1856–1865), I, iii; John Hill Wheeler, *Historical Sketches of North Carolina . . .* (2 vols.; Philadelphia, 1851), I, xvii–xviii; John Francis Hamtrack Claiborne, *Life and Times of General Sam Dale* (New York, 1860), p. viii.

[55] Jared Sparks, *The Life of Gouverneur Morris . . .* (3 vols.; Boston, 1832), I, vi.

was." [56] James Parton noted that readers could identify more easily with a human being than a paragon; they should have "not a model to copy, but a specimen to study." [57]

History was a popular discipline in the early nineteenth century because it had such useful ends. Most of all, it served society by upholding basic principles and memorializing the worthy, and as long as men agreed on these principles and were duly inspired, these aims were secure. History not only provided men with the opportunity of serving society but yielded deeply personal pleasures as well.

[56] Richard Hildreth, *The History of the United States* . . . (6 vols.; New York, 1856), I, vii; also, William Dunlap, *History of . . . Design in the United States* (2 vols.; New York, 1834), I, iii–iv; Washington Irving, *Life of George Washington* (5 vols.; New York, 1856–59), I, vi.

[57] Parton, *Andrew Jackson*, I, xi; also, Oral Sumner Coad, *William Dunlap* (New York, 1917), pp. 245–49.

X

The Personal Uses of History

ALTHOUGH ill at ease with the idea that mere amusement was an aim of history, men of the early nineteenth century eagerly embraced history as a constructive, elevated kind of pleasure. Historians readily acknowledged that their immediate purpose was to create pleasure; and critics were forced to acknowledge that the primary reason for popular interest in the past was simply that people enjoyed it. Reviewers explained that at least history provided necessary intellectual refreshment, that it was superior to most other forms of amusement, and that historians served the cause of democracy when they made knowledge entertaining. Finally, critics tried to define the ingredients of pleasure in lofty terms of human needs—the need for vicarious experience, for truth, art, ideas, and emotional enrichment.

In Quest of Pleasure

The Romantic concept of history as personal pleasure was simultaneously an outgrowth of and a revolt against the flippant eighteenth-century notion of history as light amusement. Men of the Enlightenment, with their determinedly casual attitude toward things which they really took seriously, frequently justi-

fied history in terms of entertainment, of its use, in Oliver
Goldsmith's phrase, in providing "a winter evening's amusement."
For Goldsmith, "a moderate amount of history is sufficient for
the purposes of life." Actually, most eighteenth-century historians
were far more solemn, for behind the offhand wit of Montesquieu,
Voltaire, and Gibbon lay some of the most profound thought of
the age. By their own claims, however, they were chiefly enter-
tainers, writing for the delight of the story itself, for the excitement of discovering new facts, for the pleasure produced by
sparkling language. Their readers were appropriately amused.[1]

Such lighthearted claims rankled men of the Romantic era, however. For them life was real and earnest. "Beating human hearts
were never intended to be the subject of amused speculation,"
said a critic. Good historians must avoid "the painful levity and
sardonic smiles" which characterized Voltaire and Gibbon.[2] The
past was too serious "to be taken up as a pastime," said another.
"It must be *studied*, diligently conned over." [3] The purposes of
history were as important as the purposes of life itself. "Instead
of reading . . . under the impulse of a shallow curiosity, we
should read history with the utmost serious attention." [4] Still,
the serious Romantics made their peace with history as entertainment, especially if it served other functions as well.

Educators, particularly, liked to stress the value of history as
a refreshing interval between more vigorous academic pursuits.
History, said a textbook author, "furnishes *rational* amusement,
which, relieving the mind at intervals from the fatigues of more
serious occupations, invigorates and prepares it for fresh exer-

---

[1] Oliver Goldsmith, *Dr. Goldsmith's Roman History* (Philadelphia, 1795),
pp. 1–5; also, anon., "Directions on Reading History," *American Museum*,
III (February, 1788), 183–84; Carl Becker, *The Heavenly City of the Eighteenth Century Philosophers* (New Haven, 1932), ch. IV, "The Uses of Posterity."

[2] Review, *Christian Examiner*, XXIV (July, 1838), 358.

[3] Anon., "The Philosophy of History," *North American Review*, XXXIX
(July, 1834), 41.

[4] Anon., "The Aim of History," *Princeton Review*, XXIX (April, 1857), 234;
also, review, *North American Review*, XXIX (October, 1829), 305; anon., "The
Philosophy of History," *American Magazine of Knowledge*, III (October, 1836),
14–16.

tion." [5] A critic believed that study of the past was the least objectionable diversion "for those who must find pleasures by turning aside . . . for a while from the heartless bustle of life." [6] An educator put the matter more affirmatively. History was an invigorating diversion which improved men, rescuing them from "listless, lifeless, all-devouring stupidity, idleness, inaction, ease, thoughtlessness, ennui and inattention." [7]

The great debate over the questionable effects of reading fiction was at its peak in the early decades of the century, and moralists rallied behind history as a weapon against the novel. "History, considered merely as a source of amusement, has great advantages over novels and other romances," said one, because it "elevates the imagination," while fiction "debilitates the mind by inflaming the imagination." [8] It must be made to "substitute for the works of fiction," and "supercede the necessity of recurring to frivolous pursuits" like novels.[9]

By the 1830's Americans generally accepted both history and fiction, along with their avowed purpose of entertainment. While men of the eighteenth century were sometimes more serious than they appeared, men of the nineteenth were often less earnest than they claimed. Perhaps men are most honest with themselves when they acknowledge that they study history because they like it. Critics admitted that "The mass of people read history mainly to be amused." [10] Reviewers became bolder,

[5] Alexander Fraser Tytler, *Elements of General History, Ancient and Modern* (Concord, Mass., 1825), p. 11.

[6] Anon., "Ancient and Modern History," *North American Review*, XXVIII (April, 1829), 313.

[7] Samuel Whelpley, *Lectures on Ancient History* . . . (New York, 1816), pp. iv–v; also, anon., "The Philosophy of History," *North American Review*, XXXIX (July, 1834), 53; review, *North American Review*, XLVI (January, 1838), 235.

[8] Joseph Emerson Worcester, *Elements of History* . . . (Boston, 1848), p. 1; also Jesse Olney and J. W. Barber, *The Family Book of History* . . . (Philadelphia, 1839), p. 6.

[9] Lambert Lilly [Francis Lister Hawks], *The History of New England* (Boston, 1831), p 5; Tytler, *Elements of General History*, p. 11; also, anon., "Classical Education," *Portfolio*, I (June, 1813), 567; "Historical Romances," *Portfolio*, VI (October, 1811), 357.

[10] Review, *North American Review*, XXX (January, 1830), 1.

acknowledging with delight that history "is one of the greatest pleasures," "an inexhaustible store of pleasures," and even "the most sublime entertainment." [11] Perhaps the full acceptance of both history and fiction as entertainment came with Sir Walter Scott, who delighted all but the stuffiest moralists. Said a reviewer discussing Scott's use of the past:

> Scott has not addressed our profoundest faculties, nor advocated great principles of Truth and Duty, nor extended greatly the boundaries of knowledge, nor, consequently, much advanced the fortunes of men. But he has furnished the whole world with a great amount of innocent joy. His works have been a place of recreation, accessible to all men, and forever thronged.[12]

Historians, far more than critics or readers of history, admitted that their purpose was entertainment, their aim to please the reader. William H. Prescott wrote that as far as he was concerned the aim of history was to provide a well-told story.[13] Charles Gayarré believed there was no higher aim than pleasing "the multitude." [14] Similar claims came from sober writers like Timothy Pitkin, George Ticknor, John Lothrop Motley, and Richard Hildreth.[15] "As far as possible, please the imagination of the people," James Parton reminded himself.[16] From popular historical novelists to obscure antiquarians came the acknowledgment

[11] Anon., "The Importance of Historical Knowledge," *North Carolina University Magazine,* IX (September, 1859), 98; review, *North American Review,* XCI (October, 1860), 354; Preface, *Collections Historical and Miscellaneous and Monthly Literary Journal,* I (January, 1822), iv.

[12] Review, *Christian Examiner,* XXIV (July, 1838), 360.

[13] Cited in George Ticknor, *Life of William Hickling Prescott* (Boston, 1864), p. 177.

[14] Charles Etienne Gayarré, *Romance of the History of Louisiana* (New York, 1848), pp. 16–18.

[15] Timothy Pitkin, *A Political and Civil History of the United States . . .* (2 vols.; New Haven, 1828), I, 7; George Ticknor, *History of Spanish Literature* (3 vols.; New York, 1849), I, iii–x; John Lothrop Motley, *The Correspondence of John Lothrop Motley,* ed., George William Curtis (2 vols.; New York, 1889), I, 359–70; Martha Mary Pingle, *An American Utilitarian, Richard Hildreth as a Philosopher* (New York, 1948), 201–3.

[16] Cited in Milton Embick Flower, *James Parton: The Father of Modern Biography* (Durham, N.C., 1951), p. 200.

that their history, if not all history, had as its purpose the aim
"to please," "to entertain," "to provide amusement." [17]

Historians sought to share their own pleasure in the past with
the widest possible audience. Somehow entertainment was more
acceptable if it accompanied service of democracy. David Ramsay
lamented that historical knowledge "the food for the soul, should
be . . . confined to literary and professional men." He explained that the purpose of his work was to furnish "a general
view . . . intended for popular reading." [18] It became fashion-
able to condemn "prolix disquisitions . . . too scholastic to interest the masses," "too overlaid with details and disquisitions,
and matters uninteresting to the general reader." [19] History
could impart its delights "only when read by adequate numbers." [20] If the past provided entertainment for "the few," then
it was a service to extend it also to "the *general* reader." [21] Possibly the historians' desire to popularize their writings was related to the egalitarianism of the age; probably it was related
to a desire for profits or acclaim; it was certainly unlike the
professional snobbery of later historians.

Historians liked to say that history should be in every home,

[17] Nathaniel Hawthorne, *True Stories from History and Biography* (Bos-
ton, 1851), p. iv; Charles Elliott, *History of the Great Secession from the
Methodist Episcopal Church* . . . (Cincinnati, 1855), p. v; William Buell
Sprague, *Annals of the American Pulpit* (9 vols.; New York, 1857–69), I, vi;
James Peller Malcolm, *Anecdotes of the Manners and Customs of London
during the Eighteenth Century* (2 vols.; London, 1810), I, xxix; James Mc-
Sherry, *History of Maryland* . . . (Baltimore, 1849), p. v.

[18] David Ramsay, *Universal History Americanized* (12 vols.; Philadelphia,
1819), I, xix; David Ramsay, *History of the United States* . . . (3 vols.; Philadelphia, 1816–17), I, iii–iv.

[19] William Gilmore Simms, *The History of South Carolina* . . . (Charleston, 1840), p. iii; Hawthorne, *True Stories from History*, p. iii.

[20] Humphrey Marshall, *The History of Kentucky* (2 vols.; Frankfort, 1824),
I, iii.

[21] Gayarré, *Romance of Louisiana*, p. 16; Anna Ticknor, *Life, Letters, and
Journals of George Ticknor* (2 vols.; Boston, 1857), II, 253–54; also, McSherry,
Maryland, p. v; John Warner Barber, *Interesting Events in the History of
the United States* (New Haven, 1829), pp. iv–v; Washington Irving, *Mahomet
and His Successors* (2 vols.; New York, 1850), I, x; Samuel Eliot, *History of
Liberty* (4 vols.; Boston, 1853), I, 5.

a hearthside companion for the family. Said one writer, "it ought to be on the shelf of every cottage in the land," and another urged that books about the past "should find their way . . . into the retired farm house equally with the more accessible mansion." [22] Writers reminded themselves that many of their readers were women and children who would benefit from the exalted pleasures of reading history. "Always remember," James Parton advised, "that two-thirds of the people are women and children." [23] Established historians like David Ramsay, Francis Lister Hawks, James Kirke Paulding, and William Gilmore Simms wrote histories designed to amuse children.[24] Nathaniel Hawthorne believed that one of the most purposeful books he had ever written was his *True Stories from History,* designed simply to give pleasure to "the YOUNG." [25] Even literacy need be no requisite to the enjoyment of history. "The unlearned reader, if he did not stop to peruse the volume, at least . . . could derive gratification from the pictorial representation." [26]

Ingredients of Pleasure

While historians justified entertainment in terms of invigoration and service to democracy, they were also able to define the ingredients of pleasure to show that history provided an exalted type of entertainment. History offered entertainment by providing true facts, beautiful narrative, exciting ideas, and emotional warmth. It pleased men because it satisfied natural, deeply human yearnings. Such pleasures, when properly deliniated, seemed far more lofty than idle amusement or physical indulgence.

The surest way for a historian to provide entertainment was

[22] Samuel Green Arnold, *The Life of Patrick Henry of Virginia* (Auburn, N.Y., 1854), p. 14; Henry Howe, *Historical Collections of Ohio,* (Cincinnati, 1848), p. 3.

[23] Cited in Flower, *James Parton,* p. 200.

[24] David Ramsay, *Life of George Washington* . . . (Baltimore, 1840); Lambert Lilly [Francis Lister Hawks], *The History of the Western States* (Boston, 1835); James Kirke Paulding, *A Life of Washington* (2 vols.; New York, 1836), I, v–vi; Simms, *History of South Carolina,* p. iii.

[25] Hawthorne, *True Stories from History,* p. iii.

[26] Barber, *History of the United States,* p. v; also, Howe, *Historical Collections of Ohio,* p. 3.

to offer his readers a true account of what had happened in the past. The unique quality of history was its grounding in truth. At the basest level truth was simply equated with facts, and for many antiquarians, including many members of the historical societies, the pleasure of history lay in gathering detail. Love of facts may have often been an excuse for collecting things more than a genuine interest in history, but the two were inseparable. Editors justified documentary history and reviewers welcomed it "simply for the purpose of entertainment." [27] By the 1860's facts were beginning to lose their intrinsic interest and had to be justified on the basis of their contribution to a mosaic of ultimate truth. When details ceased to be entertaining simply because they were true, the Romantic concept of history was collapsing.

Men found pleasure not only in details but in full descriptions of past ages as well. Historians chose their subject matter primarily in terms of what was new and exciting. The pleasure of knowing something that had not been known before explained the vogue for medieval history and exotic sagas of China or Peru. Even more, delight in knowing explained the popularity of American history, one of the most unknown stories to be found in the early nineteenth century.

Mystery added fascination for both historians and readers. The first men to undertake comprehensive histories of the United States—Abiel Holmes, David Ramsay, George Bancroft, and Richard Hildreth—each justified their interest in the past and the value of their work on the basis of the enjoyment of uncovering a unique and true story.[28] Local historians likewise explained their delight in discovering truth and passing it on to an avid public. "No one else has ever told the story," said one excitedly; "the barest facts have not yet appeared," said another;

[27] Review, *North American Review*, LXXX (April, 1855), 390; Abiel Holmes, "American Antiquarian Society," *Portfolio*, V (May, 1815), 470.

[28] Abiel Holmes, *The Annals of America* (2 vols.; Cambridge, Mass., 1829), I, iii; Ramsay, *History of the United States*, I, iii–iv; George Bancroft, *History of the United States . . .* (10 vols.; Boston, 1834–75), I, v–vii; Richard Hildreth, *The History of the United States of America* (6 vols.; New York, 1856), I, ix.

the outline of events "has so long been the object of public wishes," said a third.[29] In short, history was entertaining because it was fresh and true.

Historians and critics explained further that learning of the past was pleasant because it fulfilled curiosity which was an almost physiological human need. "As man is the only animal which manifests the least curiosity to know what will be *hereafter*, so he is equally distinguished by the desire to know what passed before he came into the world," said a historian.[30] John Marshall believed that curiosity about the past was "implanted in every human bosom," and another writer called it "one of the most universal emotions of the human heart." [31] Although "historick curiosity" was natural, said Peter Force, "at no former period of the world has this characteristick been so strikingly manifested." [32]

The most obvious means by which a historian provided pleasure was through the art with which he told his story—the structure, style, language, and unity of his composition. Although art, like truth, was more often a method of writing than a means of giving pleasure, historians and critics knew that the pleasure

[29] Benjamin Trumbull, *A Complete History of Connecticut . . . to the Year 1764* (2 vols.; New Haven, 1818), I, 5; Samuel Prescott Hildreth, *Pioneer History: Being An Account of the First Exploration of the Ohio Valley . . .* (Cincinnati, 1848), pp. i–iii; James Parton, *Life of Andrew Jackson* (3 vols.; New York, 1860), I, vi; also John Wesley Monette, *History of the Discovery and Settlement of the Valley of the Mississippi* (2 vols.; New York, 1846), I, iii, vii; Jabez Delano Hammond, *The History of Political Parties in the State of New York* (2 vols.; Cooperstown, N.Y., 1844), I, iv; William Hickling Prescott, *Conquest of Mexico . . .* (3 vols.; Boston, 1843), I, v–vii.

[30] Benjamin Ferris, *A History of the Original Settlements of the Delaware* (Wilmington, 1846), p. iii.

[31] J. Marshall, *Washington*, I, iii; H. Marshall, *Kentucky*, I, vii.

[32] Peter Force, ed., *American Archives . . .* (9 vols.; Washington, 1837–53), I, xiv; also Ramsay, *Universal History*, I, 2; John Leeds Bozman, *A Sketch of the History of Maryland* (Baltimore, 1811), p. v; Hugh Williamson, *The History of North Carolina* (2 vols.; Philadelphia, 1812), I, xii; Simms, *History of South Carolina*, p. vii; also John Farmer, *A Genealogical Register of the First Settlers of New England* (Lancaster, Mass., 1829), p. iii; Samuel Williams, *The Natural and Civil History of Vermont* (2 vols.; Burlington, 1809), I, 5–8; David S. Bozart, "The Importance and Utility of History," *American Museum*, II (February, 1792), 44; Jared Sparks, "History," *American Museum of Science, Literature and Art*, II (March, 1839), 123.

and popularity of history depended on artful presentation. In no period have historians lavished so much of their attention to literary presentation, and no period has been so acclaimed by contemporaries or successors for the delight which their efforts produced. Whether considered as method or purpose, it was the age of literary history.

Still another way in which history provided pleasure was in offering men a vast field for ideas. Americans who were afraid of entertainment that was merely diversion could revel in an intellectual amusement which seemed to improve the mind. Eagerly, they embraced history as a field for speculation, full of provocative ideas, in which men could wander at leisure to reflect and theorize, as they chose. "What an ample field is here opened," said an observer, "in which the daring student may enter, and expatiate to his heart's content." [33] "A philosopher pursuing his speculations upon humanity can nowhere find richer materials for the construction of his theories," said another.[34] Critics believed that history was popular in America "primarily because it presents an almost illimitable field for speculation." [35] The past would "furnish the readers with ideas," and "provide data for a philosophical investigation of all the important questions relating to man." [36]

Exercising the mind, like fulfilling curiosity or enjoying beauty, was pleasurable because it was natural and natural because it was pleasurable. "The search for truth in history," said a writer, "is the purest and most elevated ingredient of human happiness." [37] Toying with ideas and meditating on the past was "exciting," and "naturally satisfying." [38] History was "the most

[33] Anon., "The Study of History," *Southern Quarterly Review,* X (July, 1846), 147.

[34] Review, *Blackwood's Magazine,* LXXIX (April, 1856), 421.

[35] Anon., "Historic Speculations," *Southern Literary Messenger,* VI (September, 1840), 606.

[36] Review, *North American Review,* XCI (October, 1860), 302; anon., "History," *Universalist and General Review,* I (April, 1844), 166; also, anon., "Impostures of History," *Portfolio,* I (May, 1816), 369.

[37] J. L. Reynolds, *The Man of Letters* (Richmond, 1849), p. 8.

[38] Reviews, *North American Review,* XCI (October, 1860), 354; *Edinburgh Review,* LXVIII (January, 1839), 378.

delightful of intellectual recreations" because it offered the
sublime "pleasure of the mind." [39]

The final, and far the most important ingredient of pleasure
was the emotional satisfaction of contemplating time and eternity. It was the purpose of history to produce this sense of wisdom, or sublimity, or melancholy, the most profound fulfillment
of which man was capable. Educators, especially, liked to claim
that history broadened and deepened man "with the experience
of the ages." It taught "the folly of human ambition" and thus
provided "a due sense of things temporal and things eternal." [40]

The emotional thrill which history provided was closely akin
to Romantic self-indulgence in tears and melancholy. Men wandered in graveyards and gloried in ruins. Poets sighed beneath
broken columns and weeping willows, recited elegies at twilight,
wept for bygone grandeur, and spoke of footsteps in the sands
of time. Although metaphysicians found reality in the melancholy contemplation of eternity, most men simply felt fulfillment
and pleasure rather than tried to understand it. Men became
intoxicated with the sweetness of history said one writer, because
"it fills the mind with a sublime and pleasing melancholy. We
dwell with deep and tender emotions of the actions, sufferings,
and changes of those who were 'bone of our bones, and flesh of
our flesh.' " [41] Another writer believed history was attractive because "it affords a melancholy view of human nature. . . . It
furnishes us with the wisdom and experience of our ancestors
[and] has a tendency to render us contented with the condition
in life, by . . . teaching us that the highest stations are not
exempt from severe trials; that riches and power afford no

[39] Anon., "The Causes of the American Revolution," *North American Re-
view*, LXXX (April, 1855), 390; Giles F. Yates, "Ancient History," *American
Literary Magazine*, I (December, 1847), 365; also James Anthony Froude, "The
Science of History," *Hours at Home*, II (February, 1866), 323.

[40] Samuel Whelpley, *A Compend of History From the Earliest Times* . . .
(Burlington, Vt., 1808), pp. 159–61; also Barber, *History of the United States*,
p. iii.

[41] Royal Robbins, *Outlines of Ancient and Modern History* (Hartford, 1839),
p. 7.

assurances of happiness." [42] For the student "calmly seated in the shade of contemplation," history will "at once expand and enrich the soul, which feels a mournful but sublime pleasure in tracing the vestiges of exalted virtue." [43]

Although entertainment was an immediate goal of history, it was hardly a very precise one. To differentiate history from "mere amusement," nineteenth-century writers justified entertainment in terms of relaxation, democratic service, and fulfillment of natural impulses; they defined pleasure in terms of man's need for truth, art, ideas, and emotional enrichment. They never really succeeded in separating entertainment from motive and method, however, or from history's larger purposes of supporting convictions and communing with reality. Men's eagerness to be precise about purposes revealed their certainty in its utility. Their inability to separate its elements revealed the basic unity of the idea of history.

[42] Worcester, *Elements of History*, 2–3.
[43] Whelpley, *Compend of History*, p. 161; also Washington Irving, *The Sketch-Book* (New York, 1819), p. 3.

XI

History as Ultimate Reality

T HE most exalted purpose of history in the early nineteenth
century involved a fundamental probing into the reality of
life and a resulting enrichment of the soul. History was a means
of communing with ultimate truth through an understanding of
the past in the way that an artist communes with truth through
beauty or a holy man through faith. The purpose of history at
this level was to reveal far more than the events of the past; it
was to impart a mysterious knowledge of the meaning of life.
History could provide a transcendental unification of man with
eternity. The kind of history which provided the bridge from the
present to eternity was more art than philosophy, for it led men
by means of inspiration and emotion more than by reason. The
historian seeking ultimate truths was more poet than scientist or
philosopher.

The metaphysical argument for history especially interested
those poets, philosophers, and critics who were consciously
seeking a purpose for history and consciously relating the study
of the past to prevailing intellectual currents. Historians, teachers, members of historical societies, and even day-to-day browsers
in historical literature were generally content with the more immediate aims of gaining support for their convictions and enjoying a good story in the process. Even self-conscious Transcen-

dentalists like George Bancroft stopped short of claiming nearness
to heaven. Others soared on, however, especially during the middle decades of the century, to make communion with reality the
highest goal of history. More than a justification of studying the
past, unification with ultimate truth became the meaning as well
as the purpose of history, the very essence of Romantic history.
William Cullen Bryant, one of the high priests of American Romanticism, spent his life repeating the theme:

> A mighty Hand, from an exhaustless Urn,
> Pours forth the never-ending Flood of Years
> Among the nations. How the rushing waves
> Bear all before them! On their foremost edge,
> And there alone, is Life.[1]

One of the most comprehensive expressions of history as ultimate reality came from the essayist-philosopher Ralph Waldo
Emerson. To Emerson, "History rather than nature"—certainly
more than science or art—supplied "the best expositor of the divine mind." His essay, "History," originally delivered before the
Massachusetts Historical Society in 1836, was the leading essay in
his famous *Collected Essays* and the starting point for his Transcendental philosophy.[2]

His approach to history had three steps. First, he began with
the assumption, "There is one mind common to all individual
men." Each individual was a part of ultimate reality. Second,
said Emerson, the unfolding of the past was the concrete expression of the universal mind. "Of the works of this mind history
is the record." Nothing could be more complete than all that
had ever been. Here was the most complete expression of
ultimate reality, or God; and the historian was the one best
qualified to comprehend it. Finally, said Emerson, by understanding history one understands the universal mind, the meaning of life, one's total self. "Man is explicable by nothing less
than all his history." When one understands history he under-

---

[1] William Cullen Bryant, "The Flood of Years," 1876.
[2] Ralph Waldo Emerson, *The Essays of Ralph Waldo Emerson* [originally
published 1841], (Modern Library edition; New York, 1944).

stands himself; when he has come to understand history fully he has become one with the mind of God.

Emerson went to considerable lengths to show how all history existed in each man and how knowledge of the past led to self-knowledge. "The whole of history is in one man," he wrote, "there is no age or state of society or mode of action in history to which there is not something corresponding in his life." All men combine in themselves something of the Greek and something of the Gothic, something of the slave and something of the king. History teaches us this part of ourselves, this part of the universal mind. History is more than vicarious experience, for it is more than facts and entertaining stories; instead it is understanding and becoming one with past experience. "All inquiry into antiquity . . . is the desire to do away with this . . . preposterous There or Then, and introduce in its place the Here and Now." The reward is wisdom. "You shall not tell me by languages and titles a catalogue of the volumes you have read. You shall make me feel what periods you have lived." Here was history at its most sublime.[3]

History as ultimate reality was firmly grounded in European Romantic idealism, in the writing of Johann Herder in the 1780's, and in the discourses of Immanuel Kant, Johann Fichte, and Georg Wilhelm Hegel soon after. By the 1820's this German metaphysics, filtered through American Transcendentalism and Unitarianism, was fairly common in American reviews and journals.[4] A decade before Emerson's essay appeared, an anonymous American critic declared that it was the purpose of history to provide a mirror to life, allowing men to see themselves "in the silent workings and simple unfolding of the [universal] mind. . . . All the deeds and transactions of men are but expressions of this mind." In history, as in art, man sees himself. Seeing himself, he understands the past. History "cannot be understood except by self-observation, by discovering in ourselves the powers and

[3] *Ibid.*, pp. 3–25.
[4] Robert Flint, *The Philosophy of History in France and Germany* (Edinburgh, 1874), especially pp. 388–93, 457, 513; R. G. Collingwood, *The Idea of History* (Oxford, 1961), pp. 86–122.

tendencies of which history shows us the result." [5] Said another writer:

> History is the visible image of the aggregate mind of the whole human race, of which the individual is the epitome, presenting to the eye of the philosopher, on a large scale, and in well-defined, material, visible form those facts which lie concealed as mere abstractions within the bosom of human nature.[6]

This metaphysical justification of history stemmed from the assumption that the universe operated according to divine plan, and, in turn, provided the most substantial base for a providential interpretation of history. "God is the Eternal Mind," said a writer, and "a true knowledge of history is a true knowledge of God." [7] The unfolding of the past illustrated his existence and taught his lessons. History was the most important form of human knowledge, said another writer, because it was the historian's function "to trace the *mind* of God in the historic life of man." [8] George Bancroft, quoting directly from Kant and Fichte, went further than Emerson in defining history so that it became the base of a providential interpretation. While Emerson found the proof of the divine in intimations of the soul and then went on to identify the divine with history, Bancroft found his proof of God directly in the unfolding of the past.[9]

Some writers preferred to think of history as a study of life instead of a study of God; they preferred to think of the historian as an artist who depicts nature instead of a philosopher-

---

[5] Anon., "History," *American Quarterly Review*, V (March, 1829), 97–98; also anon., "The Aim of History," *Princeton Review*, XXIX (April, 1857), 234.

[6] C. C. S. Farrar, "The Science of History," *DeBow's Review*, V (March, 1848), 217; also anon., "The Study of History," *Southern Quarterly Review*, X (July, 1846), 131–32; review, *North American Review*, XL (January, 1834), 117–20.

[7] William Greenough Thayer Shedd, "The Nature and Influence of the Historic Spirit," *Bibliotheca Sacra*, XI (April, 1834), 371–75, 351; also, review, *North American Review*, XL (January, 1835), 101.

[8] Anon., "Leading Theories of the Philosophy of History," *North American Review*, XCIII (July, 1862), 167 and *passim;* also, anon., "The Mutual Relation of History and Religion," *Eclectic Magazine*, XLI (June, 1857), 158–68.

[9] Russel B. Nye, *George Bancroft: Brahmin Rebel* (New York, 1945), pp. 101–2.

theologian reaching for revelation. Although, like Thucydides, eighteenth-century historians thought of history as a study of unchanging human nature, the Romantics reached deeper into the essence of life. History was a study of man rather than of the behavior of men, a study of the human experience rather than of individual situations. As the artist distilled human experience into his creation, so did the historian.

Critics measured historians by their success in reaching this inner reality of life. "Life to the historian, if he deserves the name, wears the same aspect as it wears to the dramatic poet," explained one observer. "To both alike it is a study not of institutions, not of progress . . . but of personal character in conflict with the circumstances of life." Written history, like a painting or a poem, was "a distillation of nature." [10] A critic condemned Richard Hildreth for falling short of the ideal. "History finds its chief use," he noted, when it goes beyond facts "to the portrayal of . . . the realities of life." [11] Other critics called upon the historian to provide "the science of human nature," "the knowledge of human nature," "the larger views of human nature," "the anatomy of the human heart." [12]

Although historians tended to shy away from the grand claims for the past which critics proclaimed, the subjects they undertook and their treatment of these subjects usually revealed their concern with individual rather than social questions in the past. Men were far more likely to take up history from an interest in religion or philosophy than from an interest in public affairs. Even when historians like George Bancroft, Richard Hildreth, or

[10] Anon., "History, Its Use and Meaning," *Westminster Review*, XLII (October, 1854), 224; also, review, *North American Review*, XL (January, 1835), 117.

[11] G. H. E., "Hildreth's History of the United States," *Universalist Quarterly and General Review*, XII (October, 1855), 349.

[12] Anon., "The Philosophy of History," *North American Review*, XXXIX (July, 1834), 37; Giles F. Yates, "Ancient History," *American Literary Magazine*, I (December, 1847), 366; review, *North American Review*, XXXIX (July, 1834), 207; also, anon., "History and Its Philosophy," *Putnam's Monthly Magazine*, XI (April, 1868), 409; anon., "History," *American Quarterly Review*, I (March, 1829), 97; David S. Bozart, "The Importance and Utility of History," *American Museum*, II (February, 1792), 44.

Jared Sparks became involved in public questions such as Jacksonian politics or abolition, their interest was primarily auxiliary rather than inherent in their history. Instead, they were more often concerned with personal questions—the nature of God, the definition of morality or character or virtue, the meaning of change and decay, the opportunity for esthetic and emotional enrichment—questions which concerned the individual rather than society. To most historians, study of the past was a humanity rather than a social science, a means of self-expression and a search for values and verities.

Especially in England, critics occasionally quoted John Keats about the identity of truth and beauty in order to show that the study of the past was involvement in the essence of beauty. The past itself was beautiful in its harmony and completeness; the historian was involved in beauty when he composed a beautiful story; the reader, in turn, became immersed in the beauty of the historian's art.[13] Because of history's nearness to ultimate beauty, said a critic, "no art was ever attempted by man more elevated and ennobling." [14] The purpose of studying the past was to provide esthetic enrichment and communion with beauty. In all primitive societies, said one writer, "history was not distinguished from poetry and religion, but all were one, so, in its true form, it returns into them again." [15]

The poet did not commune with ultimate reality through the use of good grammar, and the historian could not expect to reach these heights by prosaic scholarship alone. Truth, to the Romantic, lay in the heart, to be brought forth by inspiration as well as investigation. For that reason, historians had eagerly acclaimed passion as a valuable method in finding the truth of the past. If great results were to come from history they must come

[13] Anon., "The Modern Art and Science of History," *Westminster Review*, XXXVIII (October, 1842), 369; review, *North American Review*, XL (January, 1835), 117; anon., "History and Its Philosophy," p. 407; also John Hill, "An Essay upon the Principles of Historical Composition," *Portfolio*, IX (April, 1820), 339.

[14] Anon., "The Historical Romance," *Blackwood's Edinburgh Magazine*, LVIII (September, 1845), 347.

[15] Anon., "History, Its Use and Meaning," *Westminster Review*, LXII (October, 1854), 234.

from emotion, and the Romantic was neither afraid of great results nor frightened by the voices of inspiration. History was more than a science of facts; it was grand art.

The idealist has always believed that intuition was the voice of God speaking to man, and that ultimate truths inaccessible to reason were accessible through inspiration. "On the most solemn themes the heart is wiser than the head," said a reviewer. In history, as in the other arts, "not the intellect but the soul must decide; for the soul lies near to God; in faith and prayer it receives communication from Him which it cannot distrust." [16] Historians have "not merely the senses opening to us the eternal," said Bancroft, "but an internal sense, which places us in connection with the world of intelligence and the decrees of God." [17] Emerson believed that the historian must "perceive" rather than discover truth since the deepest truths lay "fast by the soul." [18] One critic, entranced by the thought that the historian perceived ultimate truths claimed that all "the eras of human greatness have not been eras of accurate knowledge of human things; they have been eras of idealism and imagination, of credulity and dreams." [19] As men moved from Romanticism to define the purpose of history, they also moved from a concept of history to formulate definitions of the Romanticism of their age.

Critics emphasized that written history was a conduit through which the author's genius flowed; its purpose was to allow his readers to savor his divinely inspired insights. "The historian, like the poet, is not made, but born with an aptitude" for grasping truth "by inspiration and genius." [20] "Historical truth is discerned by the insight of genius . . . without any blending, or at least any show of the process of reflection, analysis, and critical judgment." [21] History was "a monument of genius," "a poetic

[16] Anon., "Hegel's Philosophy of History," *Eclectic Magazine*, XLV (September, 1858), 15.

[17] George Bancroft, *Literary and Historical Miscellanies* (New York, 1855), p. 409; also, review, *North American Review*, XL (January, 1835), 102.

[18] Emerson, *Essays*, p. 21.

[19] Anon., "History, Its Use and Meaning," p. 229.

[20] Review, *North American Review*, XL (April, 1845), 369; also, anon., "Mutual Relation of History and Religion," p. 167.

[21] Anon., "History and Its Philosophy," p. 407.

inspiration," "an attribute of the heart," a display of "the emotions and passions of the individual." [22]

History as communion with ultimates did not require total commitment or total submergence in the divine will; for most men it was enough to say that the past enriched one emotionally. Its purpose, like the purposes of art and religion, was to provide the sense of well-being that comes from communion with truth and beauty. Reviewers found hundreds of ways to explain that the purpose of history was "to move the heart . . . as in a tragedy, a painting, or an epic poem"; "to warm the soul and melt the feelings"; "to arouse the sympathetic passions and awaken generous feelings"; "to elevate and purify"; "to expand the heart . . . enlarge the sympathies . . . and make the soul more keenly sensitive"; to make man's "spirit wiser, purer, happier" and to thus fit him "for a higher and holier state of being"; to nurture "those emotional links of sympathy by which the members of the family of mankind are connected with one another." [23] History provided vicarious experience, the sense of the richness of having lived. It allowed every man to be his own Romantic hero, like Lord Byron, who boasted of having lived a hundred years at the age of twenty-one.

Finally, emotional enrichment led to wisdom. It was the purpose of history to contribute to the qualities which the wise man was supposed to possess—a philosophical spirit, sagacious

[22] Review, *New York Quarterly*, II (January, 1853), 43; anon., "The Leading Theories of the Philosophy of History," *North American Review*, XCIII (July, 1862), 188; Hill, "Historical Composition," p. 346; review, *North American Review*, XL (January, 1833), 100; also, Prospectus, *American Review of History and Politics*, I (January, 1811), ii; anon., "Buckle's History of Civilization," *North American Review*, XCIII (October, 1861), 519; anon., "The Uses of History to the Preacher," *New Englander*, XXII (July, 1863), 426; review, *American Quarterly Review*, III (March, 1828), 174.

[23] Anon., "Guizot and the Philosophy of History," *Eclectic Magazine*, IV (February, 1845), 184; G. H. E., "Hildreth's History of the United States," p. 346; anon., "The Historical Romance," pp. 343, 348; Yates, "Ancient History," p. 366; anon., "Uses of History to the Preacher," p. 425, 426; L. J. B. C., "History," *Universalist Quarterly and General Review*, I (April, 1844), 165; anon., "History, Its Use and Meaning," p. 224; also, Willie, "The Use of Imagination in the Study of History," *North Carolina University Magazine*, IX (May, 1860), 557.

understanding, a sense of eternity, a love of mankind, a sense of virtue, and a sense of sadness. Its purpose, said one writer, was to enrich "the spirit of philosophy, the spirit of virtue, wisdom and loveliness." [24] "There is something in the pictures of generations before us . . . which, going beyond the gratification of curiosity, or storing the mind with ideas, teaches us wisdom." [25] Soaring concepts led to lyric expression: "Like art, like poetry, like religion itself, [history] finds its highest use not in teaching what is good or bad . . . not in proving what good is successful . . . but in touching the heart to noble emotions; not in making us know what is good, but love what is good." [26] Romantics suspected that wisdom and sadness were related. History contributed to wisdom because it taught "the essential nothingness of all the world calls great." [27] History books were the most direct route to wisdom because they were "the saddest books in the world." [28]

When men thought of the purpose of history in terms of entertainment, in terms of supporting principles, or in terms of reality, emotional enrichment, and wisdom, they were saying in different ways that it fulfilled a deep human need. In the early nineteenth century the importance, the subject matter, the methods, interpretations, meaning, and purposes of history each possessed a coherence which men could comprehend and appreciate. This coherence was the strength of the idea of history and also its weakness. When one part of the chain was broken the entire approach and justification for history was threatened.

To a later generation already making itself heard by 1860, the

[24] Henry Laurens Pinckney, *The Spirit of the Age* (Raleigh, 1836), p. 23.

[25] Royal Robbins, *Outlines of Ancient and Modern History* (Hartford, 1839), p. 7; also John Barber, *Interesting Events in the History of the United States* (New York, 1829), p. iii.

[26] Anon., "History, Its Use and Meaning," pp. 233–34.

[27] Pinckney, *Spirit of the Age,* 23; also, anon., "The Importance of Historical Knowledge," *North Carolina University Magazine,* IX (September, 1859), 98–99; anon., "Hegel's Philosophy of History," p. 15; review, *North American Review,* XLVI (January, 1838), 277; Shedd, "Nature and Influence of the Historic Spirit," p. 352; review, *North American Review,* LXXXVIII (April, 1859), 463.

[28] Review, *North American Review,* LXX (April, 1850), 266; also, anon., "History," *American Quarterly Review,* I (March, 1829), 98; anon., "Uses of History to the Preacher," p. 427.

metaphysical purposes of history were too grand to be realistic, too vague to be scientific. In the Romantic age, history, like art and poetry, was more real than reality, more trustworthy than science. It was a noble definition of history; but then history was a noble subject.

XII

The Decline of Romantic History

Aʙᴏᴜᴛ the middle of the century the Romantic idea of history reached its peak and began to wane. Since the 1840's the amount of history in popular literature had been declining, and during the 1850's the development of historical societies, the growth in the number of history courses in the schools, and the publication of documents and historical journals reached a plateau. Most of all, the early nineteenth-century historians, self-consciously aware by the 1850's that they constituted a distinct school, realized that they were under attack. Accepted standards of historical writing—the methods, interpretations, and aims that had developed over the past half-century—were on the defensive.

During the 1850's critics began to distinguish between the older generation and a newer one. The establishment included Bancroft, Force, Gayarré, Headley, Hildreth, Howe, Hawks, Irving, Lossing, Motley, Palfrey, Paulding, Prescott, Randall, Sabine, Shurtleff, Sparks, Ticknor, and Tucker, each of whom made his major contribution before the Civil War. These men were generally regarded as out of date when their works appeared after the war. The Americans were related to a similar European school which was also becoming dated. "Herder, Kant, Hegel, Guizot, Michelet, Cousin, and even Carlyle and Macaulay," said a disillusioned critic in 1852, "none of them give us genuine history, or even their own views of history; they merely give us their speculations about what history ought to be." [1] The appearance of an identifiable new group of writers, at least in Europe, confirmed the generation gap. Henry Thomas Buckle, Jacob Burckhardt, H. A. Taine, and especially Leopold von Ranke were generating the controversy and excitement that Scott and Irving had created a generation earlier. [2] In America critics recognized transitional figures, of course, men who were hailed before and after the war. These included Lyman C. Draper, James Parton, and Francis Parkman, but after the war most of them were making an effort to divorce themselves from the principles of the earlier period. [3] Particularly after the four-year hiatus in historical publication that came with the Civil War, the line dividing the generations appeared deeper to contemporaries than it in fact was.

Behind the change from Hegelian Romanticism to Ranke's empirical idealism were all of the ideas and forces boiling in the world of the mid-century—industrialization, democracy, professionalism, sectionalism, and others. Accompanying industrialization were materialism, the vogue of science, and the concomitant rise of critical realism in the arts, all of which threatened the Romantic faith that passion was a more truthful guide than observation and that men could reach beyond objective facts to intuitive truth. With the continuing growth of the democratic dogma, educators were now transforming history into civics and social studies. With increasing vocational specialization, the amateur historian who was concerned with truth yielded to the professional who was concerned with method. Antiquarian col-

---

[1] Review, *Brownson's Quarterly Review*, IX (October, 1852), 423.

[2] For example, reviews, *Museum of Foreign Literature, Science and Art*, XL (September, 1840), 35; *Living Age*, LVIII (September, 1858), 883–904; *North American Review*, XCIII (July, 1861), 99–107; *North American Review*, CII (January, 1866), 275–80; *North American Review*, CXVII (July, 1873), 223–29; *Living Age*, LXXIV (August, 1862), 160–62; *Atlantic*, XI (January, 1863), 27–42; *Nation*, XVI (April, 1873), 270–73.

[3] William B. Hesseltine, *Pioneer's Mission: The Story of Lyman C. Draper* (Madison, Wisc., 1954), p. 193 and *passim*; Howard Dougherty, *Francis Parkman* (New York, 1962), pp. 167, 338, 398.

lectors like Lyman Draper became professional archivists, finding in Ranke's empiricism a philosophical justification they had always lacked.[4]

The Problem of Contradiction

More demonstrably damaging to the early nineteenth-century concept of history were the new contradictions appearing in historical works. Often they were related to growing sectional hostility and they cast doubt on the basic assumption that history illustrated truth. The first important sectional outburst among historians came in 1847 when New England historian Lorenzo Sabine cast aspersion on Southern efforts in the Revolution, and Southern critics angrily replied that he had abused the facts. Senator Charles Sumner's citation from Sabine was part of the incendiary speech that led to Sumner's caning by Preston Brooks. Sectional feeling appeared in Richard Hildreth's six-volume *History of the United States* (1849–56) and George Tucker's four-volume *History of the United States* (1856–57). Hildreth was an abolitionist who disliked the Puritans, and Tucker was a slavery advocate who disliked nullification, so that, for the first time since the works of Thomas Hutchinson, almost every critic was bound to find both works biased. Sectional politicians began calling for schoolbooks by historians "loyal to our own institutions."[5] Not all of the new scholarly contention was sectional, however. Edmund Bailey O'Callaghan disputed Washington Irving's caustic treatment of the Dutch; Peter Oliver and John Wingate Thornton debated the virtues of the Puritans; and Richard Frothingham reopened old Federalist–Republican wounds by his treatment of the generalship at Bunker Hill. In the critical fervor surrounding each work the feeling grew that history itself was no longer reliable.[6]

[4] Draper, "Annual Report of the Wisconsin Historical Society," *Wisconsin Historical Collections*, V (1860), 2.

[5] Anon., "Southern School Books," *DeBow's Review*, XIII (September, 1852), 259.

[6] For a summary of these disputes, see David D. Van Tassel, *Recording America's Past: An Interpretation of the Development of Historical Studies in America, 1607–1884* (Chicago, 1960), pp. 123–25; 134–41.

Controversy was especially damaging to early nineteenth-century historical concepts because men had come to believe so firmly in the existence of absolute truth and definitive historical accounts. During the early decades of the century men witnessed such remarkable strides in the field of historical writing that perfection seemed the next logical step. Intuition as a means of capturing the past further guaranteed that truth was fixed, since intuition was the voice of God. Emerson maintained that men felt the truths of the past better than they knew them. Almost every critic who considered methodology acclaimed the historian's intuitive penetration of facts as a means of assuring that history would become "fixed like chemistry." [7] When critics and historians talked about the purpose of history they again expressed faith in absolutes. Since it was the purpose of history to illustrate a fixed truth, historical facts presumably could be set forth definitively. Of course, everything depended on agreement about fundamental principles. When contradictions appeared in historical accounts, not only did this indicate that the methods of research were faulty, but the aim of illustrating truth was faulty as well.

The most outspoken defender of absolute history was George Bancroft, a man who saw his historical writing outdated before it was complete. "They speak falsely who say truth is the daughter of time," he wrote. "It is the child of eternity, as old as the Divine mind. The perception of it takes place in the order of time; truth itself knows nothing of the succession of the ages." [8] At first critics considered Bancroft so perfect "as to supercede the necessity of any future work of the same kind." [9] John Adams

[7] "Editor's Table," *Harper's Magazine*, X (May, 1855), 835, cited in Van Tassel, *Recording America's Past*, p. 141.

[8] George Bancroft, *Literary and Historical Miscellanies* (New York, 1855), p. 404.

[9] Review, *North American Review*, XL (January, 1835), 99; also, reviews, *Eclectic Magazine*, XLI (May, 1857), 26; *Edinburgh Review*, CV (January, 1857), 24; anon., "Ancient and Modern History," *North American Review*, XXVIII (April, 1829), 332–33; anon., "The Uses of History to the Preacher," *New Englander*, XXII (July, 1863), 429; Giles F. Yates, "Ancient History," *American Literary Magazine*, I (December, 1847), 368; anon., "History of Our Own Times," *Eclectic Magazine*, IX (October, 1846), 165.

believed that the past could be set forth definitively for all time. Once a subject had been "done" it seemed "patently unnecessary to write it over again."[10] It took Washington Irving to see both the pervasiveness and the absurdity of the concept, having his Diedrich Knickerbocker label his *History of New York, the only authentic history of the times that ever hath been, or ever will be published.*[11]

The Problem of Law

At the same time that historical controversy was breaking down methods and aims, the public was yearning for the appearance of laws in history to explain the past and predict the future. Americans had long embraced grand interpretations of the past, and European positivists such as Auguste Comte and Henry Thomas Buckle insisted upon the existence of law in history. Enthusiasts were ready to believe that history could accomplish almost anything. Increasingly, the desire for fixed law became the supposition that it must exist, and critics called for historians to give up established methods and aims to look for it, like scientists.

The concept of scientific history was ahead of the reality. During the 1850's, well before most historians had embraced the methods of the positivists or the search for law, critics claimed that "no abstract question has of late years attracted greater attention than the inquiry whether history is or is not capable of being studied as a science."[12] Other observers noted that the question of law in history "has been rather a pet subject for a

[10] Benjamin Trumbull, *A Complete History of Connecticut . . . to the Year 1764* (2 vols.; New Haven, 1818), I, 7; also Henry Reed Stiles, *The History of Ancient Windsor, Connecticut . . .* (New York, 1859), p. vi; James Peller Malcolm, *Anecdotes of the Manners and Customs of London during the Eighteenth Century* (2 vols.; London, 1810), I, vii.

[11] Diedrich Knickerbocker [Washington Irving], *A History of New York . . .* in Washington Irving, *Works* (27 vols.; Geoffrey Crayon edition; New York, 1880–82), I, i.

[12] Anon., "The Study of History," *Cornhill Magazine*, III (June, 1861), 666; also Orestes Augustus Brownson, "Remarks on Universal History," *United States Magazine and Democratic Review*, XII (May, 1843), 458; E. D. Sanborn, "Partisanship in History," *Bibliotheca Sacra*, XVI (July, 1859), 603.

few years past"; "it has become as fruitful in controversy as
polemics or politics." [13] By 1857, said a reviewer, Buckle's *History
of Civilization* "was the book of the day. . . . It was admired,
criticised, discussed, assailed in every class-room here and in England. Ladies and gentlemen who had never mastered the annals
of a single country discovered 'historical laws.' Fanatical ad-
mirers fancied that Mr. Buckle had opened a new era in historical speculation, and timid opponents thought he had shaken
the basis of morals." [14] At least until the Civil War, however,
the antipositivists remained dominant. "Those who oppose the
notion that history can be treated as a science," said an observer,
"are on the popular side." [15] The first American scholar who
actually called himself a positivist and consciously tried to write
history according to its precepts was probably the New York
scientist-historian John William Draper, whose *Intellectual Development of Europe* appeared in 1863.[16]

As the new group rallied around the word "science," the old
school rallied around the word "art." During the 1850's, more
than at any time since the beginning of the century, historians
had the sense of belonging to a school and critics felt obliged
to pledge allegiance to one side or the other. Aware that an entire
concept of history was at stake, defenders formulated their best
definitions of what that concept was and was not. Eagerly, the
establishment set out to defend the proposition that history was
more than objectivity and less than law.

The most frequent defense centered around method: the

[13] Review, *North American Review*, LXXX (April, 1855), 392; Sanborn,
"Partisanship in History," p. 603; see also William T. Thornton, "History and
Its Scientific Pretensions," *Macmillian's Magazine*, VIII (May, 1863), 25; E. A.
Lawrence, "The Problem of History," *American Presbyterian Review*, XIX
(November, 1870), 478; anon., "Primary Laws of Political Development in
Civil History," *North American Review*, LXXXVIII (April, 1859), 388; C. C. S.
Farrar, "The Science of History," *DeBow's Review*, V (March, 1848), 216; also
anon., "The Leading Theories on the Philosophy of History," *North American
Review*, XCIII (July, 1862), 163.

[14] Review, *Nation*, XVI (April, 1873), 270.

[15] Anon., "Study of History," p. 666.

[16] Donald Fleming, *John William Draper and the Religion of Science* (Philadelphia, 1950), pp. 56–64, 74–94.

search for predictive law required objectivity, and objectivity was not sufficient for comprehending the past. The historian could not be objective, and even if he could, objectivity was not worth the sacrifice. "Giving up enthusiasm . . . we gain nothing in its place, for the temper has yet been wanting among us to regard facts with reverence." [17] Applying scientific methods to a study of man is a contradiction, for "man is essentially not subject to science." [18] "A science of history would imply an exact analysis . . . a logical separation of all the elements which are inseparably blended together. . . . In the history of human events . . . how are you going to comply with the rigorous demands which science implies?" [19] Historical truth came from inspiration. "Whenever history would teach lessons beyond what poetry teaches, it transcends its proper functions." [20] The historian could "no more ask for a theory of this or that period of history, than we should ask for a theory of Macbeth or Hamlet." [21]

A more subtle rejection of law in history came from Ralph Waldo Emerson. Since history was the mind of God—the totality of all that had happened and would happen in the universe—one could not hope to understand it until all history had occurred. History was infinite, and if man ever came to understand it, he would be outside of it, united with God. The most the historian could do, said Emerson, was to understand the past so completely that he understood its inevitability. Such understanding, however, provided no law and could not be predictive. "No man can antedate his experience." [22] Other writers claimed

[17] Anon., "History, Its Use and Meaning," *Westminster Review*, LXII (October, 1854), 230; also C. R., "Impostures of History," *Portfolio*, I (May, 1816), 369; anon., "Ancient and Modern History," p. 338.

[18] Anon., "Buckle's History of Civilization," *North American Review*, XCIII (October, 1861), 519–20.

[19] Anon., "History and Its Philosophy," *Putnam's Monthly Magazine*, XI (April, 1868), 409; also, C. R., "Impostures of History," p. 369.

[20] Anon., "History, Its Use and Meaning," p. 224; also, anon., "Primary Laws of Development," p. 388; anon., "History," *American Quarterly Review*, V (March, 1829), 95.

[21] James Anthony Froude, "The Science of History," *Hours At Home*, II (February, 1868), 329.

[22] Ralph Waldo Emerson, *The Essays of Ralph Waldo Emerson*, (Modern Library edition; New York, 1944), p. 24; also William Cooke Taylor, *A Man-*

that God had specifically forbidden to man the key to history and thus the knowledge of the future. While men might find patterns in the past—and indeed they had—he could never find law because "the historian can never predict the future." [23] Thomas Carlyle put it in more secular terms. Any historian who found law or useful lessons in the past, he said, would use his knowledge to rule the world.[24]

Another argument against law, and consequently against the scientific approach to history, appeared in a defense of free will against determinism. Immanuel Kant had made free will central to early nineteenth-century philosophy, and Americans were deeply committed to man's ability to control fate. The problem of law in history "is the old controversy of free will and necessity," critics noted.[25] If Buckle and the rest were correct in their proffered laws of history, "what does . . . human free will amount to? What in this case becomes of man's liberty?" [26] "If there is law, morality is overturned. Man has no power over his actions and is subject neither to praise nor blame; he is a helpless puppet, not an individual at all." [27] Defenders of history as art lined up in support of "individual character," "the free determination of man," "man's uniqueness and originality," "human choice." [28]

ual of Ancient History (New York, 1855), p. vi; Samuel Griswold Goodrich, Pictorial History of Ancient Rome (New York, 1850), p. vi; Emma Willard, Universal History in Perspective (New York, 1858), p. v; Alexander Fraser Tytler, Elements of General History (Concord, N.H., 1825), p. 11.

[23] Anon., "The Causes of History," New Englander, XXII (April, 1863), 157; anon., "History and Its Philosophy," p. 408, 415–16; also, anon., "Lectures on the History of France," North American Review, LXXV (July, 1852), 250; anon., "History," p. 93; review, Christian Examiner, XLIII (September, 1847), 261; anon., "The Study of History," Southern Quarterly Review, X (July, 1846), 144; anon., "The Philosophy of History," North American Review, XXXIX (July, 1834), 50.

[24] Anon., "The Dignity of History," Nation, IV (May, 1867), 417.

[25] Anon., "Study of History," p. 666.

[26] Anon., "History and Its Philosophy," p. 409; also, C. C. S. Farrar, "The Science of History," DeBow's Review, V (May, 1848), 450.

[27] Anon., "Study of History," p. 672.

[28] Anon., "History," pp. 93, 97; also, anon., "Philosophy of History," p. 50; anon., "Guizot and the Philosophy of History," Eclectic Magazine, IV (February, 1845), 181; anon., "Buckle's History of Civilization," p. 519.

The clinching argument against the scientific method and the search for law was that all the laws thus far suggested were hopelessly contradictory. Attempts to fit events into a comprehensive pattern had caused them "to be twisted and distorted a thousand ways." [29] "History swarms with . . . theorists." [30] To select one "out of a hundred equally probable hypotheses . . . commits all sorts of violence on common sense and history." [31] Explained one bewildered writer: "I have known, and now know, many historians; they are all honorable characters and are generally esteemed. . . . But they have . . . each attained a diametrically opposite result . . . and yet all conscientiously believe they have written the truth." [32]

Although the logic of the defenders of the old order may have been sound, the inadequacies of their interpretation of history remained, and for the first time in America some men were saying that history was bunk. Contradictions have been "fatal to the credibility of history," said a writer.[33] "History can tell us little of the past and nothing of the future." [34] Perhaps it would be better if the whole study were abandoned. "Leaving aside the matter of amusement, we do not know that the writer of history has been of any considerable service to his fellow creatures except as a collector and chronicler of fact." [35] Sadly, observers noted that "history is not the subject it once was. . . . The results of the past ten or fifteen years in historical investigation are exceedingly mortifying to any one who has been proud to call himself a student of history. . . . Our beloved dates, our easy explanations, and popular narration are half dissolved

[29] C. C. S. Farrar, "The Science of History," *DeBow's Review*, V (January, 1848), 60.

[30] Sanborn, "Partisanship in History," p. 621.

[31] Anon., "Providential and Prophetical Histories," *Edinburgh Review*, L (January, 1830), 293.

[32] Anon., "Thoughts on the Manner of Writing History," *Southern Literary Messenger*, III (February, 1837), 163; also, anon., "Hints upon History," *Eclectic Magazine*, XII (January, 1848), 92–100.

[33] Sanborn, "Partisanship in History," p. 649.

[34] Froude, "Science of History," p. 326.

[35] Anon., "Dignity of History," p. 417.

under the touch of modern investigation." [36] "From enthusiasm there is reaction into doubt," noted another observer. "That all history is contradictory, untrue and useless . . . is becoming more and more the latent conviction of many reflecting persons." [37]

Disillusionment with what history had so far accomplished only intensified the desire for something new. History had reached its unprecedented level of popularity because men believed it could explain life on earth, and it had succeeded in proportion to its boldness. Its failure, then, lay in timidity. While defenders of the old methods foresaw dangers in aspiring for more, the expectation of grander explanations was built into all that history had so far accomplished.

The success of early nineteenth-century historians in compiling quantities of information also pointed to the need for laws which would explain the data. "We want a principle to organize this huge chaos into significance and tell us what it means," the critics insisted.[38] "The materials of modern history are accumulating so rapidly." "The human mind wants to simplify history into a system." [39] If the old methods could not provide comprehensive explanations, perhaps other methods would. "History without a law is like a vast almanac of the ages, mere juxtaposition without connection." [40]

Clearly the desire for law was growing. "How urgent," said one critic, "is the necessity for arranging facts into a scientific classification whose teachings shall be as infallible as the teaching of any other of the positive sciences." [41] Even when they generally agreed that "no Newton has yet appeared," many were

[36] Anon., "American Antiquity," *Atlantic Monthly*, I (May, 1858), 769–770.

[37] Anon., "History, Its Use and Meaning," pp. 230, 223.

[38] Anon., "Hegel's Philosophy of History," *Eclectic Magazine*, XLV (September, 1858), 2.

[39] Review, *North American Review*, LXXX (January, 1855), 89; C. C. S. Farrar, "The Science of History," *DeBow's Review*, V (March, 1848), p. 216; also, anon., "Philosophy of History," p. 37.

[40] Anon., "Hegel's Philosophy of History," p. 2; also, anon., "Thoughts on Writing History," p. 157.

[41] C. C. S. Farrar, "The Science of History," *DeBow's Review*, V (March, 1848), 218.

coming to believe that the day was not far off.[42] It was only a matter of time until history would "reveal all the laws . . . and enable us . . . to predict the future." [43]

Scientific history excited men with the promise of the answers it might provide. Enthusiasts hailed it as "the greatest science that has yet blessed the world," the science which would not only explain "what has been . . . but with equal facility it foretells what is to be." [44] Men related the new history to the technology of the railroad and factory and felt immensely modern in championing its fresh approach. "The science of history . . . has only become possible in our own time." [45] New techniques promised "to do nothing less than lift history from its present humble condition, and erect it into a *pure science*." [46]

During the early nineteenth century men liked to say that the most profound understanding of history was the understanding of how events could not have been otherwise. Perhaps it was inevitable at the beginning of the century that revolutionary change and emerging nationalism brought with them a keen awareness of time. Perhaps it was inevitable that in an era of restless individualism men would soar beyond a cool rationalism to penetrate truth intuitively and seek support in history for all of their beliefs and desires. Perhaps too it was inevitable that this history would evolve into overblown rhetoric and contradiction and that in an age of science men would react to cultivate objectivity and search for law. When Romantic history emerged it was new and beautiful, and when it faded around the time of the Civil War it was out of date.

[42] Anon., "Philosophy of History," p. 37.

[43] Review, *North American Review*, LXXIII (October, 1851), 411.

[44] C. C. S. Farrar, "The Science of History," *DeBow's Review*, V (January, 1848), 61.

[45] Anon., "Hegel's Philosophy of History," pp. 1–2; also, anon., "Study of History," p. 25; Brownson, "Remarks on Universal History," p. 457; anon., "The Modern Art and Science of History," *Westminster Review*, XXXVIII (October, 1842), 344.

[46] C. C. S. Farrar, "The Science of History," *DeBow's Review*, V (January, 1848), 58.

Bibliographical Note

Since this whole book is about the history written and read in America from 1800 to 1860, a really complete bibliography would include all of the works published during the period; however that would be too formidable. Many times I have wished for a library such as must exist in some Latin country where the history books are simply arranged according to the date of publication. In part, I had to be guided by the list of 625 works published by the 145 historians of the period who are listed in Allen Johnson and Dumas Malone, eds., *Dictionary of American Biography* (22 vols.; New York, 1928–44). Frank Luther Mott, *Golden Multitudes: The Story of Best Sellers in the United States* (New York, 1947), provides a list of the most popular history books, and Agnew O. Roorbach, *The Development of the Social Studies in American Secondary Education Before 1861* (Philadelphia, 1937), provides the most complete list of history textbooks. James Westfall Thompson, *A History of Historical Writing* (2 vols., New York, 1942), lists the most important European historical works of the period, and the Library of Congress catalogues provide a fair index to the availability of American editions of these works. Government-supported historical publications are most easily identified in Benjamin Pearley Poore, *Descriptive Catalogue of the Government Publications of the*

United States (Washington, 1885). An important guide to publications of historical societies is Appleton Prentiss Clark Griffin,
Bibliography of American Historical Societies (Washington,
1907). Finally, for a kind of random sample check, I found it
useful to comb through a particular section of library stacks,
picking out the history books with early nineteenth-century bind-
ings and browsing in them as a man of 1860 might have done.
Many of these works—as nearly as possible, the most important
and represenative ones—are discussed in the text and cited in
footnotes, especially in chapter five.

The book reviews of the period are almost as valuable as the
books themselves for determining what history meant in the
early nineteenth century, for critics are often more astute than
authors in defining the subjects, methods, interpretations, and
aims which men expect of their historians. The most valuable
source of critical judgment is the *North American Review*
(1815–65). Other periodicals providing good reviews include
Atlantic Monthly (1857–61), *Christian Examiner* (1824–69),
DeBow's Review (1846–60), *Eclectic Magazine* (1844–60), *Harper's Magazine* (1850–61), *Living Age* (1844–61), *Monthly Anthology* (1803–11), *Museum of Foreign Literàture, Science and
Art* (1822–42), *New York Mirror* (1823–42), *Portfolio* (1801–
27), and *Southern Literary Messenger* (1834–64). A guide to
reviews, especially for the better-known historians, is Samuel
Austin Allibone, *A Critical Dictionary of English Literature and
British and American Authors* (3 vols.; Philadelphia, 1899).

An enormous number of articles, essays, and lectures were
written during the period about the study and purpose of the
past. More then one hundred of these articles are listed in *Poole's
Index to Periodical Literature* under the heading "History," or
some variation. This includes articles from English periodicals,
which I occasionally used, particularly when they were widely
circulated in the United States. Statements about the study of
history are abundant in the reports and annual addresses before
historical societies. Most issues of the historical journals listed
on p. 46, contain articles of this type. The introductions of
many books, especially textbooks, provide comprehensive state-

ments, and the annual reports of state school commissioners often go to some length to explain the rise of historical studies. Among the most elaborate discussions are Ralph Waldo Emerson, "History," in *The Essays of Ralph Waldo Emerson* (Modern Library edition, New York, 1944); George Bancroft, *Literary and Historical Miscellanies* (New York, 1855); William H. Prescott, *Biographical and Critical Miscellanies* (New York, 1845); and William Greenough Thayer Shedd, *Lectures Upon the Philosophy of History* (Andover, N.H., 1856).

Recent scholars have dealt with many particular aspects of history in the United States during the early nineteenth century. David D. Van Tassel, *Recording America's Past: An Interpretation of the Development of Historical Studies in America, 1607–1884* (Chicago, 1960), is the most comprehensive, but it is limited to the American study of American history. David Levin, *History as Romantic Art: Bancroft, Prescott, Motley, and Parkman* (Stanford, 1959), is a brilliant analysis of the method and themes running through the works of the four most important American Romantic historians. Michael Kraus, *The Writing of American History* (Norman, Okla., 1953), is a comprehensive guide to the writings of major historians. John Spencer Bassett, *The Middle Group of American Historians* (New York, 1917), still offers useful insights. Harvey Wish, *The American Historian* (New York, 1960), is largely biographical. A forthcoming book by Richard C. Vitzhum deals perceptively with the Romantic historians' use of sources. John Higham, with Leonard Krieger and Felix Gilbert, *History* (Englewood Cliffs, N.J., 1965), includes material on the development of historical thinking in America. Richard Hofstadter, *The Progressive Historians: Turner, Beard, Parrington* (New York, 1968), contains a fine introductory chapter. Useful works of a more specific nature include Leslie W. Dunlap, *American Historical Societies, 1790–1860* (Madison, Wis., 1944); Ernest Erwin Leisy, *The American Historical Novel* (Norman, Okla., 1950); Edward H. O'Neill, *A History of American Biography, 1800–1935* (Philadelphia, 1935); and Bessie Louise Pierce, *Public Opinion and the Teaching of History in the United States* (New York, 1926).

Among the most valuable treatments of individual historians are Russel B. Nye, *George Bancroft: Brahmin Rebel* (New York, 1944); Donald Fleming, *John William Draper and the Religion of Science* (Philadelphia, 1950); William B. Hesseltine, *Pioneer's Mission: The Story of Lyman Copeland Draper* (Madison, Wis., 1954); Donald Eugene Emerson, *Richard Hildreth* (Baltimore, 1946); Frank O. Gatell, *John Gorham Palfrey and the New England Conscience* (Cambridge, Mass., 1963); Howard Doughty, *Francis Parkman* (New York, 1962); Milton Embick Flower, *James Parton: The Father of Modern Biography* (Durham, N.C., 1951); C. Harvey Gardiner, *The Literary Memoranda of William H. Prescott* (2 vols.; Norman, Okla., 1961); and Herbert Baxter Adams, *The Life and Writings of Jared Sparks* (2 vols.; Boston, 1893).

A particularly distinguished body of material exists on the intellectual bases of American historical attitudes, though it is sometimes difficult to establish the connection between philosophical thought and the attitudes which seem to lie behind the study of history. Probably the most important work is Robin George Collingwood, *The Idea of History* (New York, 1946). Trygve R. Tholfsen, *Historical Thinking: An Introduction* (New York, 1967), is brief and superbly lucid. The two most thorough accounts of the European tradition of historical writing are James Westfall Thompson, *A History of Historical Writing* (2 vols.; New York, 1942), and George Peabody Gooch, *History and Historians in the Nineteenth Century* (Boston, 1959). Harry Elmer Barnes, *A History of Historical Writing* (Norman, Okla., 1937), is very readable. More specialized studies include John Bennett Black, *The Art of History* (London, 1926), on the leading eighteenth-century historians, and Thomas Preston Peardon, *The Transition in English Historical Writing, 1760–1830* (New York, 1933). A suggestive study of the early period in America is Peter Gay, *A Loss of Mastery: The Puritan Historians in Colonial America* (Berkeley, 1966). Two outstanding studies of late-nineteenth-century American historical thought are W. Stull Holt, "The Idea of Scientific History in America," *Journal of the History of Ideas,* I (June, 1940), 352–

62, and William H. Jordy, *Henry Adams, Scientific Historian* (New Haven, 1952). The most successful interpretations of the American sense of time and the past are the brilliant study of R. W. B. Lewis, *The American Adam: Innocence, Tragedy, and Tradition in the Nineteenth Century* (Chicago, 1955), and the equally stimulating work by Fred Somkin, *Unquiet Eagle: Memory and Desire in the Idea of American Freedom, 1815–1860* (Ithaca, 1967). To all of these authors, to others listed in the footnotes, and to many others besides, I am indebted and grateful.

Index

 THE JOHNS HOPKINS PRESS

Designed by Arlene J. Sheer

*Composed in Baskerville text with Goudy Light Face Roman display
by The Colonial Press Inc.*

*Printed on Warren's "1854"
by The Colonial Press Inc.*

*Bound in Interlaken Arco Vellum
by The Colonial Press Inc.*